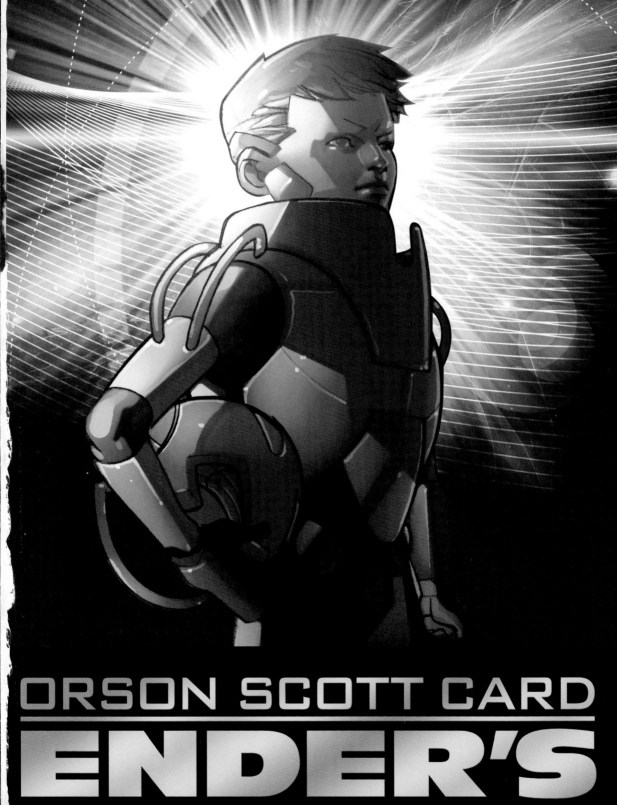

ORSON SCOTT CARD
ENDER'S GAME
COMMAND SCHOOL

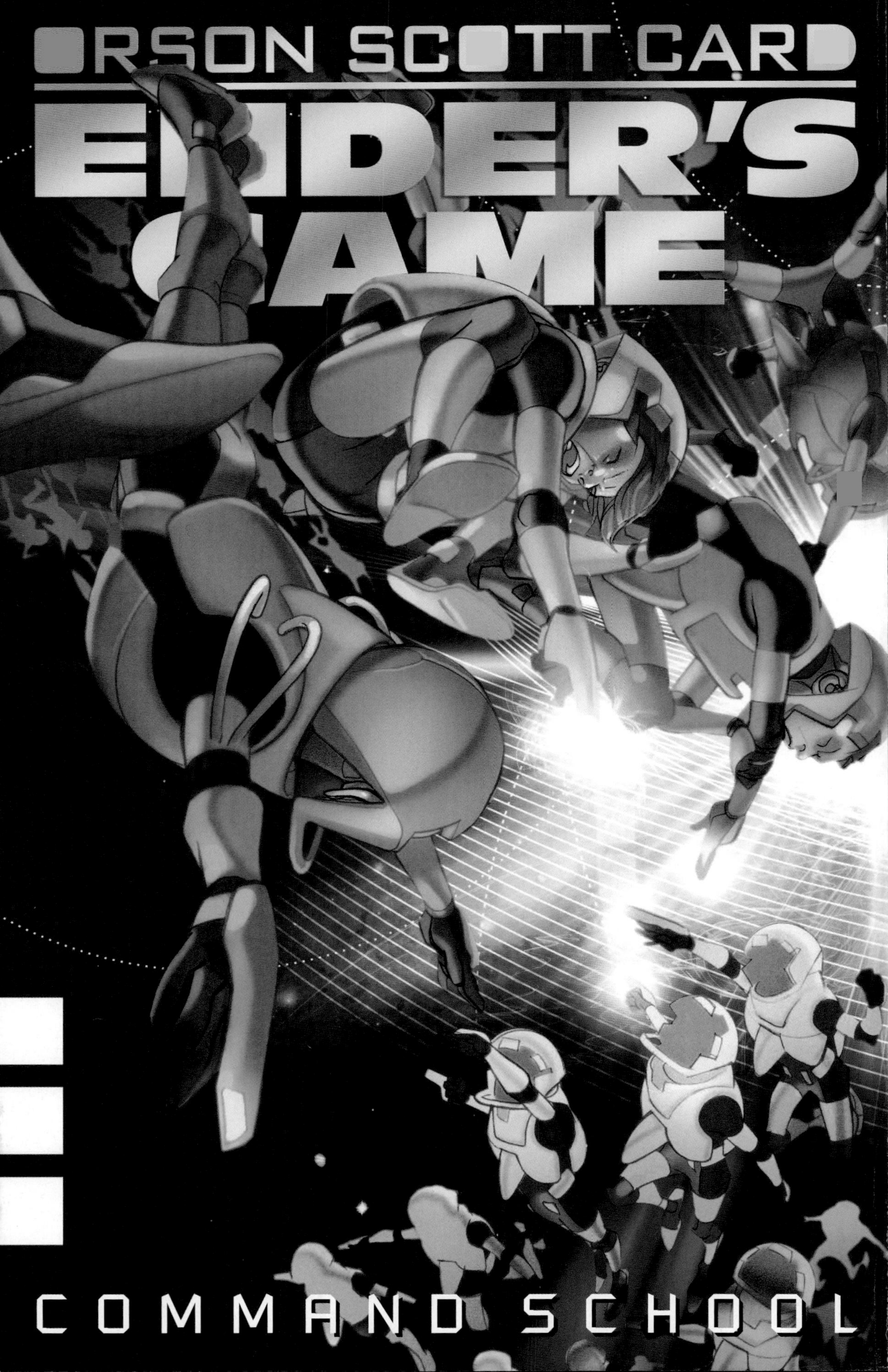
ORSON SCOTT CARD
ENDER'S GAME
COMMAND SCHOOL

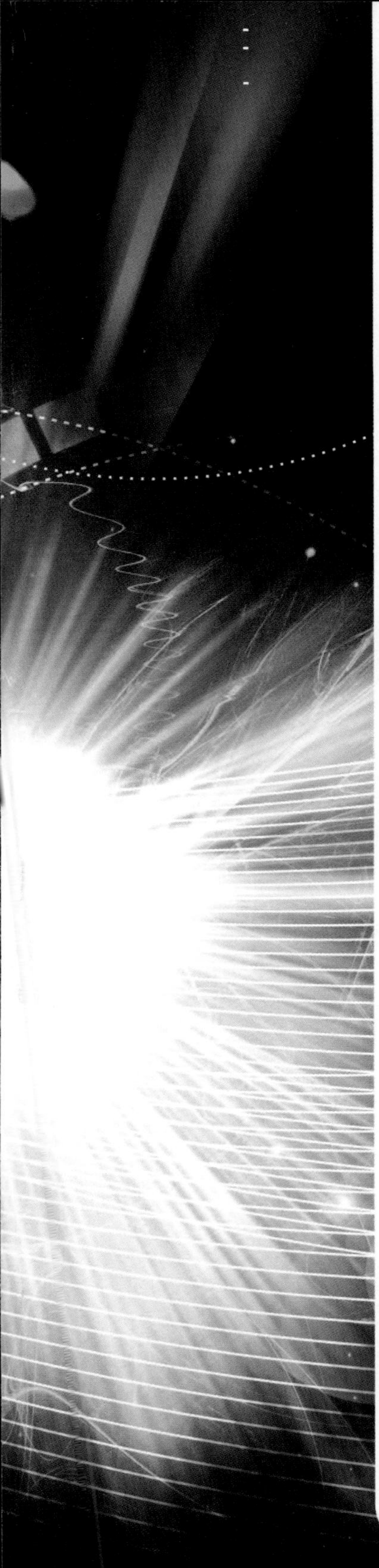

Creative Director & Executive Director:
ORSON SCOTT CARD
Script: **CHRISTOPHER YOST**
Art: **PASQUAL FERRY**
Color Art: **FRANK D'ARMATA**
Lettering: **VC'S CORY PETIT**
Story Consultant: **JAKE BLACK**
Cover Art: **PASQUAL FERRY**
& FRANK D'ARMATA
Editor: **JORDAN D. WHITE**
Supervising Editor: **NICK LOWE**
Senior Editor: **MARK PANICCIA**

Special thanks to
KRISTINE CARD,
KATHLEEN BELLAMY,
DARIAN ROBBINS,
ANDREW BAUGHAN,
RALPH MACCHIO,
LAUREN SANKOVITCH,
JIM NAUSEDAS,
JIM MCCANN,
ARUNE SINGH,
CHRIS ALLO
& JEFF SUTER

Collection Editor: **JENNIFER GRÜNWALD**
Assistant Editor: **ALEX STARBUCK**
Associate Editor: **JOHN DENNING**
Editor, Special Projects:
MARK D. BEAZLEY
Senior Editor, Special Projects:
JEFF YOUNGQUIST
Senior Vice President of Sales:
DAVID GABRIEL
Senior Vice President of Strategic
Development: **RUWAN JAYATILLEKE**
Vice President of Creative: **TOM MARVELLI**
Book designer: **RODOLFO MURAGUCHI**

Editor in Chief: **JOE QUESADA**
Publisher: **DAN BUCKLEY**
Executive Producer: **ALAN FINE**

ENDER'S GAME: COMMAND SCHOOL. Contains material originally published in magazine form as ENDER'S GAME: COMMAND SCHOOL #1-5. First printing 2010. ISBN# 978-0-7851-3582-1. Published by MARVEL WORLDWIDE, INC., a subsidiary of MARVEL ENTERTAINMENT, LLC. OFFICE OF PUBLICATION: 417 5th Avenue, New York, NY 10016. **Manufactured between 1/25/10 and 2/24/10 by R.R. DONNELLEY, INC., SALEM, VA, USA.**

10 9 8 7 6 5 4 3 2 1

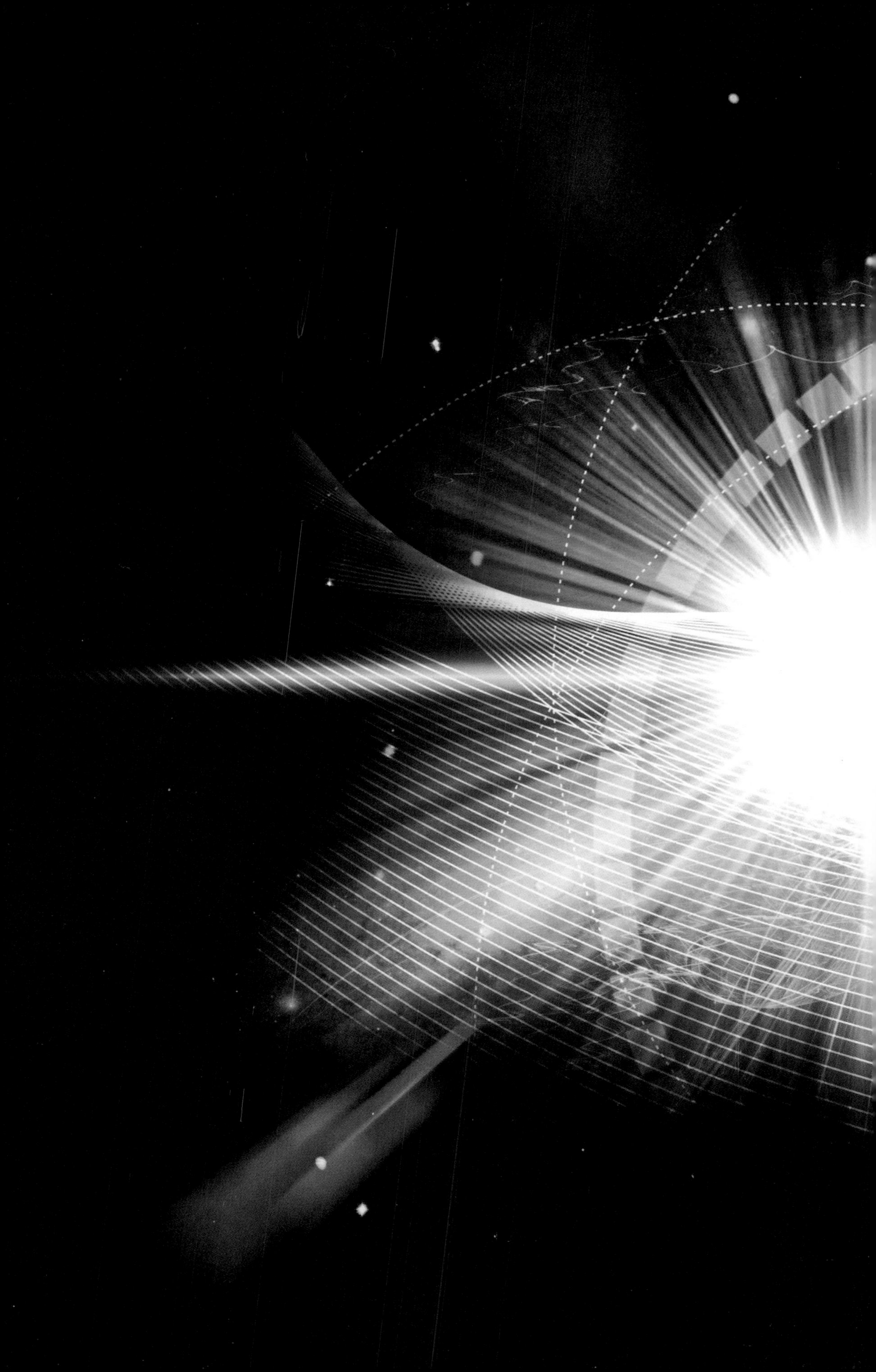

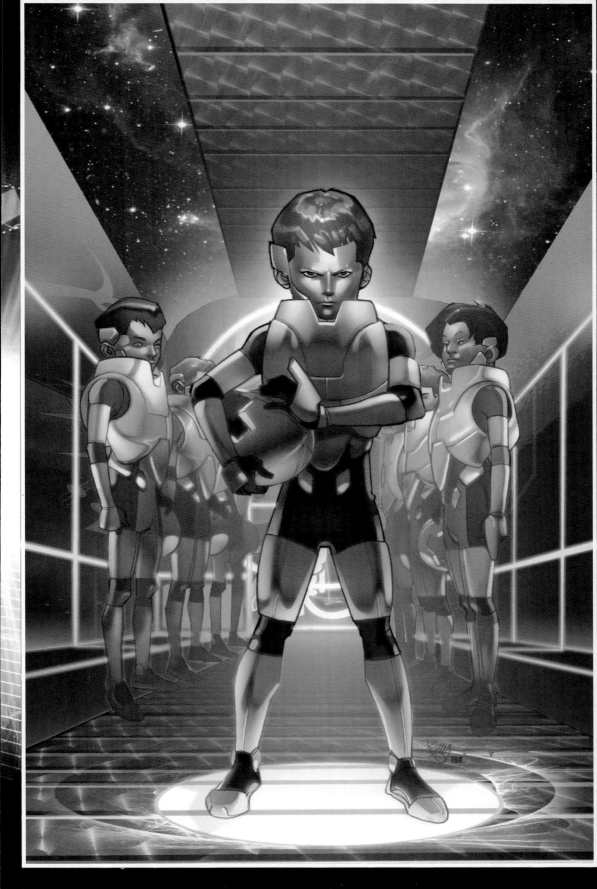

O N E

INTERNATIONAL FLEET MONITORED COMMUNICATIONS
PARTICIPANTS: COLONEL H. GRAFF, MAJOR J. ANDERSON
REF ID # 22457-86422, KEYWORD SEARCH: 'DRAGON'

<<<THIS CONVERSATION WAS RECORDED FOLLOWING THE PROMOTION OF ANDREW WIGGIN TO COMMANDER OF DRAGON ARMY>>>

GRAFF: For a few minutes there, it actually occurred to me to wonder what kind of a man would heal a broken child of some of his hurt, just so he could throw him back into battle again. A little private moral dilemma. Please overlook it. I was tired.

ANDERSON: Saving the world, remember?

G: Call him in.

A: We're doing what must be done, Colonel Graff.

G: Come on, Anderson, you're just dying to see how he handles all those rigged games I had you work out.

A: That's a pretty low thing to--

G: So I'm a low kind of guy. Come on, Major. We're both the scum of the earth. I'm dying to see how he handles them, too. After all, our lives depend on him doing real well. Neh?

A: You're not starting to use the boys' slang, are you?

G: Call him in, Major. I'll dump the rosters into his files and give him his security system. What we're doing to him isn't all bad, you know. He gets his privacy again.

A: Isolation, you mean.

G: The lonliness of power. Go call him in.

A: Yes, sir. I'll be back with him in fifteen minutes.

G: Welcome, little boy. Your dear Uncle Graff has plans for you.

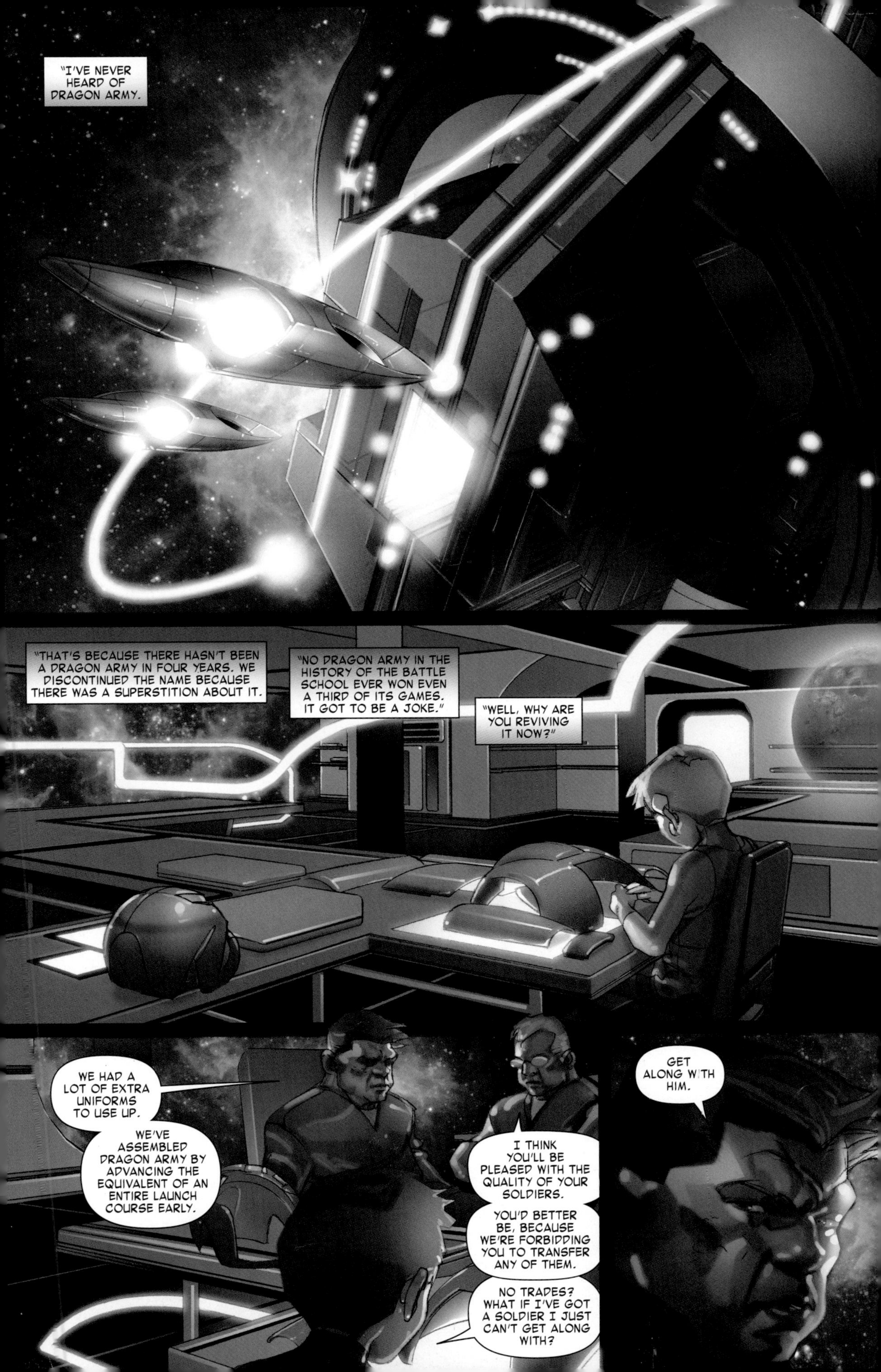
"I'VE NEVER HEARD OF DRAGON ARMY.
"THAT'S BECAUSE THERE HASN'T BEEN A DRAGON ARMY IN FOUR YEARS. WE DISCONTINUED THE NAME BECAUSE THERE WAS A SUPERSTITION ABOUT IT.
"NO DRAGON ARMY IN THE HISTORY OF THE BATTLE SCHOOL EVER WON EVEN A THIRD OF ITS GAMES. IT GOT TO BE A JOKE."
"WELL, WHY ARE YOU REVIVING IT NOW?"
WE HAD A LOT OF EXTRA UNIFORMS TO USE UP.
WE'VE ASSEMBLED DRAGON ARMY BY ADVANCING THE EQUIVALENT OF AN ENTIRE LAUNCH COURSE EARLY.
I THINK YOU'LL BE PLEASED WITH THE QUALITY OF YOUR SOLDIERS.
YOU'D BETTER BE, BECAUSE WE'RE FORBIDDING YOU TO TRANSFER ANY OF THEM.
NO TRADES? WHAT IF I'VE GOT A SOLDIER I JUST CAN'T GET ALONG WITH?
GET ALONG WITH HIM.

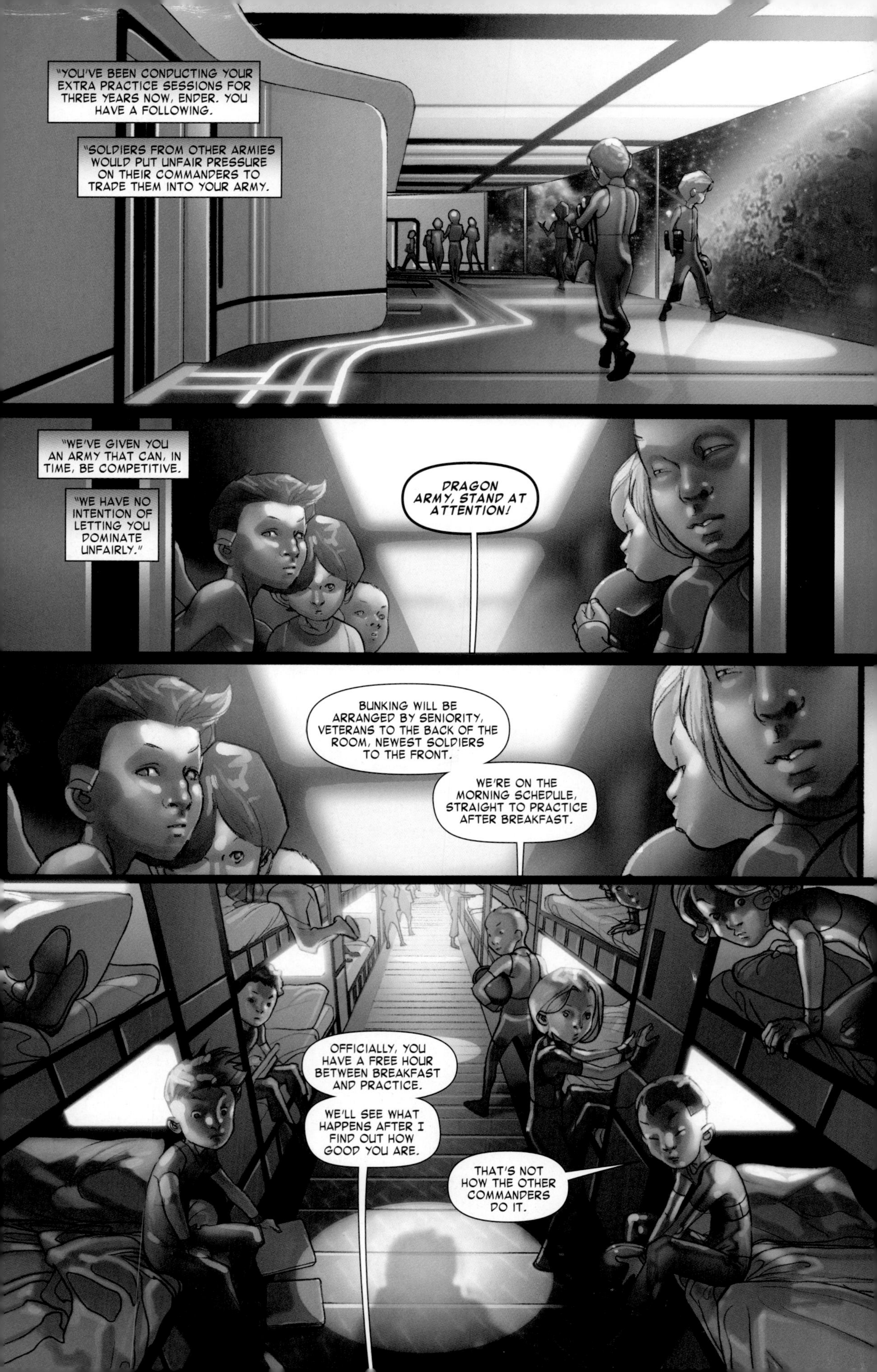
"YOU'VE BEEN CONDUCTING YOUR EXTRA PRACTICE SESSIONS FOR THREE YEARS NOW, ENDER. YOU HAVE A FOLLOWING.
"SOLDIERS FROM OTHER ARMIES WOULD PUT UNFAIR PRESSURE ON THEIR COMMANDERS TO TRADE THEM INTO YOUR ARMY.
"WE'VE GIVEN YOU AN ARMY THAT CAN, IN TIME, BE COMPETITIVE.
"WE HAVE NO INTENTION OF LETTING YOU DOMINATE UNFAIRLY."
DRAGON ARMY, STAND AT ATTENTION!
BUNKING WILL BE ARRANGED BY SENIORITY, VETERANS TO THE BACK OF THE ROOM, NEWEST SOLDIERS TO THE FRONT.
WE'RE ON THE MORNING SCHEDULE, STRAIGHT TO PRACTICE AFTER BREAKFAST.
OFFICIALLY, YOU HAVE A FREE HOUR BETWEEN BREAKFAST AND PRACTICE.
WE'LL SEE WHAT HAPPENS AFTER I FIND OUT HOW GOOD YOU ARE.
THAT'S NOT HOW THE OTHER COMMANDERS DO IT.

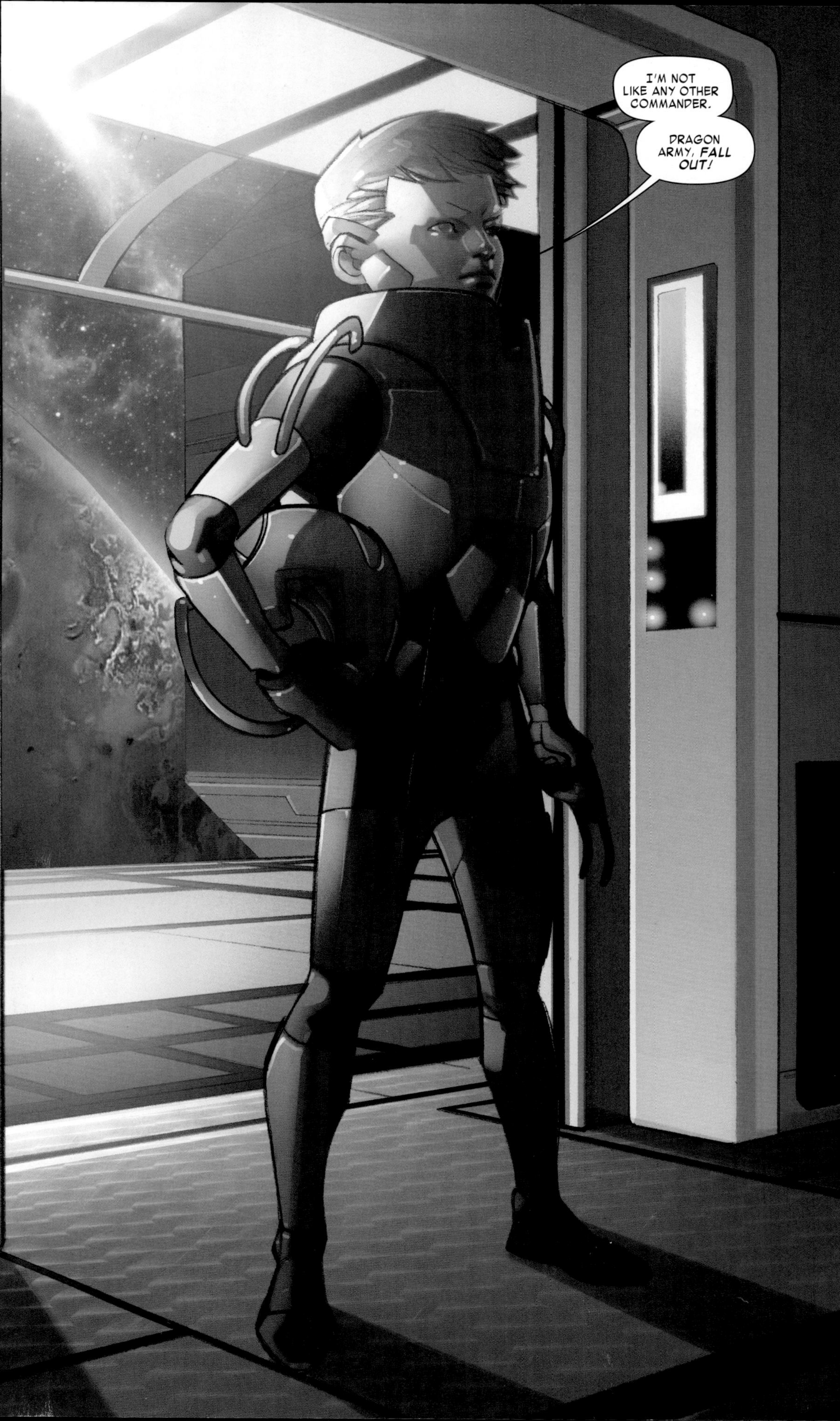
I'M NOT LIKE ANY OTHER COMMANDER.
DRAGON ARMY, FALL OUT!

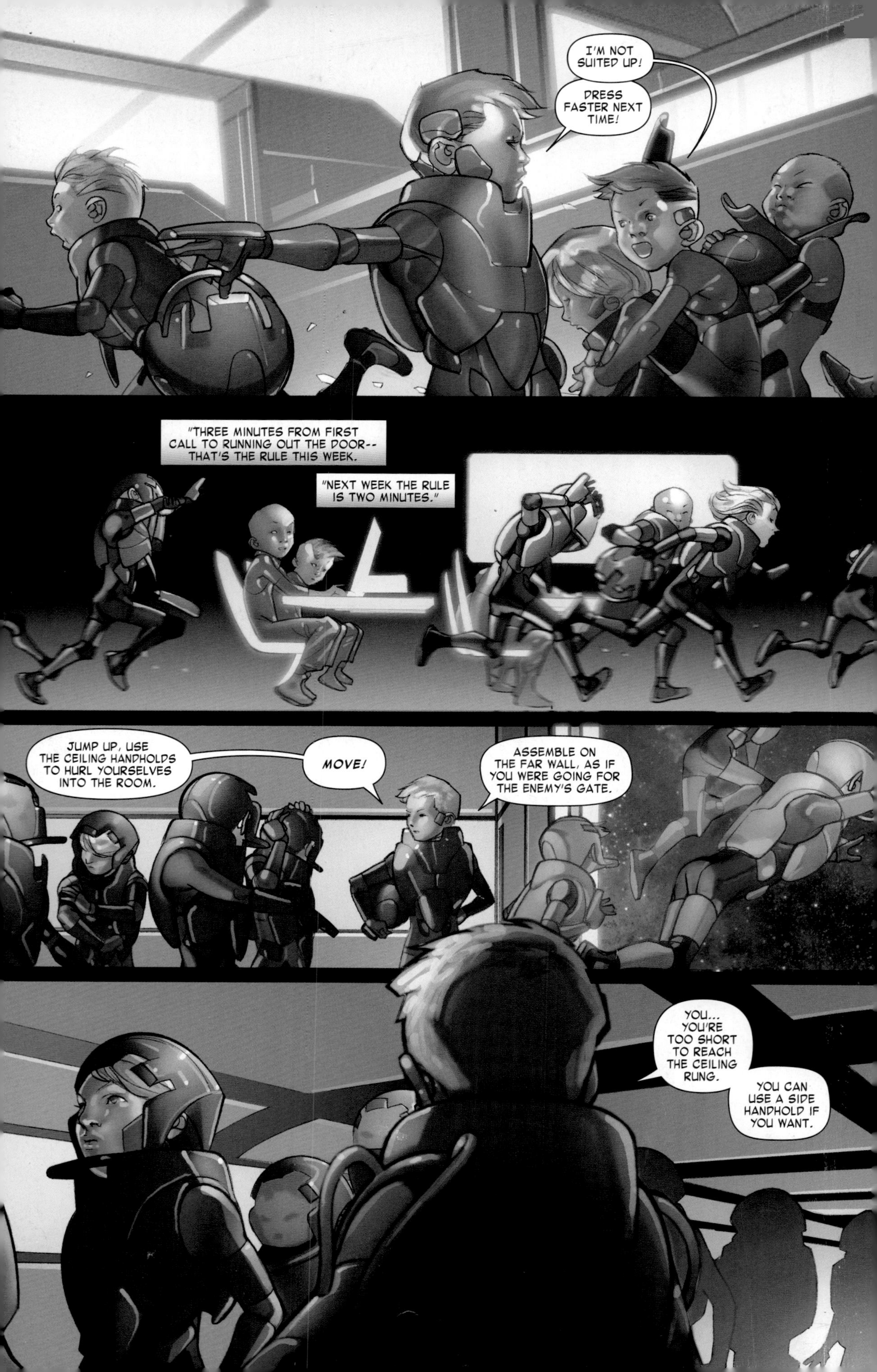
I'M NOT SUITED UP!
DRESS FASTER NEXT TIME!
"THREE MINUTES FROM FIRST CALL TO RUNNING OUT THE DOOR-- THAT'S THE RULE THIS WEEK.
"NEXT WEEK THE RULE IS TWO MINUTES."
JUMP UP, USE THE CEILING HANDHOLDS TO HURL YOURSELVES INTO THE ROOM.
MOVE!
ASSEMBLE ON THE FAR WALL, AS IF YOU WERE GOING FOR THE ENEMY'S GATE.
YOU... YOU'RE TOO SHORT TO REACH THE CEILING RUNG.
YOU CAN USE A SIDE HANDHOLD IF YOU WANT.

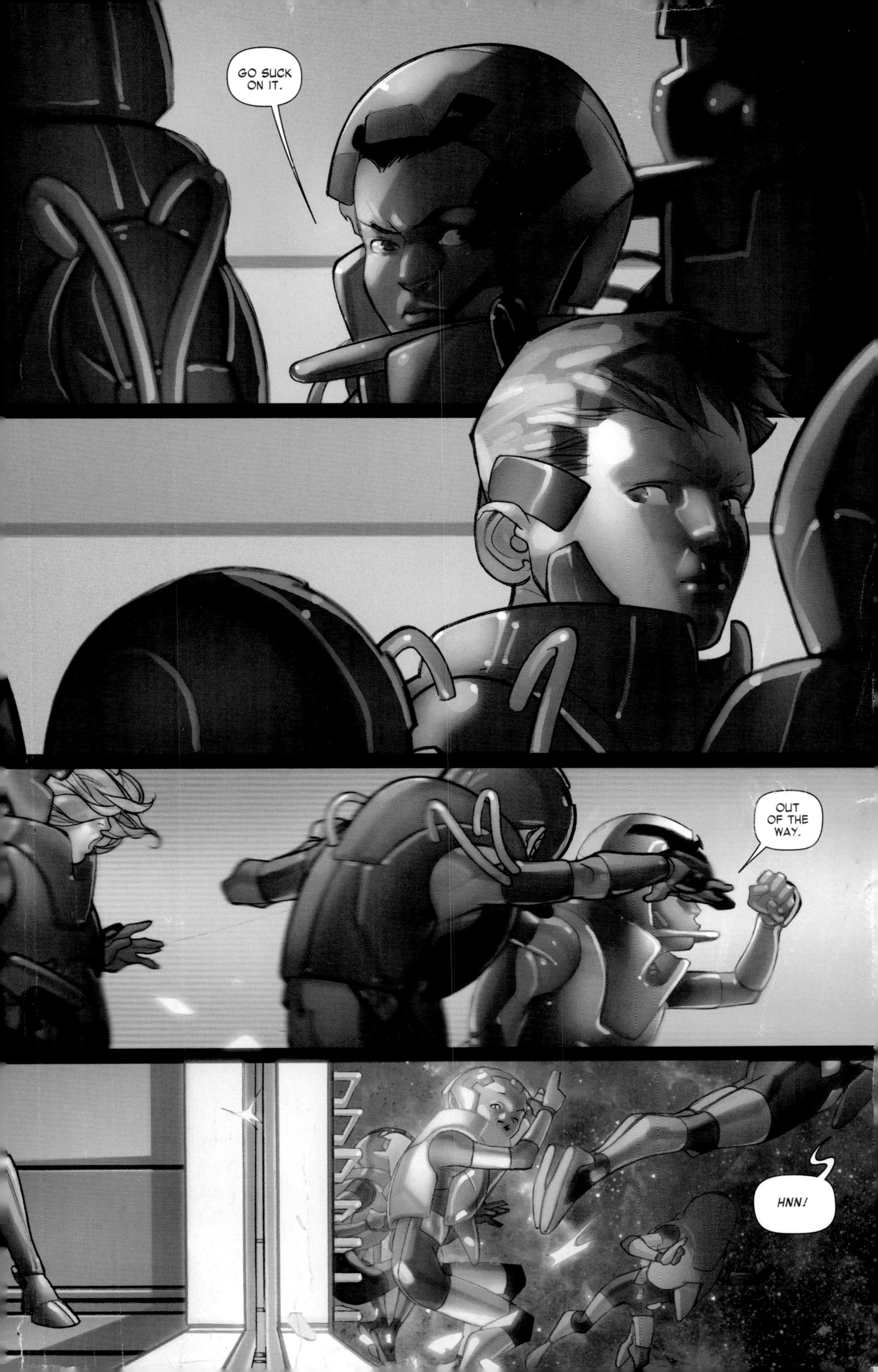
GO SUCK ON IT.
OUT OF THE WAY.
HNN!

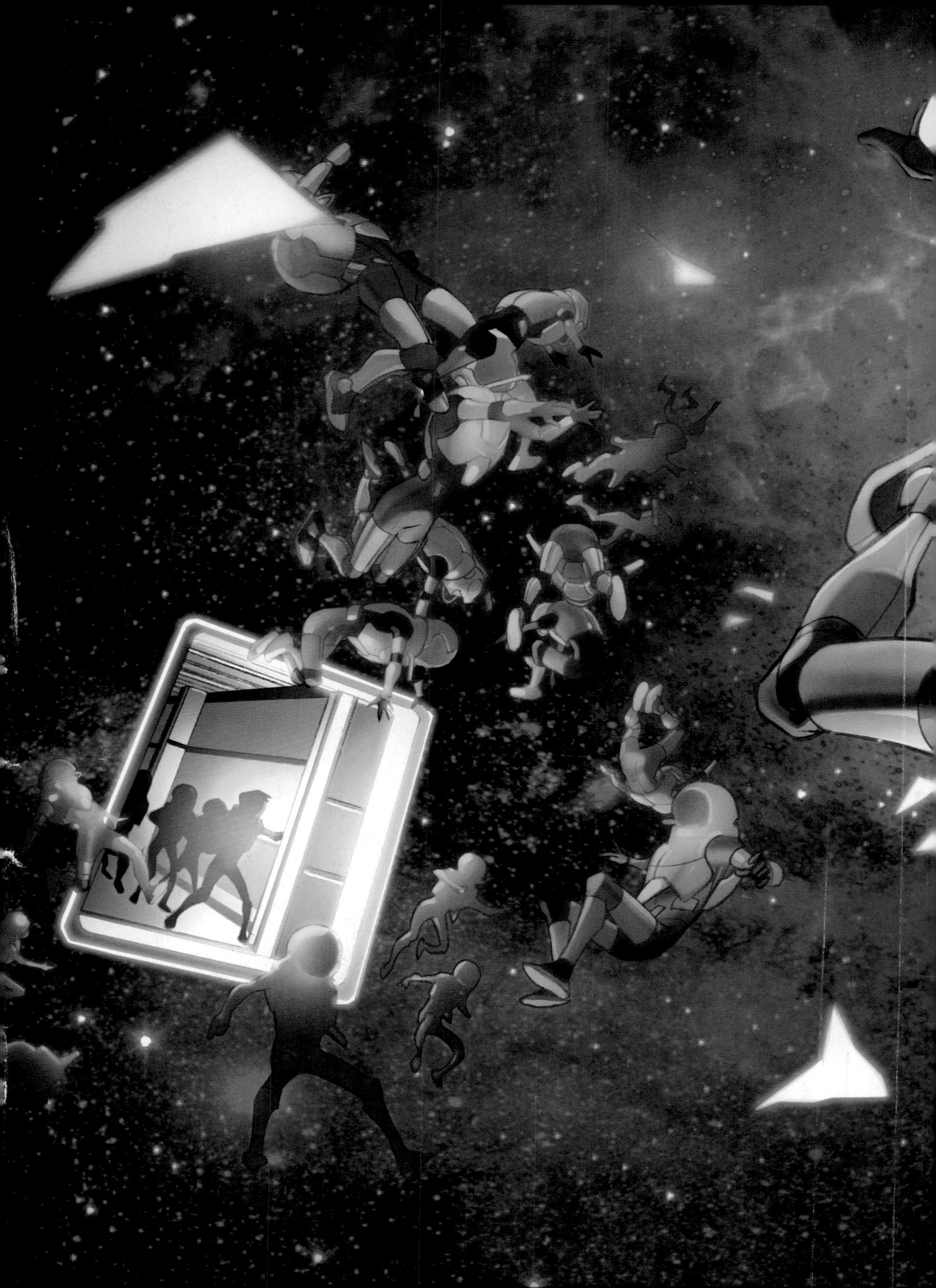

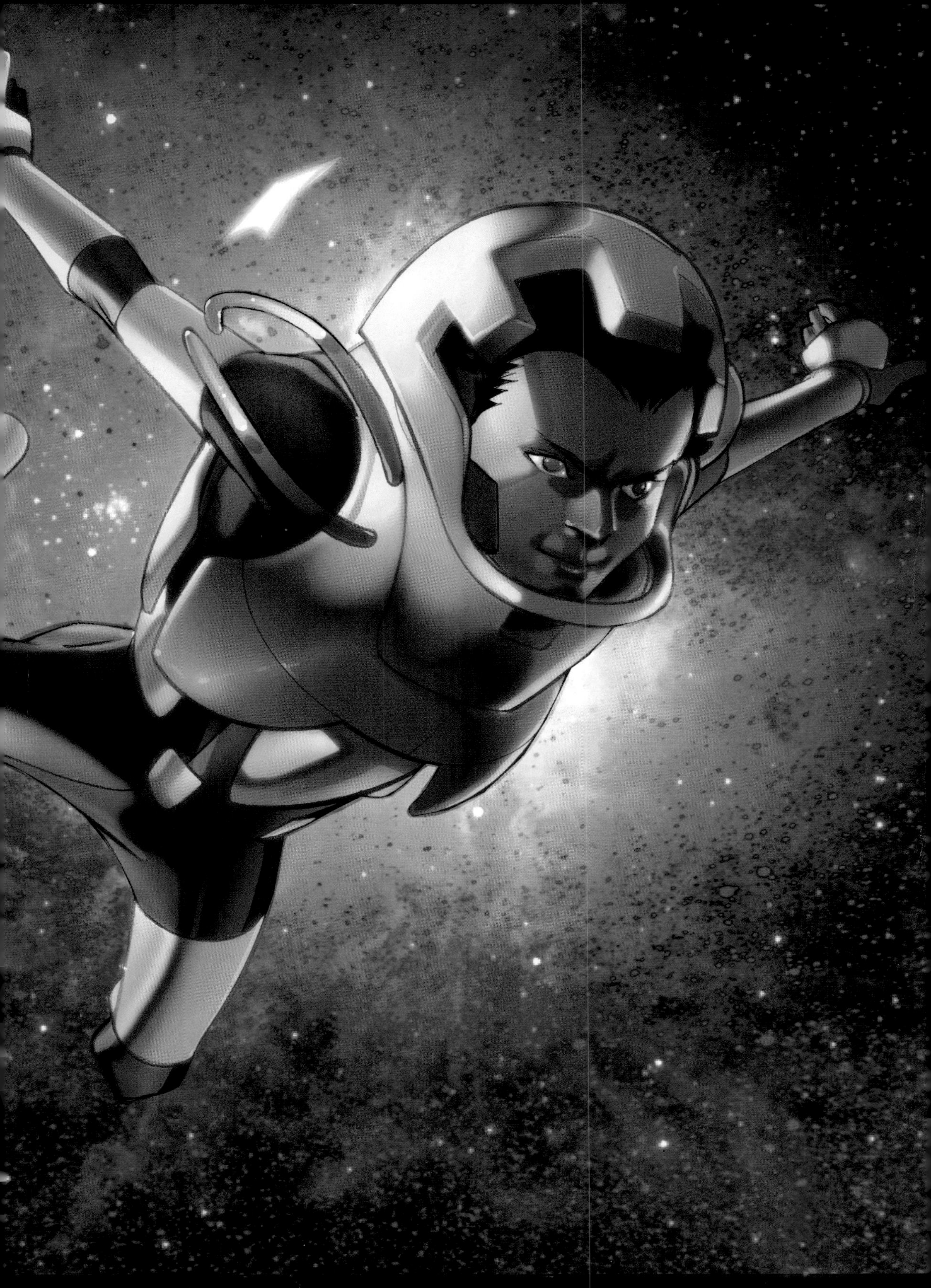

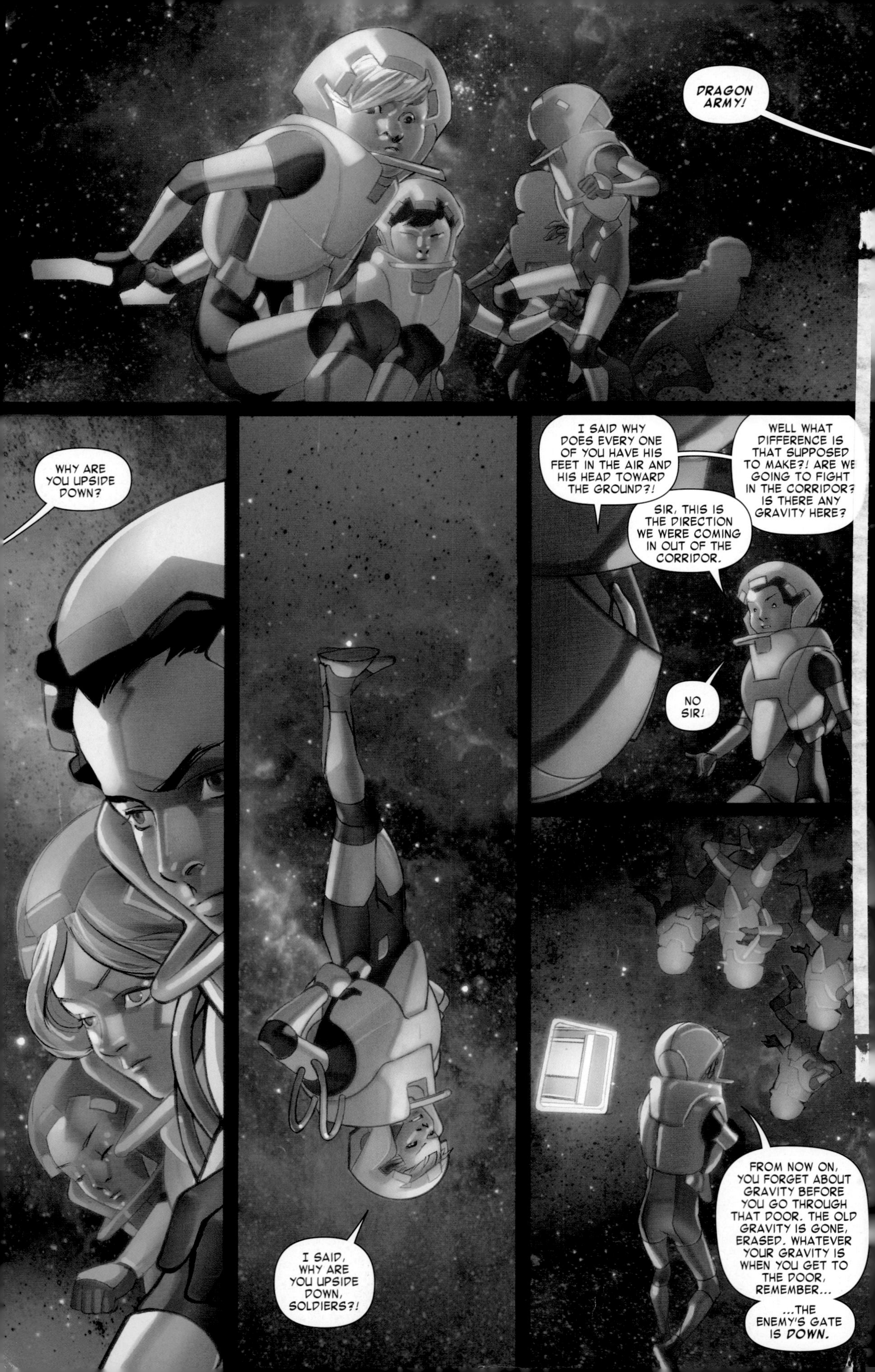
DRAGON ARMY!
WHY ARE YOU UPSIDE DOWN?
I SAID, WHY ARE YOU UPSIDE DOWN, SOLDIERS?!
I SAID WHY DOES EVERY ONE OF YOU HAVE HIS FEET IN THE AIR AND HIS HEAD TOWARD THE GROUND?!
WELL WHAT DIFFERENCE IS THAT SUPPOSED TO MAKE?! ARE WE GOING TO FIGHT IN THE CORRIDOR? IS THERE ANY GRAVITY HERE?
SIR, THIS IS THE DIRECTION WE WERE COMING IN OUT OF THE CORRIDOR.
NO SIR!
FROM NOW ON, YOU FORGET ABOUT GRAVITY BEFORE YOU GO THROUGH THAT DOOR. THE OLD GRAVITY IS GONE, ERASED. WHATEVER YOUR GRAVITY IS WHEN YOU GET TO THE DOOR, REMEMBER...
...THE ENEMY'S GATE IS DOWN.

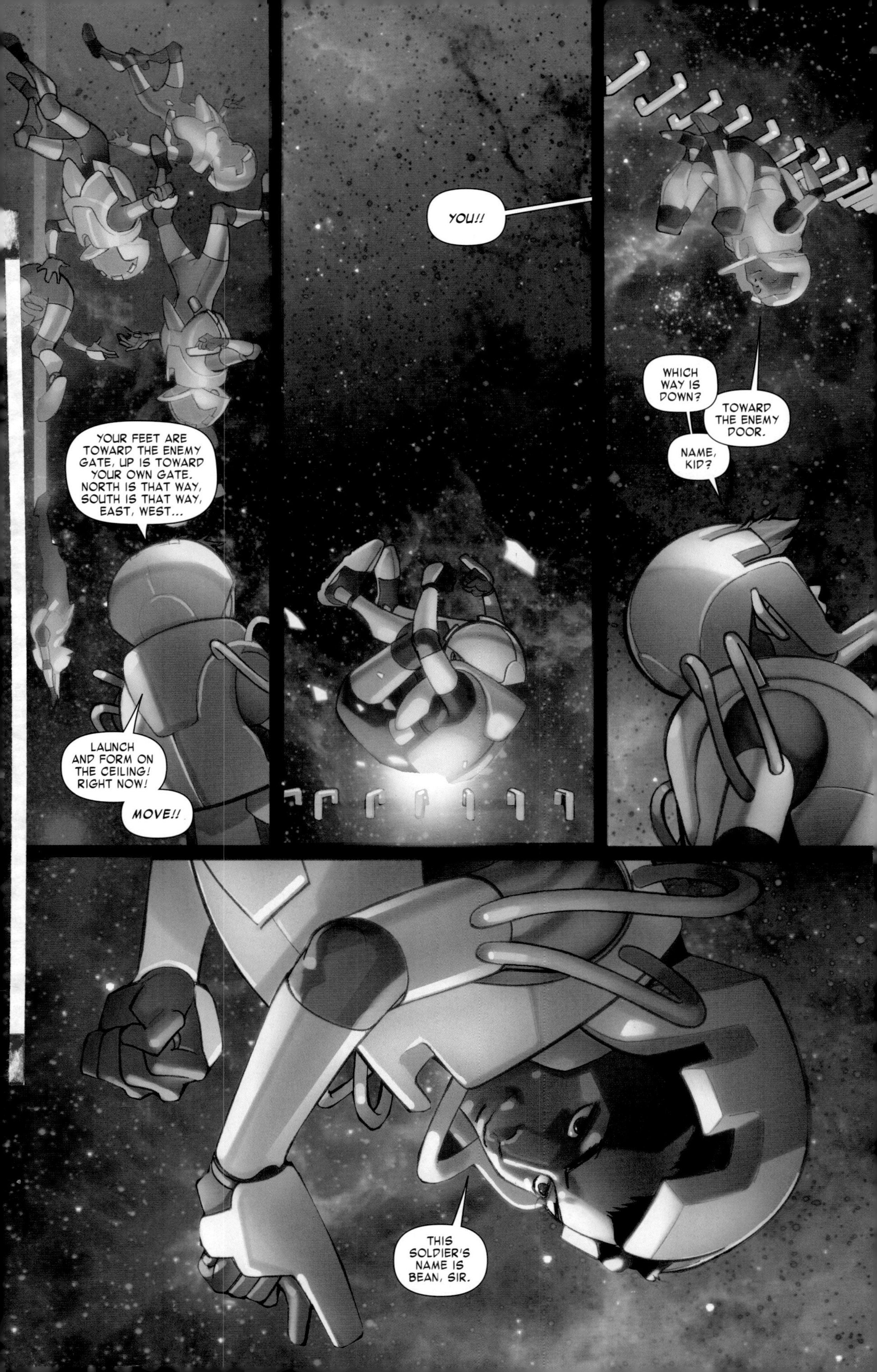
YOUR FEET ARE TOWARD THE ENEMY GATE, UP IS TOWARD YOUR OWN GATE. NORTH IS THAT WAY, SOUTH IS THAT WAY, EAST, WEST...
LAUNCH AND FORM ON THE CEILING! RIGHT NOW!
MOVE!!
YOU!!
WHICH WAY IS DOWN?
TOWARD THE ENEMY DOOR.
NAME, KID?
THIS SOLDIER'S NAME IS BEAN, SIR.

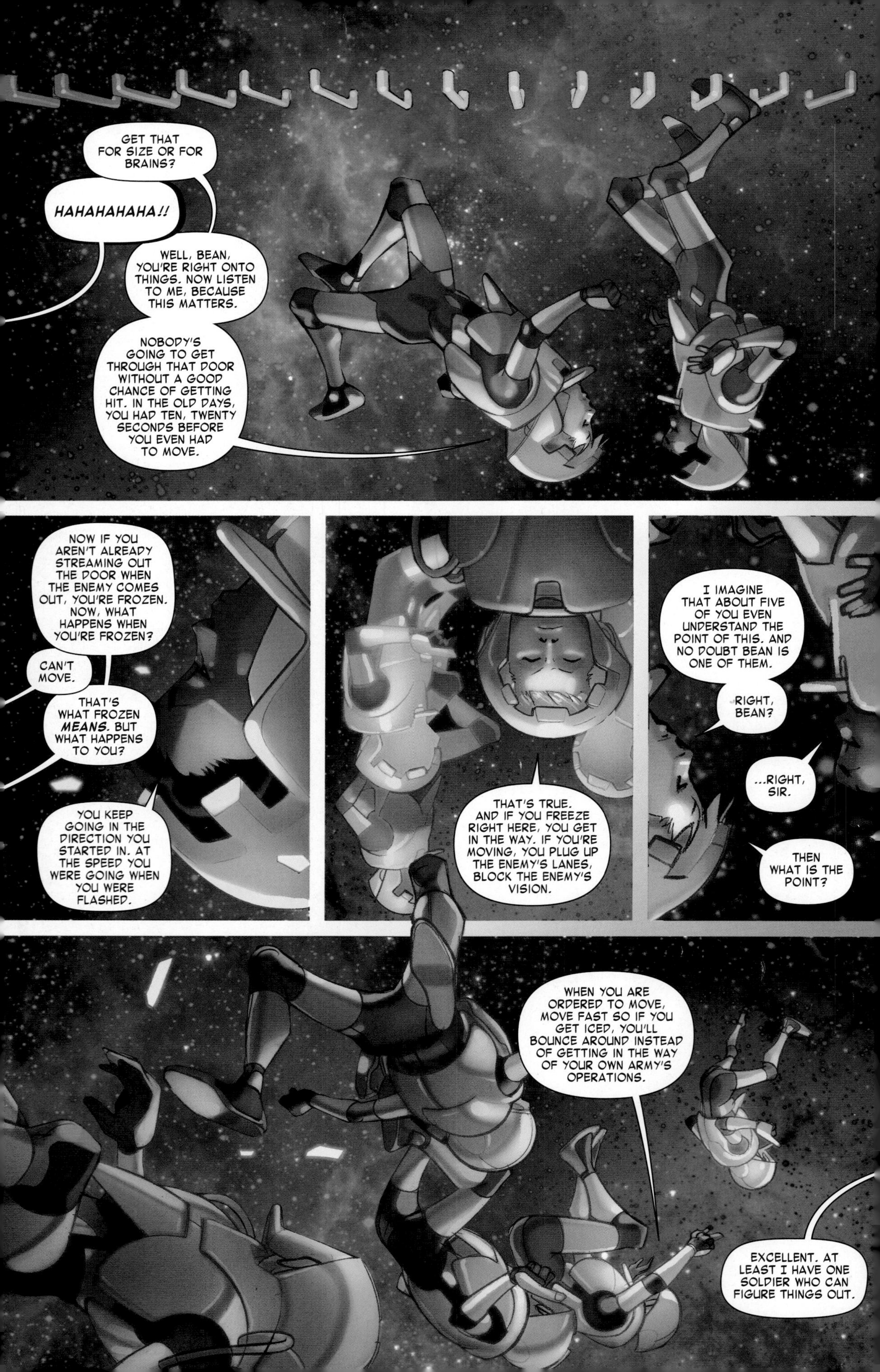
GET THAT FOR SIZE OR FOR BRAINS?
HAHAHAHAHA!!
WELL, BEAN, YOU'RE RIGHT ONTO THINGS. NOW LISTEN TO ME, BECAUSE THIS MATTERS.
NOBODY'S GOING TO GET THROUGH THAT DOOR WITHOUT A GOOD CHANCE OF GETTING HIT. IN THE OLD DAYS, YOU HAD TEN, TWENTY SECONDS BEFORE YOU EVEN HAD TO MOVE.
NOW IF YOU AREN'T ALREADY STREAMING OUT THE DOOR WHEN THE ENEMY COMES OUT, YOU'RE FROZEN. NOW, WHAT HAPPENS WHEN YOU'RE FROZEN?
CAN'T MOVE.
THAT'S WHAT FROZEN *MEANS.* BUT WHAT HAPPENS TO YOU?
YOU KEEP GOING IN THE DIRECTION YOU STARTED IN. AT THE SPEED YOU WERE GOING WHEN YOU WERE FLASHED.
THAT'S TRUE. AND IF YOU FREEZE RIGHT HERE, YOU GET IN THE WAY. IF YOU'RE MOVING, YOU PLUG UP THE ENEMY'S LANES, BLOCK THE ENEMY'S VISION.
I IMAGINE THAT ABOUT FIVE OF YOU EVEN UNDERSTAND THE POINT OF THIS. AND NO DOUBT BEAN IS ONE OF THEM.
RIGHT, BEAN?
...RIGHT, SIR.
THEN WHAT IS THE POINT?
WHEN YOU ARE ORDERED TO MOVE, MOVE FAST SO IF YOU GET ICED, YOU'LL BOUNCE AROUND INSTEAD OF GETTING IN THE WAY OF YOUR OWN ARMY'S OPERATIONS.
EXCELLENT. AT LEAST I HAVE ONE SOLDIER WHO CAN FIGURE THINGS OUT.

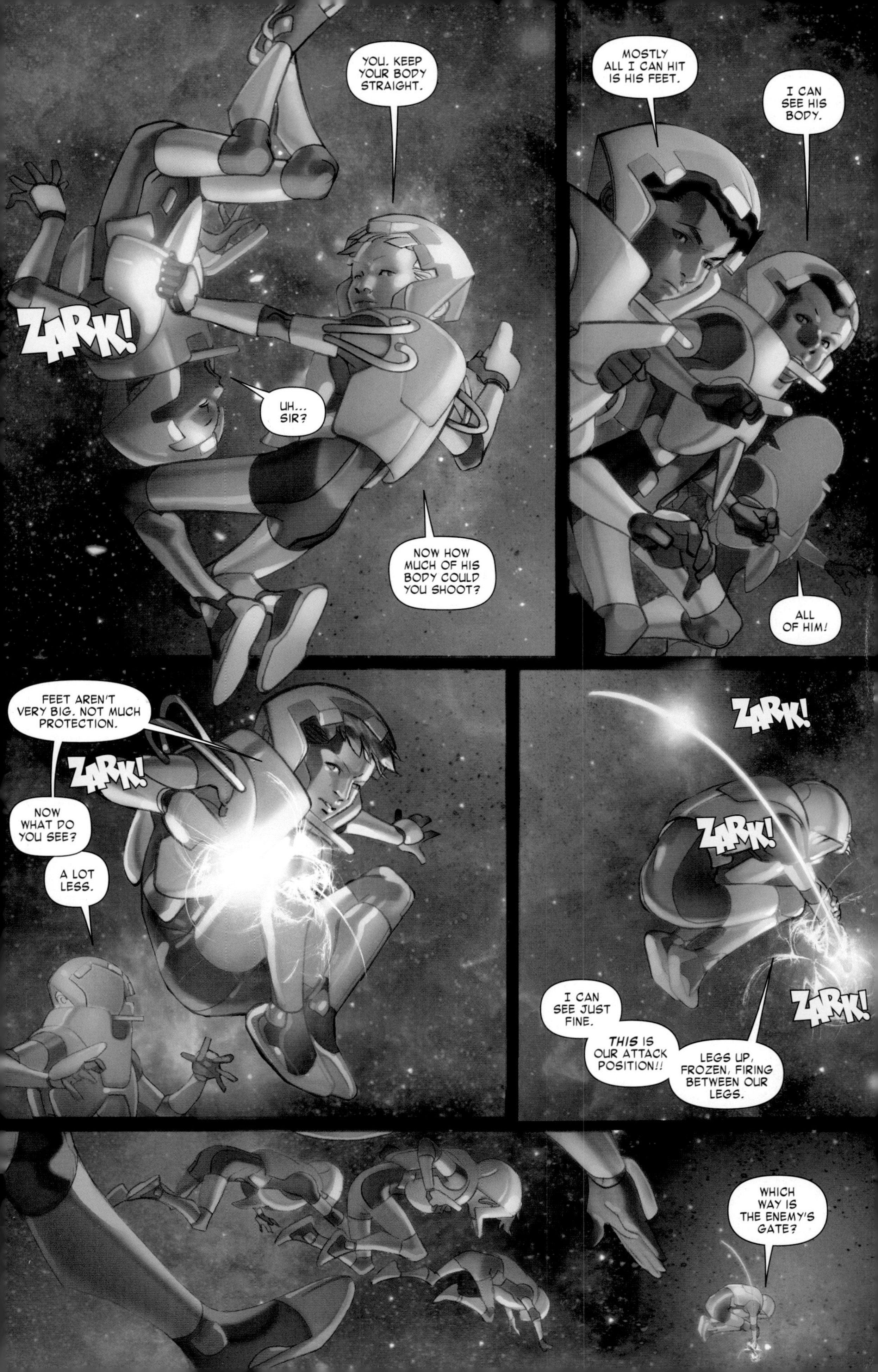
YOU. KEEP YOUR BODY STRAIGHT.
ZARK!
UH... SIR?
NOW HOW MUCH OF HIS BODY COULD YOU SHOOT?
MOSTLY ALL I CAN HIT IS HIS FEET.
I CAN SEE HIS BODY.
ALL OF HIM!
FEET AREN'T VERY BIG. NOT MUCH PROTECTION.
ZARK!
NOW WHAT DO YOU SEE?
A LOT LESS.
ZARK!
ZARK!
ZARK!
I CAN SEE JUST FINE.
THIS IS OUR ATTACK POSITION!!
LEGS UP, FROZEN, FIRING BETWEEN OUR LEGS.
WHICH WAY IS THE ENEMY'S GATE?

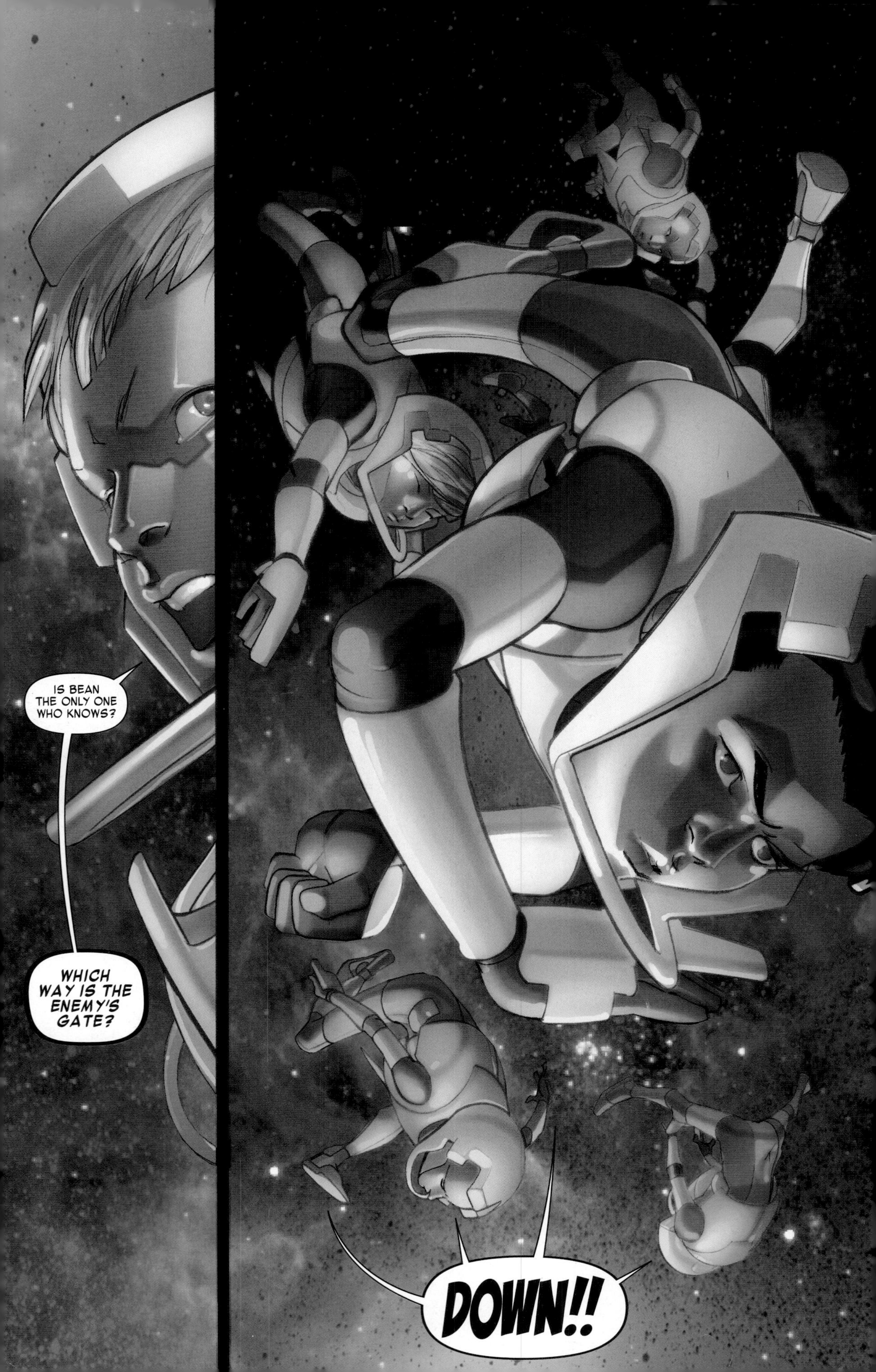
IS BEAN THE ONLY ONE WHO KNOWS?
WHICH WAY IS THE ENEMY'S GATE?
DOWN!!

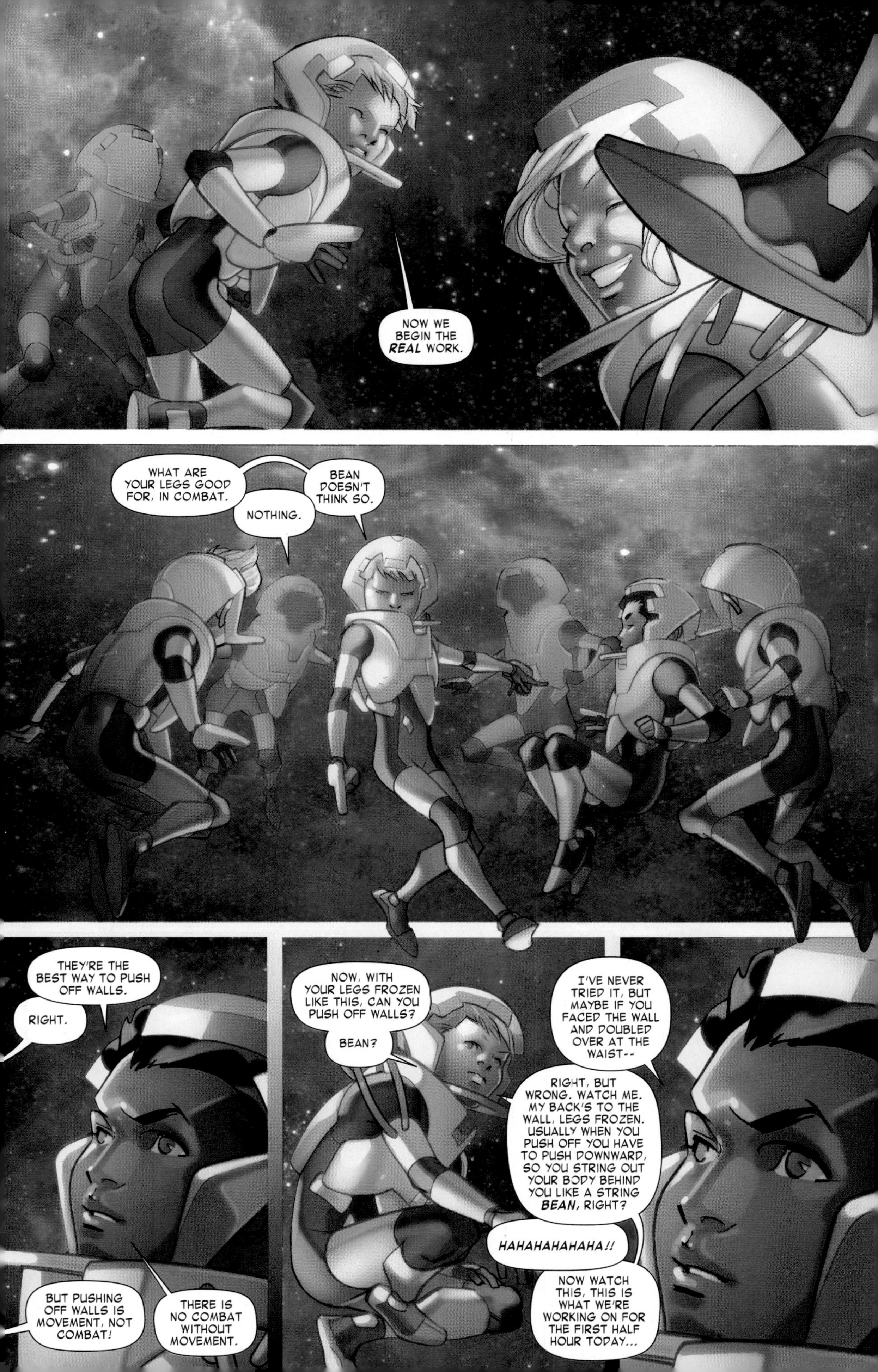
NOW WE BEGIN THE *REAL* WORK.
WHAT ARE YOUR LEGS GOOD FOR, IN COMBAT.
BEAN DOESN'T THINK SO.
NOTHING.
THEY'RE THE BEST WAY TO PUSH OFF WALLS.
RIGHT.
BUT PUSHING OFF WALLS IS MOVEMENT, NOT COMBAT!
THERE IS NO COMBAT WITHOUT MOVEMENT.
NOW, WITH YOUR LEGS FROZEN LIKE THIS, CAN YOU PUSH OFF WALLS?
BEAN?
I'VE NEVER TRIED IT, BUT MAYBE IF YOU FACED THE WALL AND DOUBLED OVER AT THE WAIST--
RIGHT, BUT WRONG. WATCH ME. MY BACK'S TO THE WALL, LEGS FROZEN. USUALLY WHEN YOU PUSH OFF YOU HAVE TO PUSH DOWNWARD, SO YOU STRING OUT YOUR BODY BEHIND YOU LIKE A STRING *BEAN*, RIGHT?
HAHAHAHAHAHA!!
NOW WATCH THIS, THIS IS WHAT WE'RE WORKING ON FOR THE FIRST HALF HOUR TODAY...

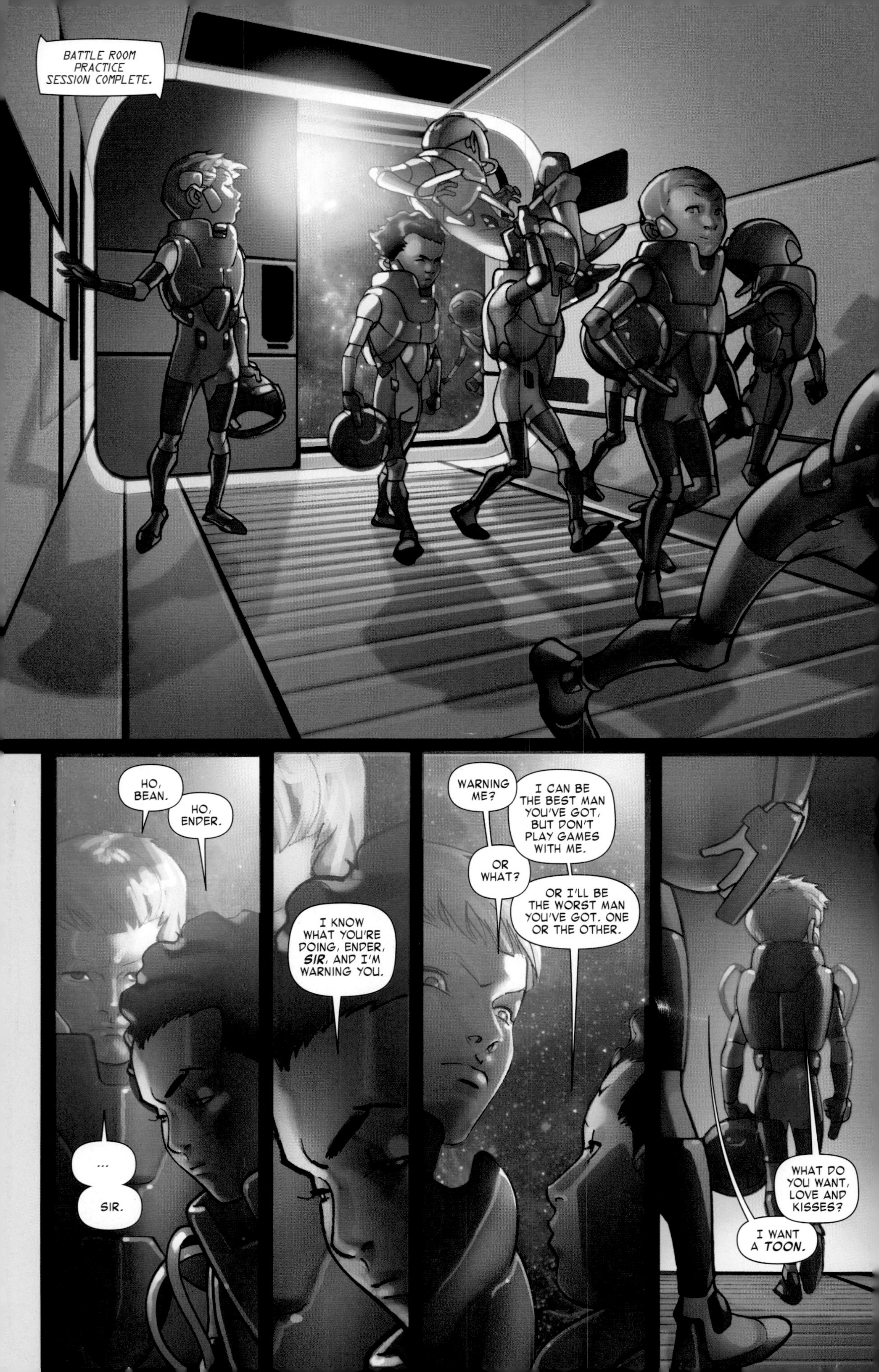
BATTLE ROOM PRACTICE SESSION COMPLETE.
HO, BEAN.
HO, ENDER.
...
SIR.
I KNOW WHAT YOU'RE DOING, ENDER, SIR, AND I'M WARNING YOU.
WARNING ME?
I CAN BE THE BEST MAN YOU'VE GOT, BUT DON'T PLAY GAMES WITH ME.
OR WHAT?
OR I'LL BE THE WORST MAN YOU'VE GOT. ONE OR THE OTHER.
WHAT DO YOU WANT, LOVE AND KISSES?
I WANT A TOON.

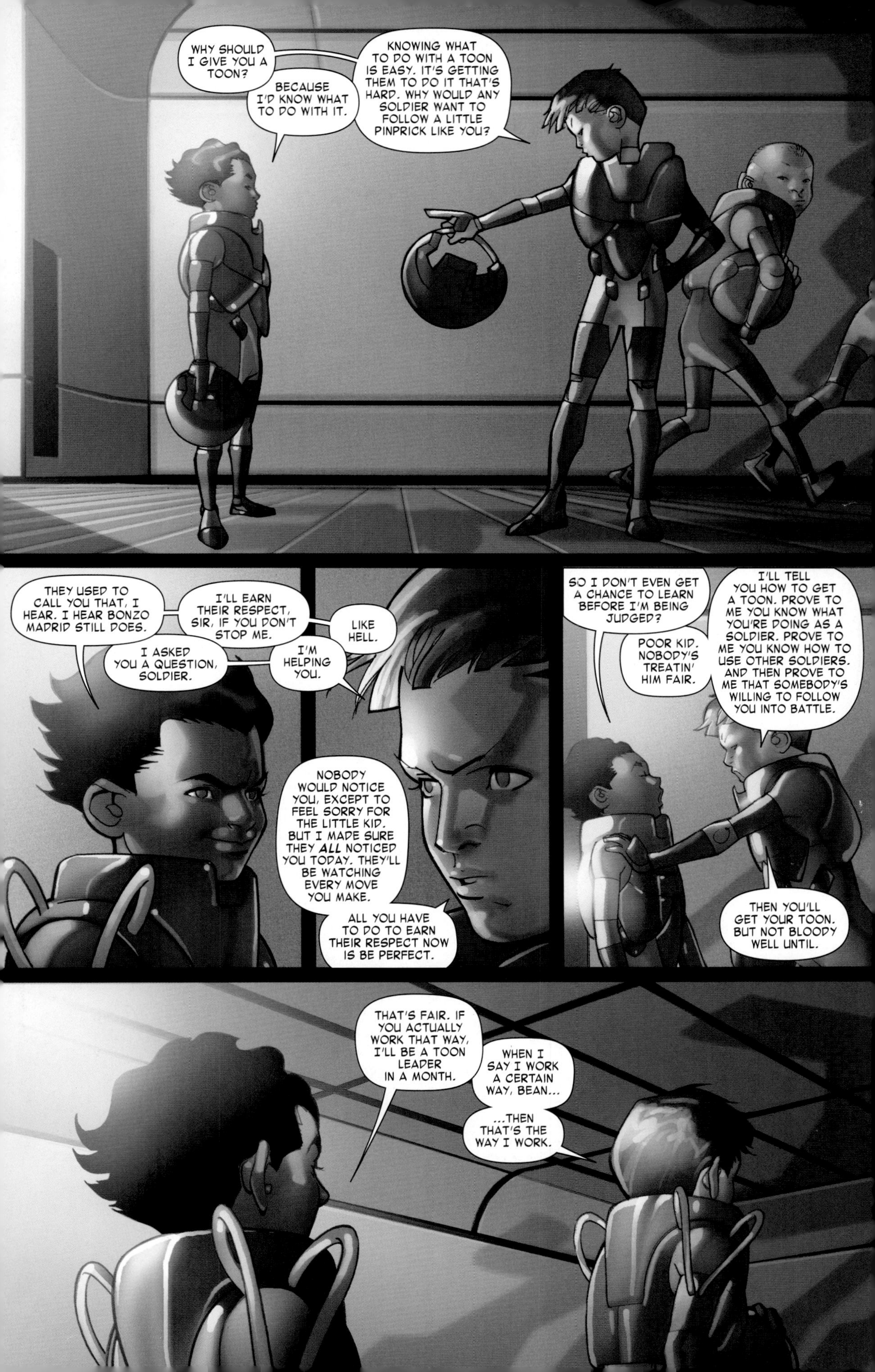
WHY SHOULD I GIVE YOU A TOON?
BECAUSE I'D KNOW WHAT TO DO WITH IT.
KNOWING WHAT TO DO WITH A TOON IS EASY. IT'S GETTING THEM TO DO IT THAT'S HARD. WHY WOULD ANY SOLDIER WANT TO FOLLOW A LITTLE PINPRICK LIKE YOU?
THEY USED TO CALL YOU THAT, I HEAR. I HEAR BONZO MADRID STILL DOES.
I'LL EARN THEIR RESPECT, SIR, IF YOU DON'T STOP ME.
LIKE HELL.
I ASKED YOU A QUESTION, SOLDIER.
I'M HELPING YOU.
NOBODY WOULD NOTICE YOU, EXCEPT TO FEEL SORRY FOR THE LITTLE KID. BUT I MADE SURE THEY ALL NOTICED YOU TODAY. THEY'LL BE WATCHING EVERY MOVE YOU MAKE.
ALL YOU HAVE TO DO TO EARN THEIR RESPECT NOW IS BE PERFECT.
SO I DON'T EVEN GET A CHANCE TO LEARN BEFORE I'M BEING JUDGED?
POOR KID. NOBODY'S TREATIN' HIM FAIR.
I'LL TELL YOU HOW TO GET A TOON. PROVE TO ME YOU KNOW WHAT YOU'RE DOING AS A SOLDIER. PROVE TO ME YOU KNOW HOW TO USE OTHER SOLDIERS. AND THEN PROVE TO ME THAT SOMEBODY'S WILLING TO FOLLOW YOU INTO BATTLE.
THEN YOU'LL GET YOUR TOON. BUT NOT BLOODY WELL UNTIL.
THAT'S FAIR. IF YOU ACTUALLY WORK THAT WAY, I'LL BE A TOON LEADER IN A MONTH.
WHEN I SAY I WORK A CERTAIN WAY, BEAN...
...THEN THAT'S THE WAY I WORK.

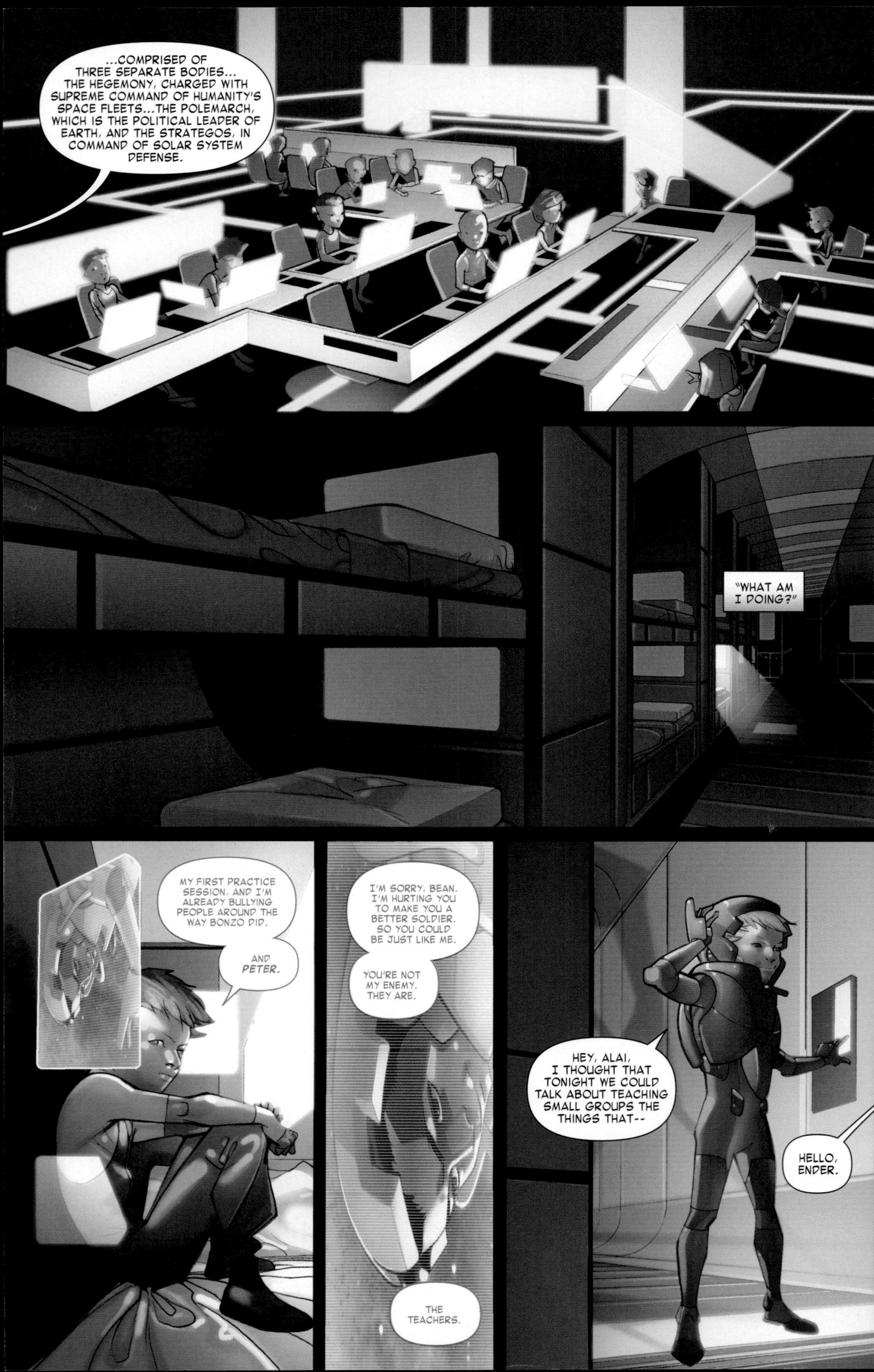
...COMPRISED OF THREE SEPARATE BODIES... THE HEGEMONY, CHARGED WITH SUPREME COMMAND OF HUMANITY'S SPACE FLEETS...THE POLEMARCH, WHICH IS THE POLITICAL LEADER OF EARTH, AND THE STRATEGOS, IN COMMAND OF SOLAR SYSTEM DEFENSE.
"WHAT AM I DOING?"
MY FIRST PRACTICE SESSION, AND I'M ALREADY BULLYING PEOPLE AROUND THE WAY BONZO DID.
AND *PETER*.
I'M SORRY, BEAN. I'M HURTING YOU TO MAKE YOU A BETTER SOLDIER. SO YOU COULD BE JUST LIKE ME.
YOU'RE NOT MY ENEMY. THEY ARE.
THE TEACHERS.
HEY, ALAI, I THOUGHT THAT TONIGHT WE COULD TALK ABOUT TEACHING SMALL GROUPS THE THINGS THAT--
HELLO, ENDER.

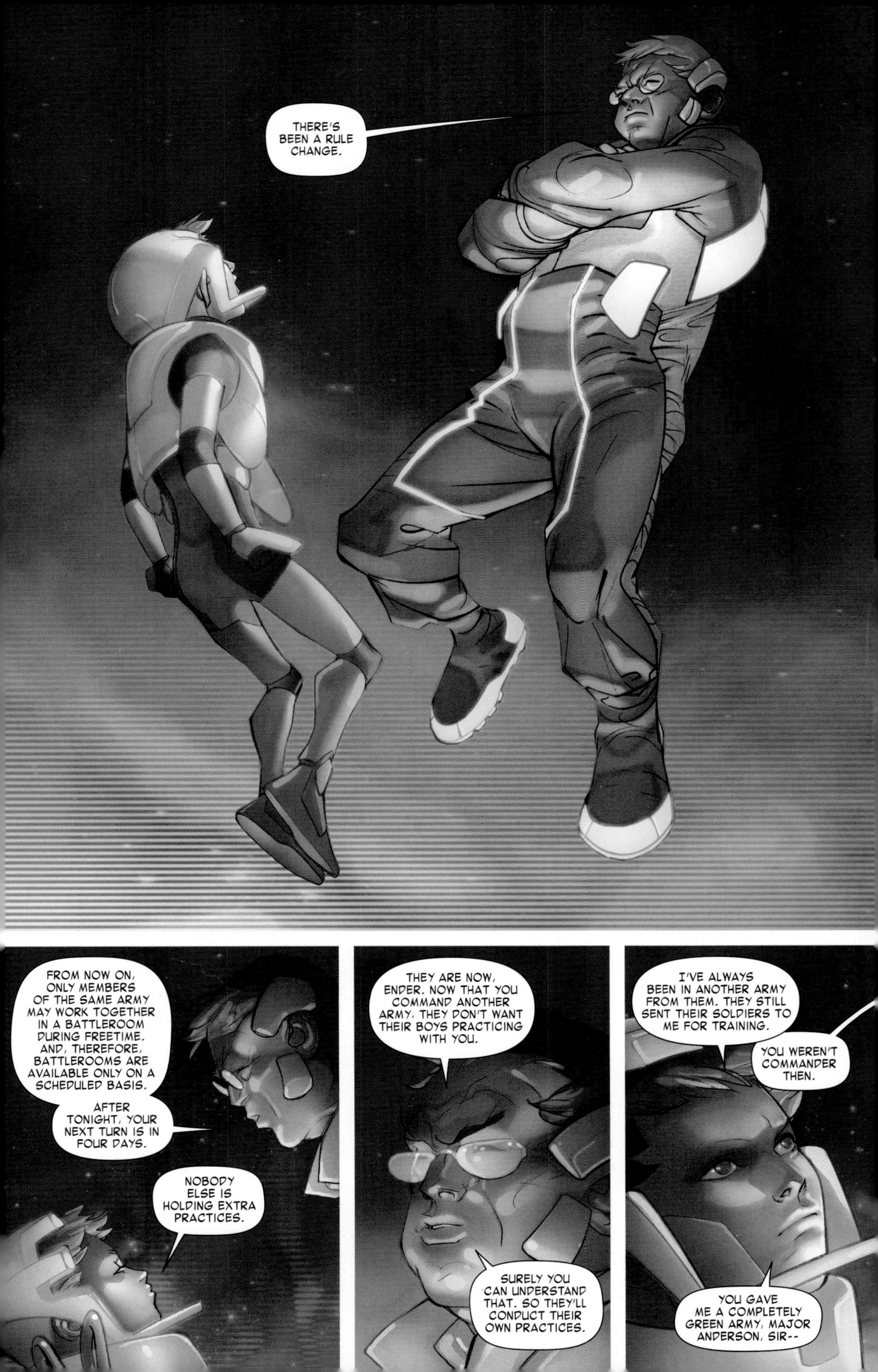
THERE'S BEEN A RULE CHANGE.
FROM NOW ON, ONLY MEMBERS OF THE SAME ARMY MAY WORK TOGETHER IN A BATTLEROOM DURING FREETIME. AND, THEREFORE, BATTLEROOMS ARE AVAILABLE ONLY ON A SCHEDULED BASIS.
AFTER TONIGHT, YOUR NEXT TURN IS IN FOUR DAYS.
NOBODY ELSE IS HOLDING EXTRA PRACTICES.
THEY ARE NOW, ENDER. NOW THAT YOU COMMAND ANOTHER ARMY, THEY DON'T WANT THEIR BOYS PRACTICING WITH YOU.
SURELY YOU CAN UNDERSTAND THAT. SO THEY'LL CONDUCT THEIR OWN PRACTICES.
I'VE ALWAYS BEEN IN ANOTHER ARMY FROM THEM. THEY STILL SENT THEIR SOLDIERS TO ME FOR TRAINING.
YOU WEREN'T COMMANDER THEN.
YOU GAVE ME A COMPLETELY GREEN ARMY, MAJOR ANDERSON, SIR--

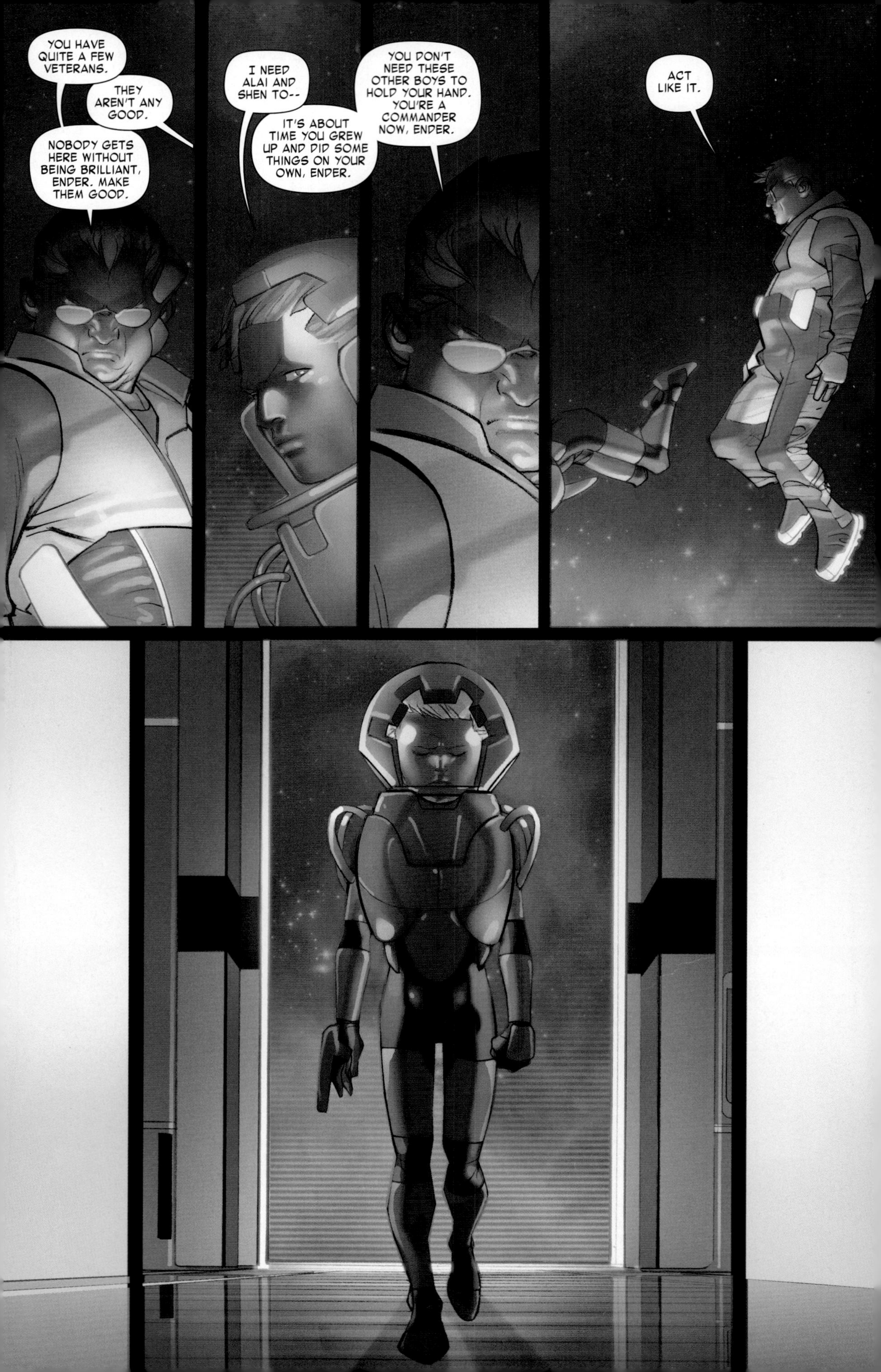
YOU HAVE QUITE A FEW VETERANS.
THEY AREN'T ANY GOOD.
NOBODY GETS HERE WITHOUT BEING BRILLIANT, ENDER. MAKE THEM GOOD.
I NEED ALAI AND SHEN TO--
IT'S ABOUT TIME YOU GREW UP AND DID SOME THINGS ON YOUR OWN, ENDER.
YOU DON'T NEED THESE OTHER BOYS TO HOLD YOUR HAND. YOU'RE A COMMANDER NOW, ENDER.
ACT LIKE IT.

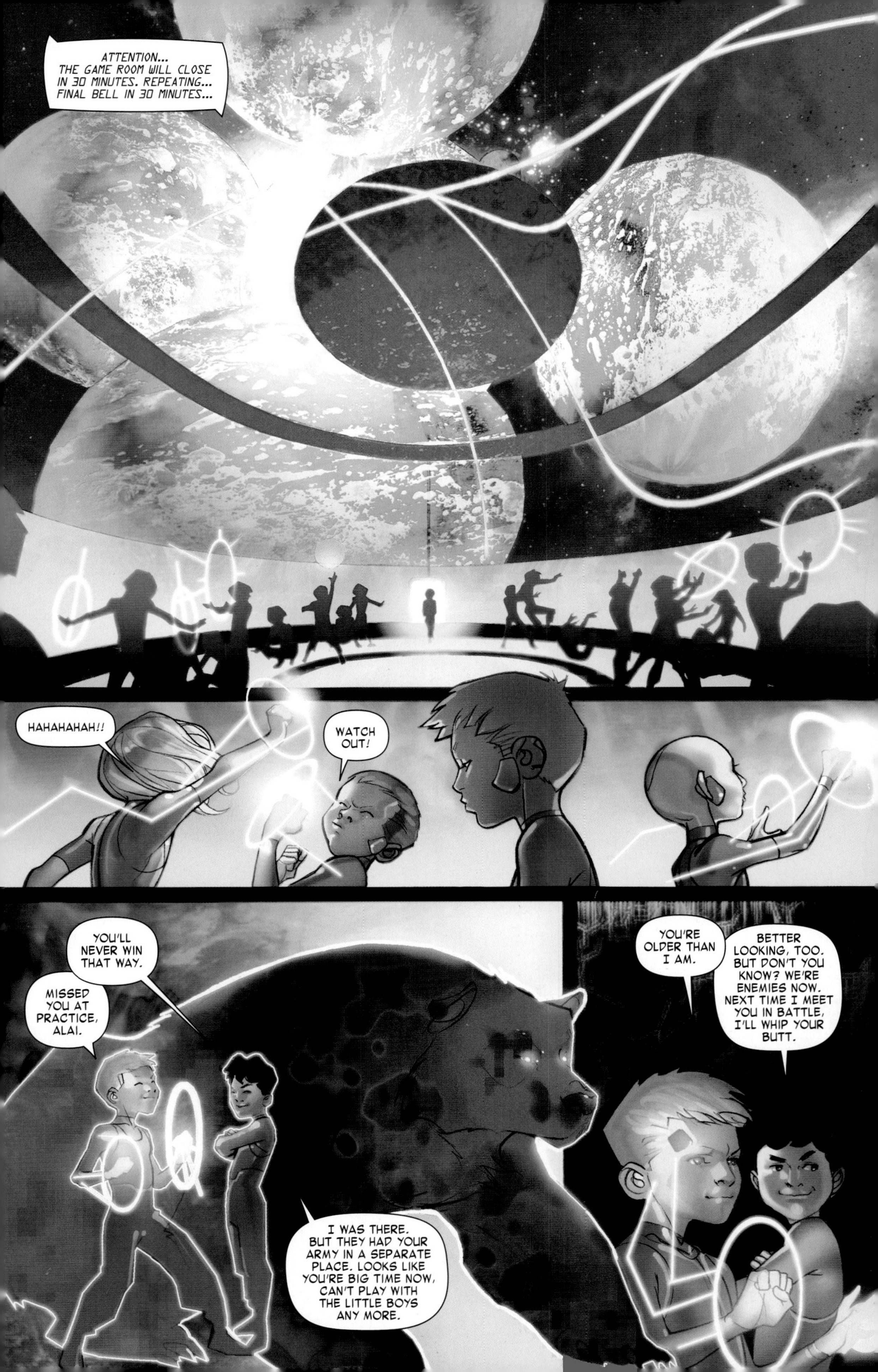
ATTENTION... THE GAME ROOM WILL CLOSE IN 30 MINUTES. REPEATING... FINAL BELL IN 30 MINUTES...
HAHAHAHAH!!
WATCH OUT!
YOU'LL NEVER WIN THAT WAY.
MISSED YOU AT PRACTICE, ALAI.
I WAS THERE. BUT THEY HAD YOUR ARMY IN A SEPARATE PLACE. LOOKS LIKE YOU'RE BIG TIME NOW, CAN'T PLAY WITH THE LITTLE BOYS ANY MORE.
YOU'RE OLDER THAN I AM.
BETTER LOOKING, TOO. BUT DON'T YOU KNOW? WE'RE ENEMIES NOW. NEXT TIME I MEET YOU IN BATTLE, I'LL WHIP YOUR BUTT.

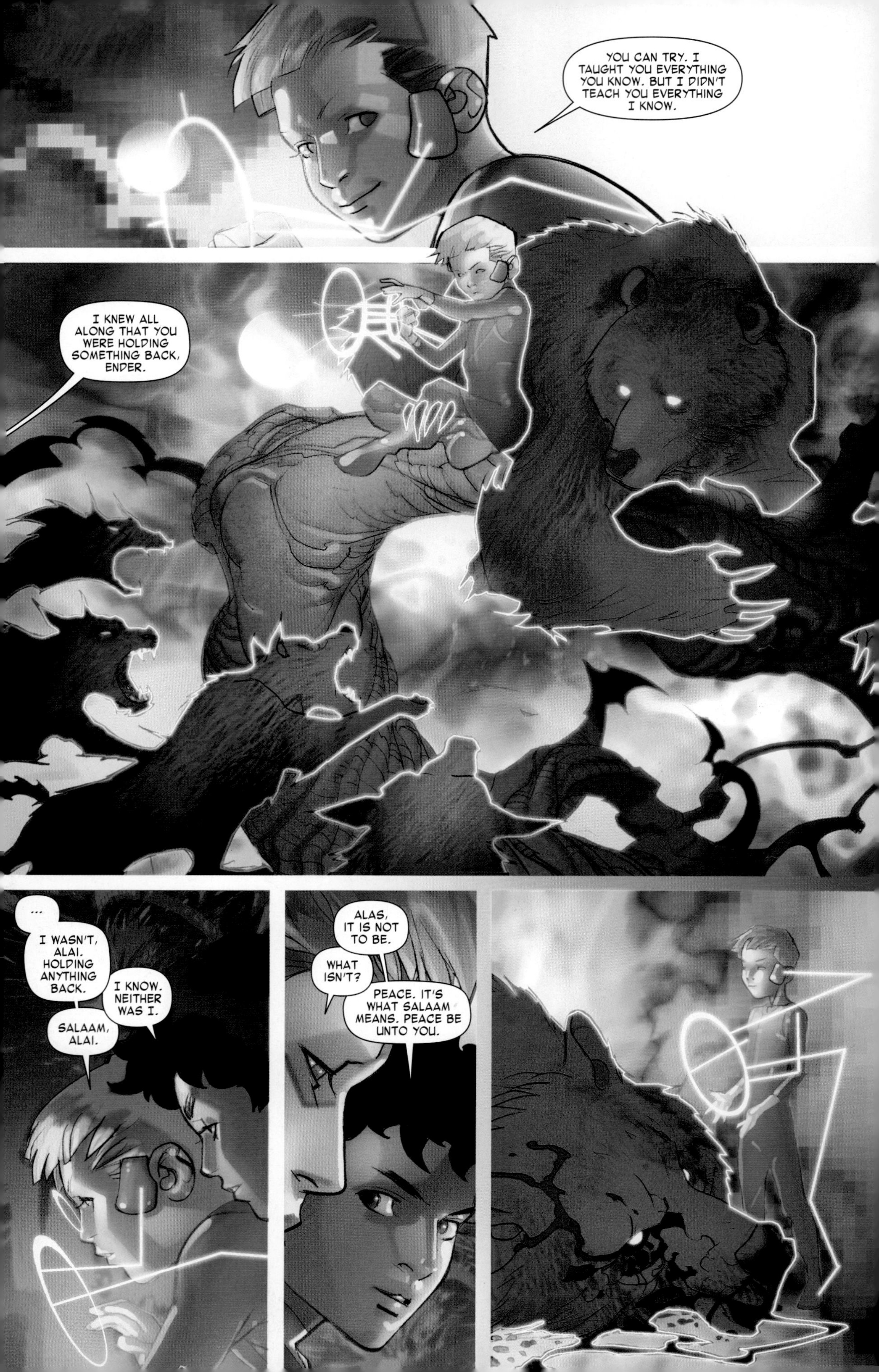
YOU CAN TRY. I TAUGHT YOU EVERYTHING YOU KNOW. BUT I DIDN'T TEACH YOU EVERYTHING I KNOW.
I KNEW ALL ALONG THAT YOU WERE HOLDING SOMETHING BACK, ENDER.
...
I WASN'T, ALAI. HOLDING ANYTHING BACK.
I KNOW. NEITHER WAS I.
SALAAM, ALAI.
ALAS, IT IS NOT TO BE.
WHAT ISN'T?
PEACE. IT'S WHAT SALAAM MEANS. PEACE BE UNTO YOU.

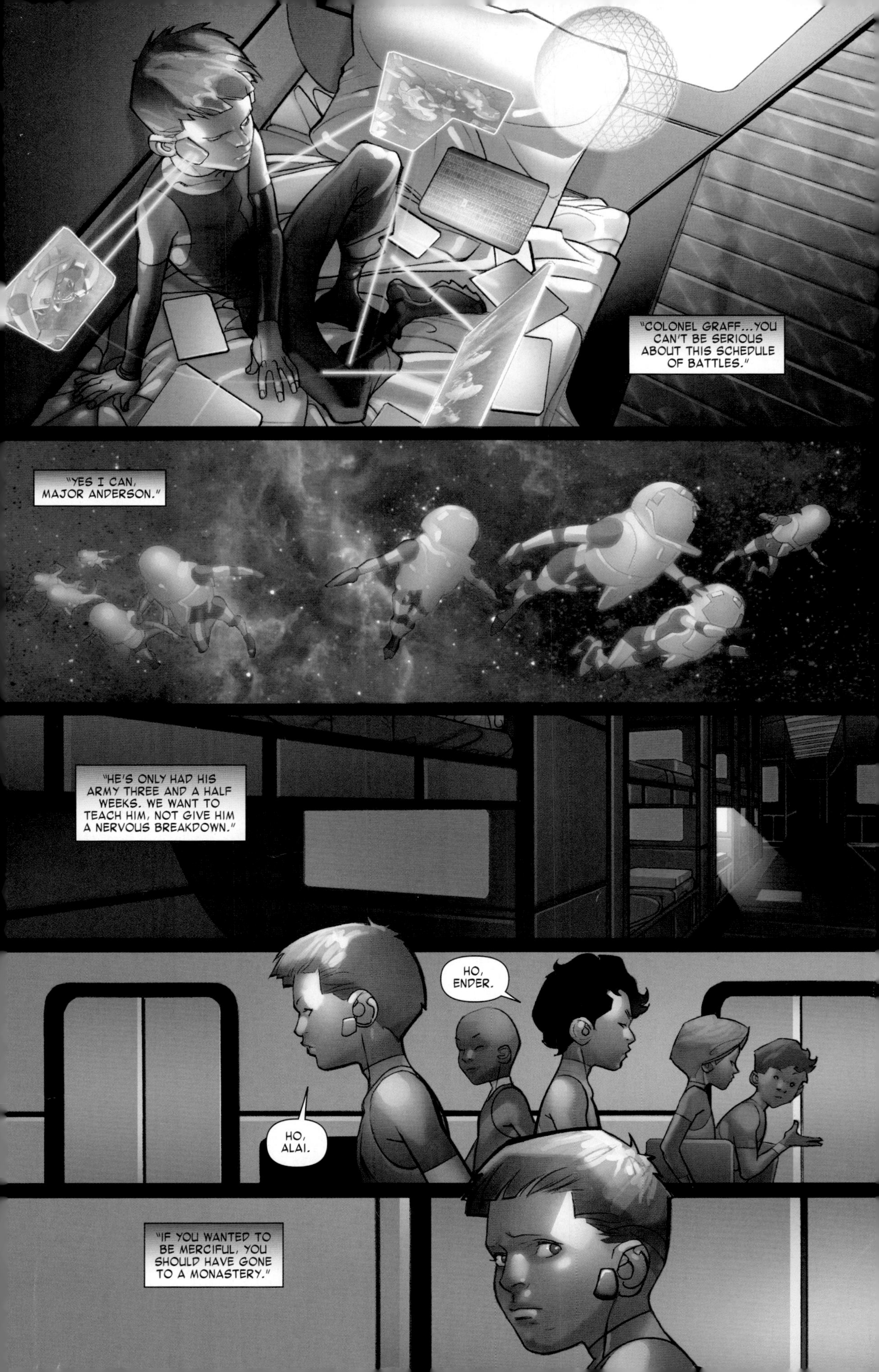
"COLONEL GRAFF...YOU CAN'T BE SERIOUS ABOUT THIS SCHEDULE OF BATTLES."
"YES I CAN, MAJOR ANDERSON."
"HE'S ONLY HAD HIS ARMY THREE AND A HALF WEEKS. WE WANT TO TEACH HIM, NOT GIVE HIM A NERVOUS BREAKDOWN."
HO, ENDER.
HO, ALAI.
"IF YOU WANTED TO BE MERCIFUL, YOU SHOULD HAVE GONE TO A MONASTERY."

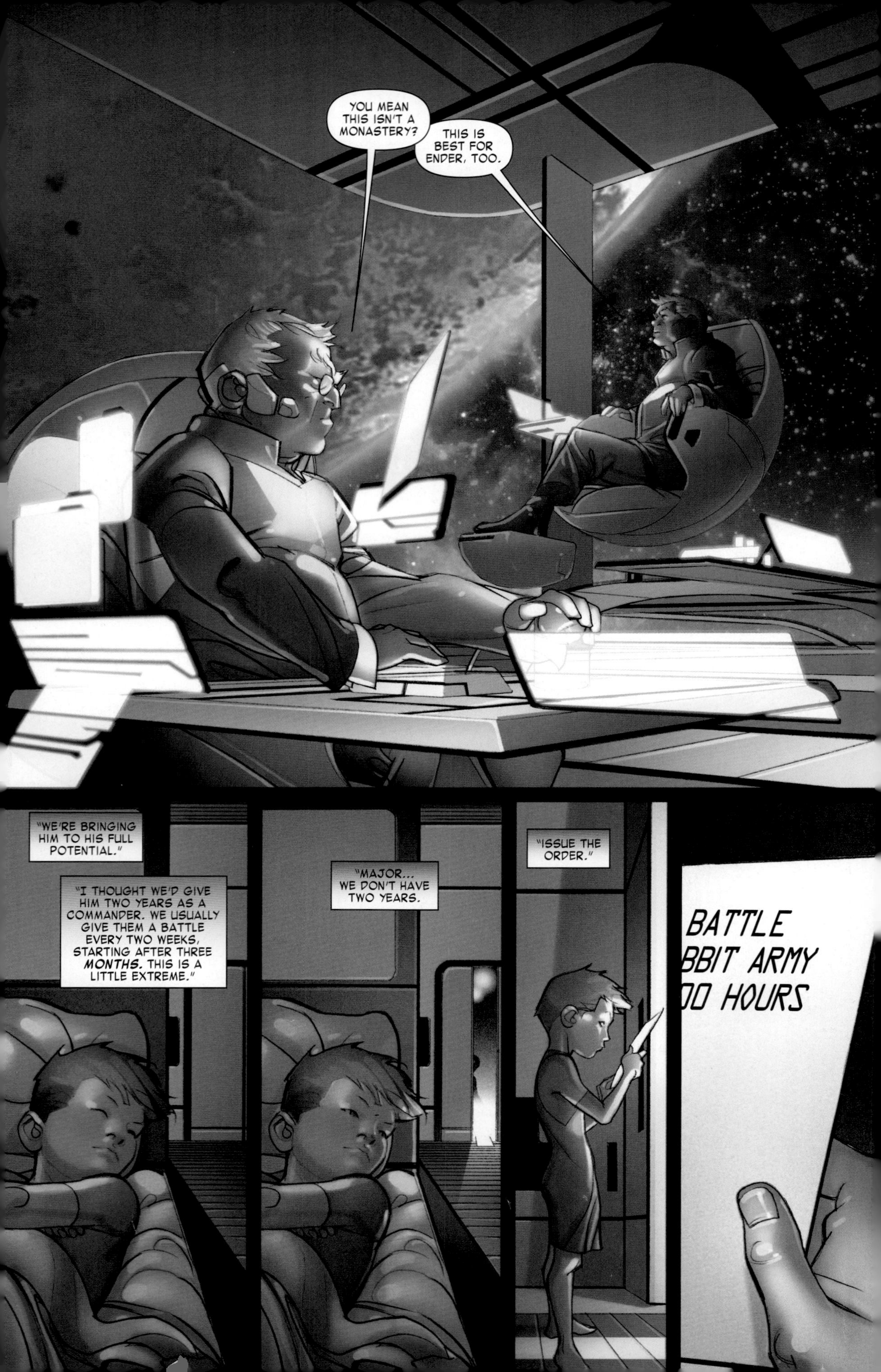
YOU MEAN THIS ISN'T A MONASTERY?
THIS IS BEST FOR ENDER, TOO.
"WE'RE BRINGING HIM TO HIS FULL POTENTIAL."
"I THOUGHT WE'D GIVE HIM TWO YEARS AS A COMMANDER. WE USUALLY GIVE THEM A BATTLE EVERY TWO WEEKS, STARTING AFTER THREE MONTHS. THIS IS A LITTLE EXTREME."
"MAJOR... WE DON'T HAVE TWO YEARS.
"ISSUE THE ORDER."
BATTLE
BBIT ARMY
00 HOURS

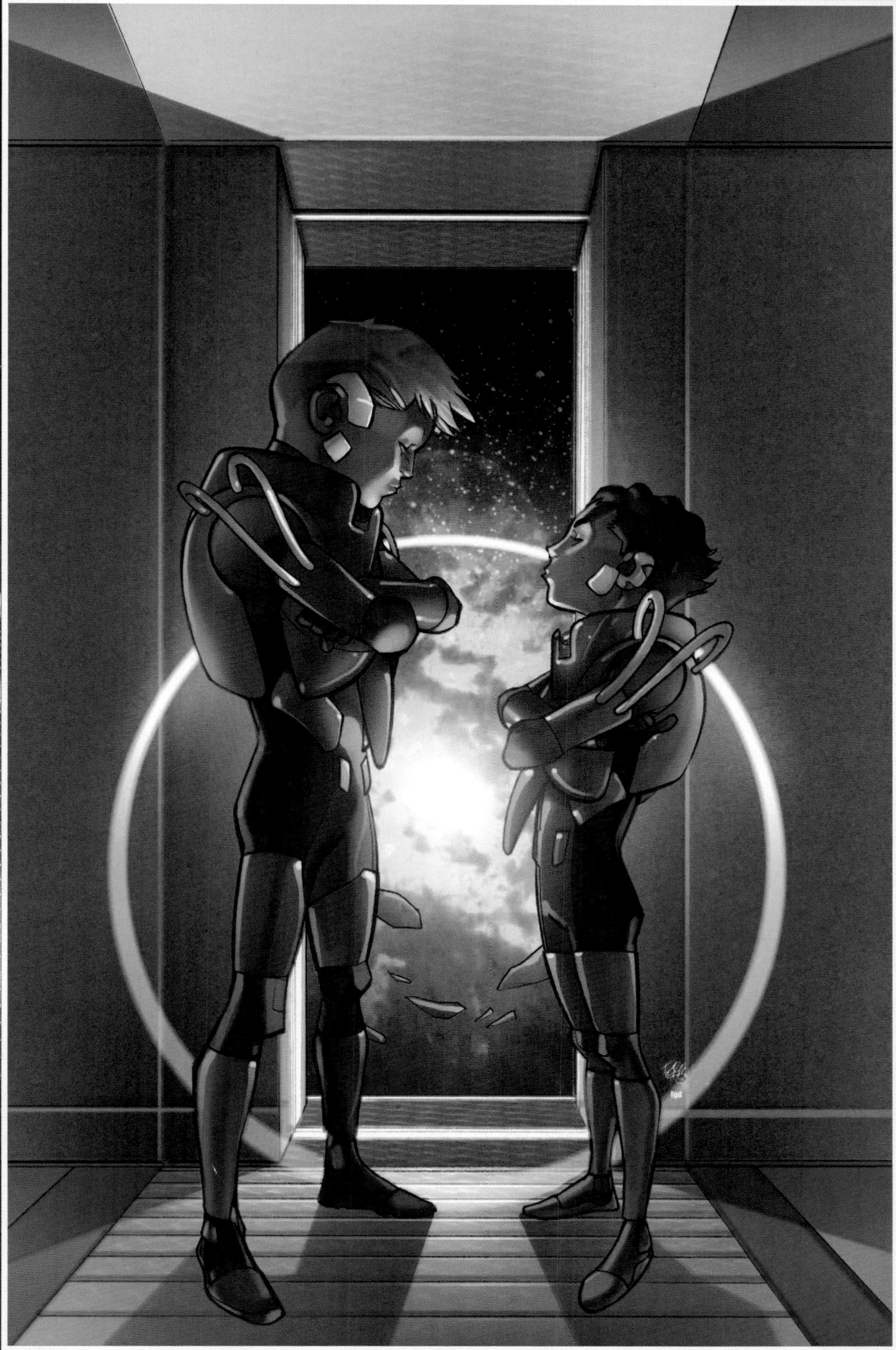

T W O

INTERNATIONAL FLEET MONITORED COMMUNICATIONS
PARTICIPANTS: COLONEL H. GRAFF, MAJOR J. ANDERSON
REF ID # 22457-86431, KEYWORD SEARCH: 'SCHEDULE'

<<<THIS CONVERSATION WAS RECORDED PRIOR TO BEGINNING OF THE
DRAGON ARMY SCHEDULE OF BATTLES>>>

GRAFF: I have this picture of Ender a year from now. Completely worn
out, because he was pushed farther than he or any living person could go.

ANDERSON: We told the computer that our highest priority was having
the subject remain useful after the training program.

G: Well, as long as he's useful—

A: Look, Colonel Graff, you're the one who made me prepare this, over
my protests if you'll remember.

G: I know, you're right, I shouldn't burden you with my conscience.
But my eagerness to sacrifice little children in order to save mankind is
wearing thin. There are people already figuring how children should be
used as soon as the Formics are destroyed.

A: Seems premature.

G: It seems insane. And it's for those people that we're pushing Ender to
the edge of human endurance.

A: I think you underestimate Ender.

G: But I fear that I also underestimate the stupidity of the rest of
mankind. Are we absolutely certain that we ought to win this war?

A: Sir, those words sound like treason.

G: It was black humor.

A: It wasn't funny. When it comes to the Formics, nothing—

G: Nothing is funny, I know.

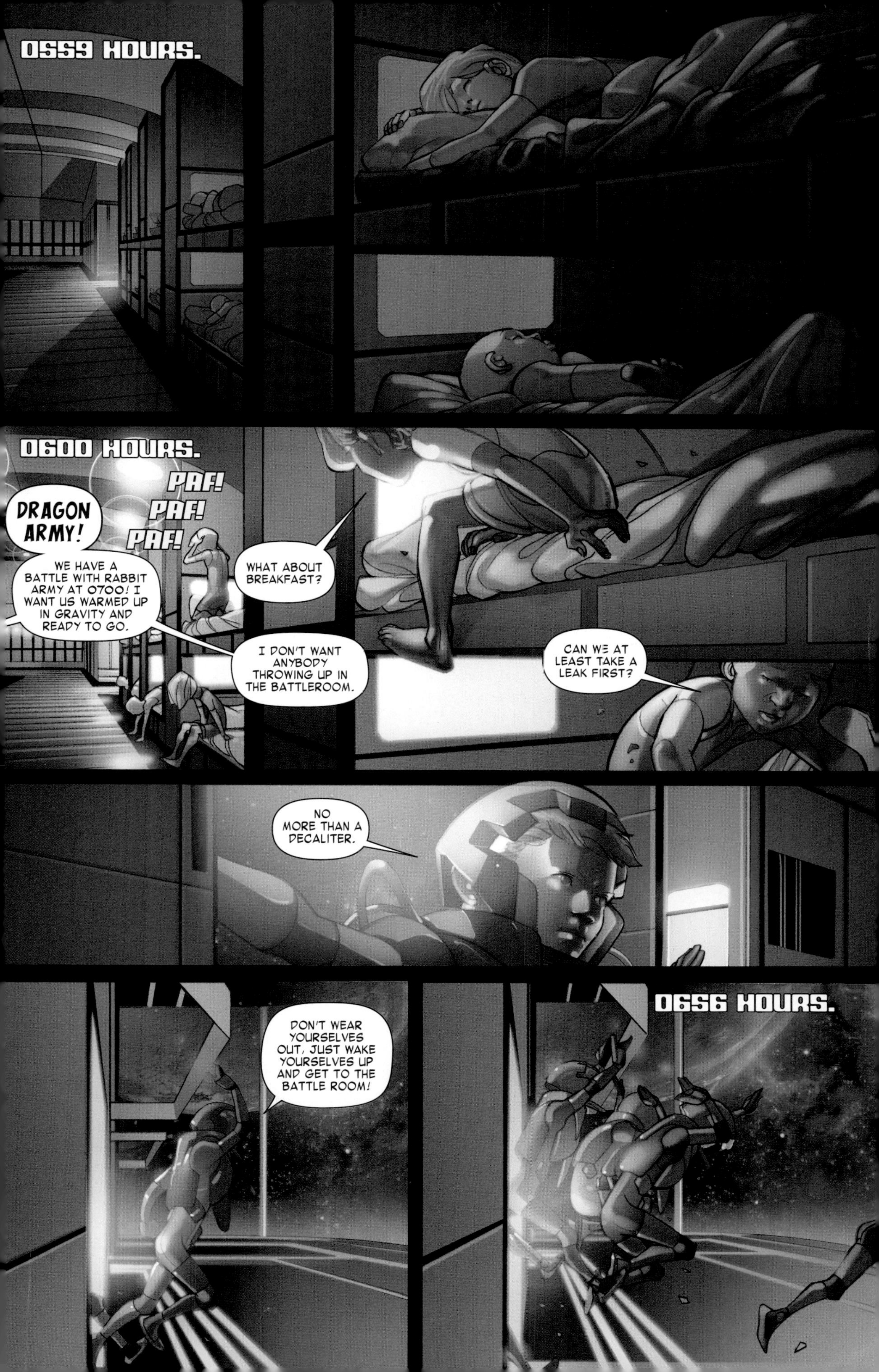

0559 HOURS.
0600 HOURS.
PAF!
PAF!
PAF!
DRAGON ARMY!
WE HAVE A BATTLE WITH RABBIT ARMY AT 0700! I WANT US WARMED UP IN GRAVITY AND READY TO GO.
WHAT ABOUT BREAKFAST?
I DON'T WANT ANYBODY THROWING UP IN THE BATTLEROOM.
CAN WE AT LEAST TAKE A LEAK FIRST?
NO MORE THAN A DECALITER.
DON'T WEAR YOURSELVES OUT, JUST WAKE YOURSELVES UP AND GET TO THE BATTLE ROOM!
0656 HOURS.

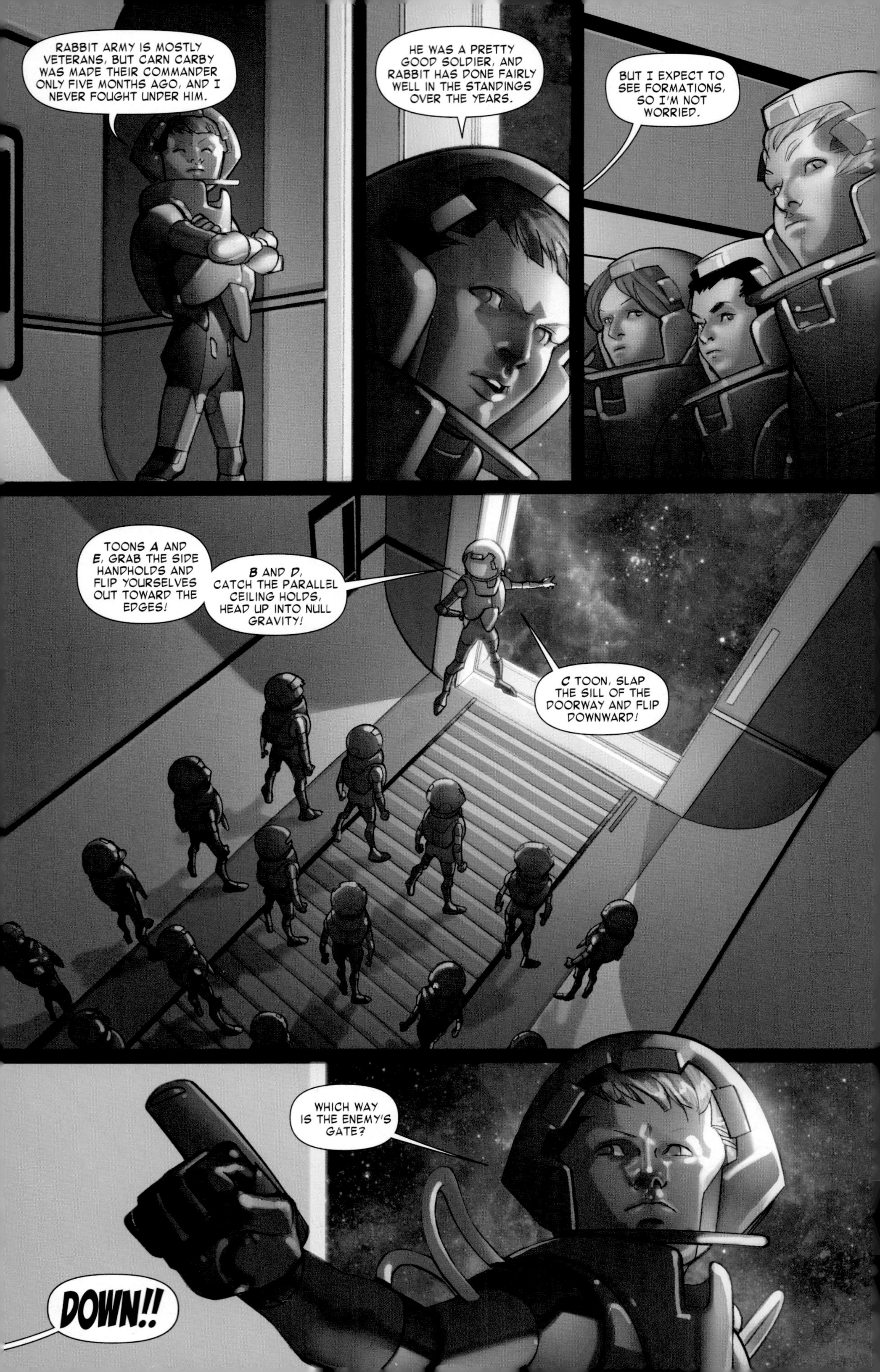
RABBIT ARMY IS MOSTLY VETERANS, BUT CARN CARBY WAS MADE THEIR COMMANDER ONLY FIVE MONTHS AGO, AND I NEVER FOUGHT UNDER HIM.
HE WAS A PRETTY GOOD SOLDIER, AND RABBIT HAS DONE FAIRLY WELL IN THE STANDINGS OVER THE YEARS.
BUT I EXPECT TO SEE FORMATIONS, SO I'M NOT WORRIED.
TOONS A AND E, GRAB THE SIDE HANDHOLDS AND FLIP YOURSELVES OUT TOWARD THE EDGES!
B AND D, CATCH THE PARALLEL CEILING HOLDS, HEAD UP INTO NULL GRAVITY!
C TOON, SLAP THE SILL OF THE DOORWAY AND FLIP DOWNWARD!
WHICH WAY IS THE ENEMY'S GATE?
DOWN!!

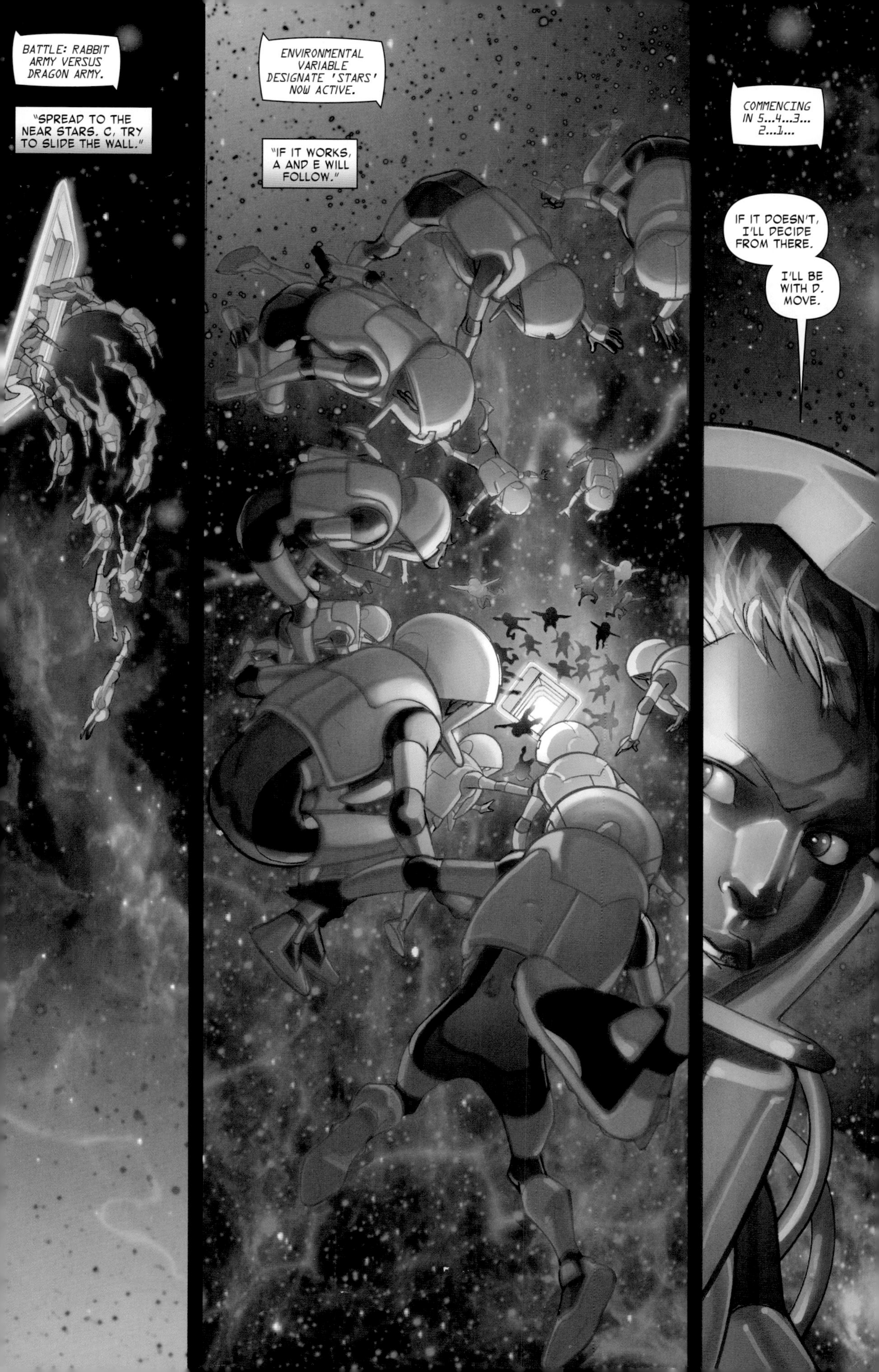
BATTLE: RABBIT ARMY VERSUS DRAGON ARMY.
"SPREAD TO THE NEAR STARS. C, TRY TO SLIDE THE WALL."
ENVIRONMENTAL VARIABLE DESIGNATE 'STARS' NOW ACTIVE.
"IF IT WORKS, A AND E WILL FOLLOW."
COMMENCING IN 5...4...3... 2...1...
IF IT DOESN'T, I'LL DECIDE FROM THERE.
I'LL BE WITH D. MOVE.

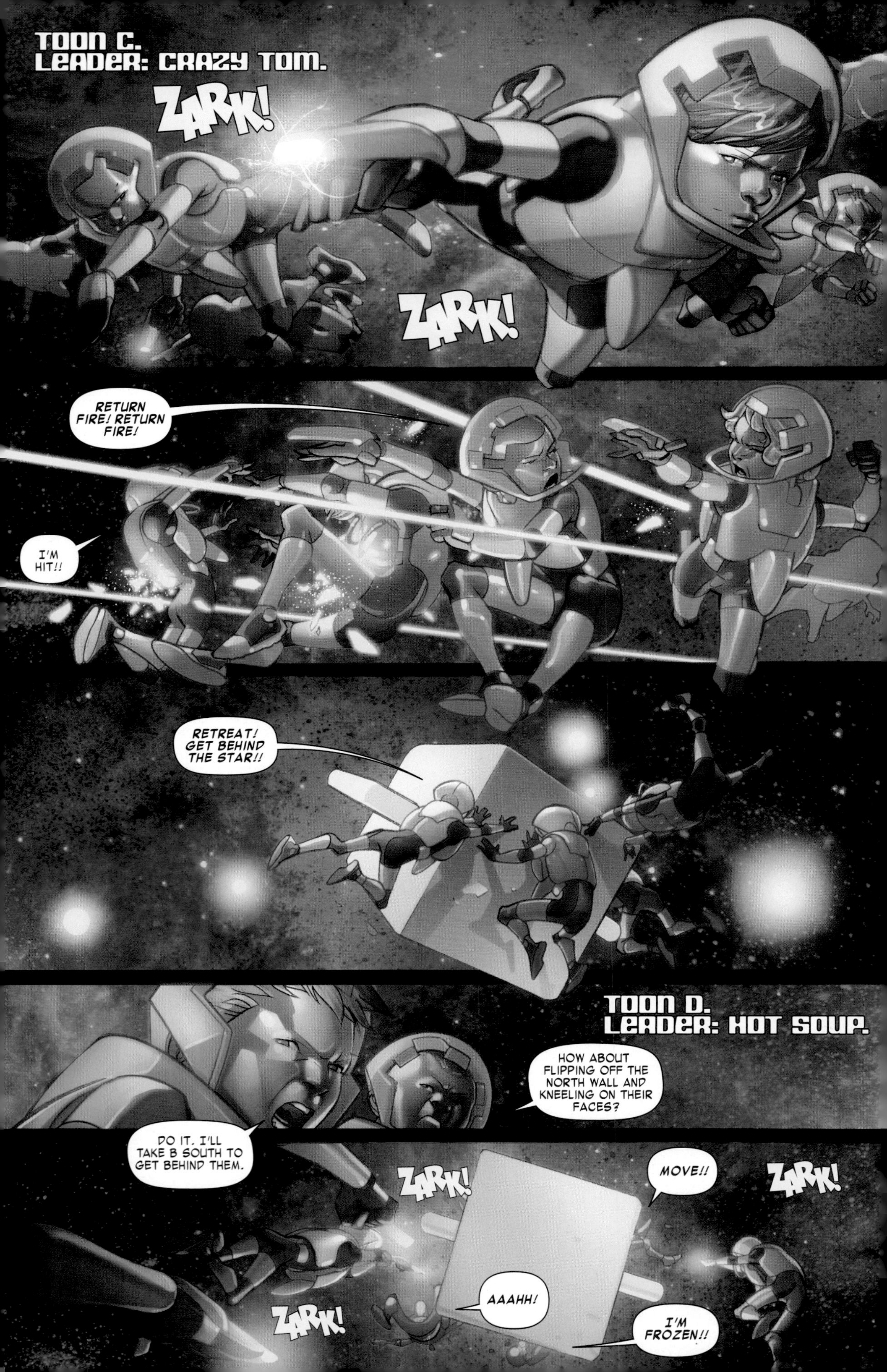
TOON C.
LEADER: CRAZY TOM.
ZARK!
ZARK!
RETURN FIRE! RETURN FIRE!
I'M HIT!!
RETREAT! GET BEHIND THE STAR!!
TOON D.
LEADER: HOT SOUP.
HOW ABOUT FLIPPING OFF THE NORTH WALL AND KNEELING ON THEIR FACES?
DO IT. I'LL TAKE B SOUTH TO GET BEHIND THEM.
ZARK!
MOVE!!
ZARK!
ZARK!
AAAHH!
I'M FROZEN!!

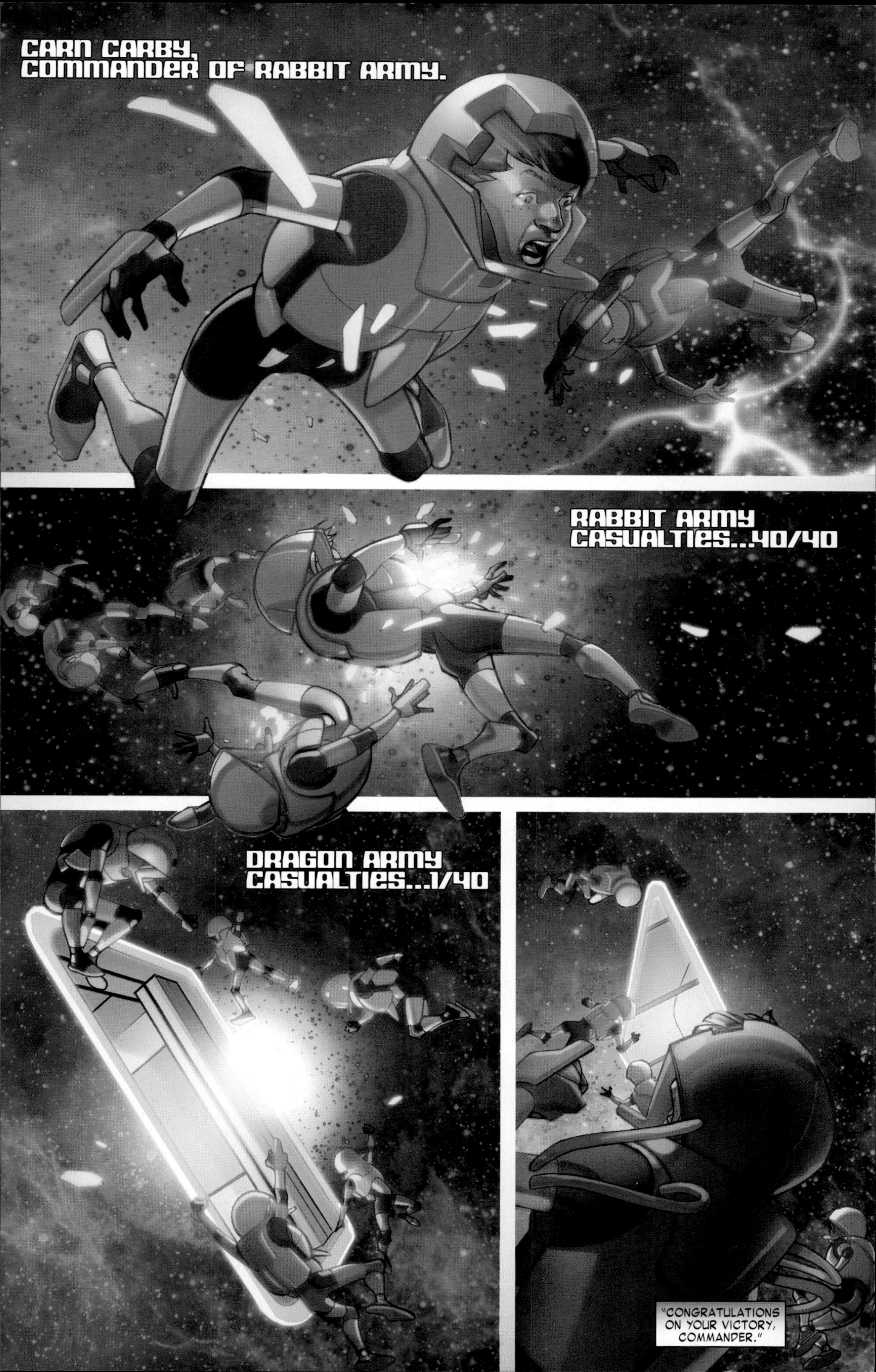

CARN CARBY,
COMMANDER OF RABBIT ARMY.
RABBIT ARMY
CASUALTIES...40/40
DRAGON ARMY
CASUALTIES...1/40
"CONGRATULATIONS ON YOUR VICTORY, COMMANDER."

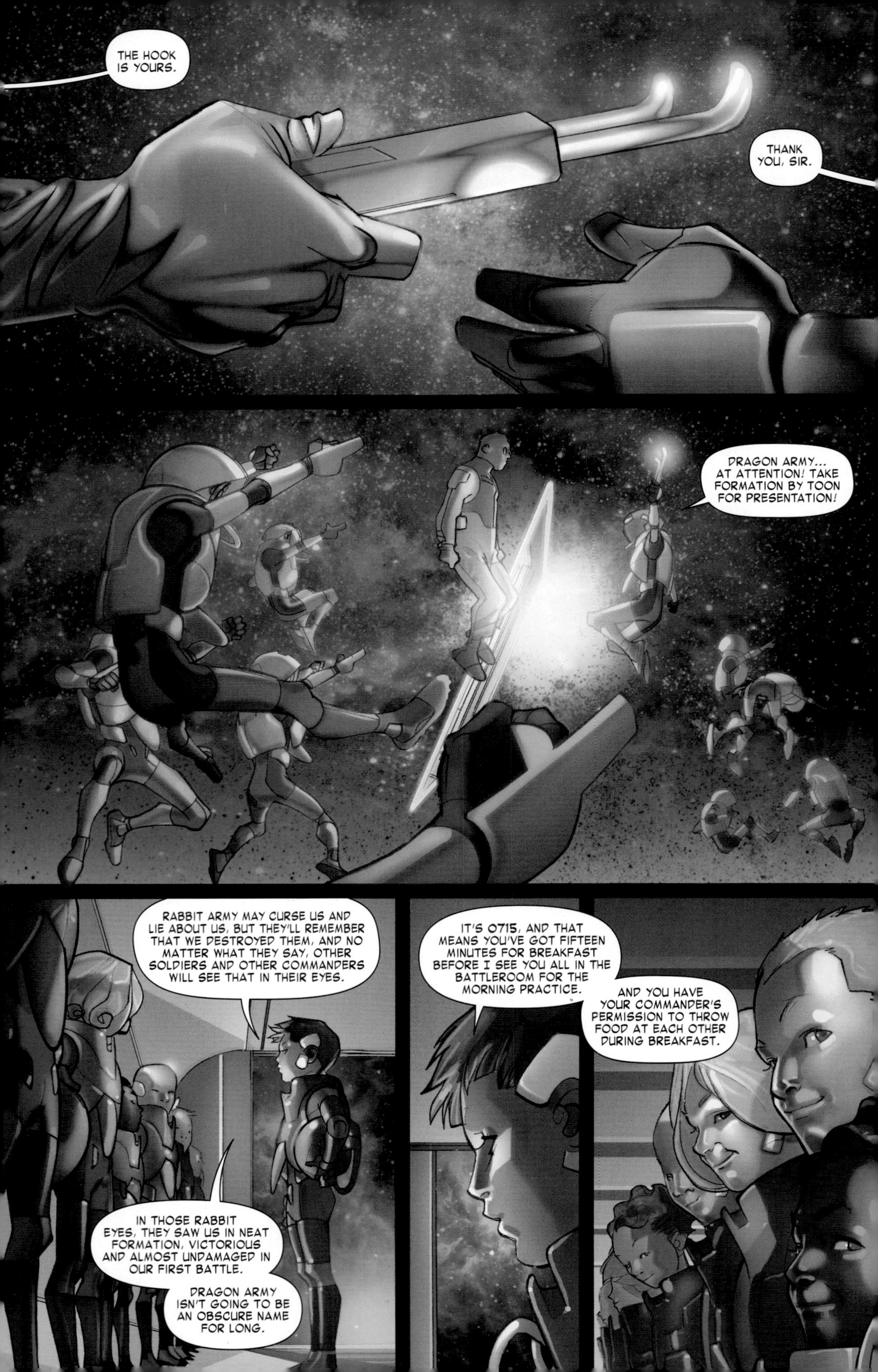
THE HOOK IS YOURS.
THANK YOU, SIR.
DRAGON ARMY... AT ATTENTION! TAKE FORMATION BY TOON FOR PRESENTATION!
RABBIT ARMY MAY CURSE US AND LIE ABOUT US, BUT THEY'LL REMEMBER THAT WE DESTROYED THEM, AND NO MATTER WHAT THEY SAY, OTHER SOLDIERS AND OTHER COMMANDERS WILL SEE THAT IN THEIR EYES.
IN THOSE RABBIT EYES, THEY SAW US IN NEAT FORMATION, VICTORIOUS AND ALMOST UNDAMAGED IN OUR FIRST BATTLE.
DRAGON ARMY ISN'T GOING TO BE AN OBSCURE NAME FOR LONG.
IT'S 0715, AND THAT MEANS YOU'VE GOT FIFTEEN MINUTES FOR BREAKFAST BEFORE I SEE YOU ALL IN THE BATTLEROOM FOR THE MORNING PRACTICE.
AND YOU HAVE YOUR COMMANDER'S PERMISSION TO THROW FOOD AT EACH OTHER DURING BREAKFAST.

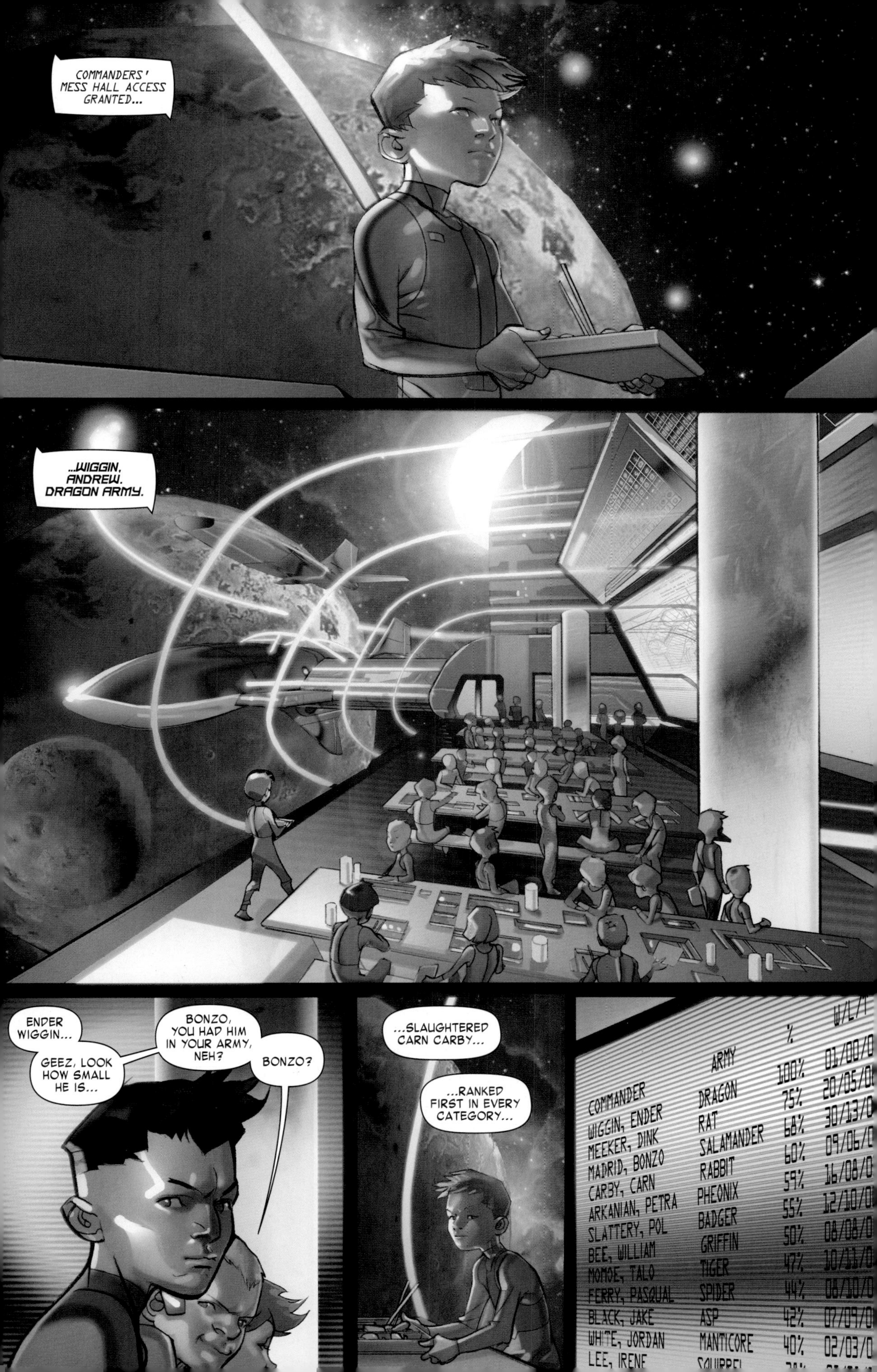

COMMANDERS' MESS HALL ACCESS GRANTED...
...WIGGIN, ANDREW. DRAGON ARMY.
ENDER WIGGIN...
GEEZ, LOOK HOW SMALL HE IS...
BONZO, YOU HAD HIM IN YOUR ARMY, NEH?
BONZO?
...SLAUGHTERED CARN CARBY...
...RANKED FIRST IN EVERY CATEGORY...
COMMANDER
ARMY
%
W/L/T
WIGGIN, ENDER DRAGON 100% 01/00/0
MEEKER, DINK RAT 75% 20/05/0
MADRID, BONZO SALAMANDER 68% 30/13/0
CARBY, CARN RABBIT 60% 09/06/0
ARKANIAN, PETRA PHEONIX 59% 16/08/0
SLATTERY, POL BADGER 55% 12/10/0
BEE, WILLIAM GRIFFIN 50% 08/08/0
MOMOE, TALO TIGER 47% 10/11/0
FERRY, PASQUAL SPIDER 44% 08/10/0
BLACK, JAKE ASP 42% 07/09/0
WHITE, JORDAN MANTICORE 40% 02/03/0
LEE, IRENE

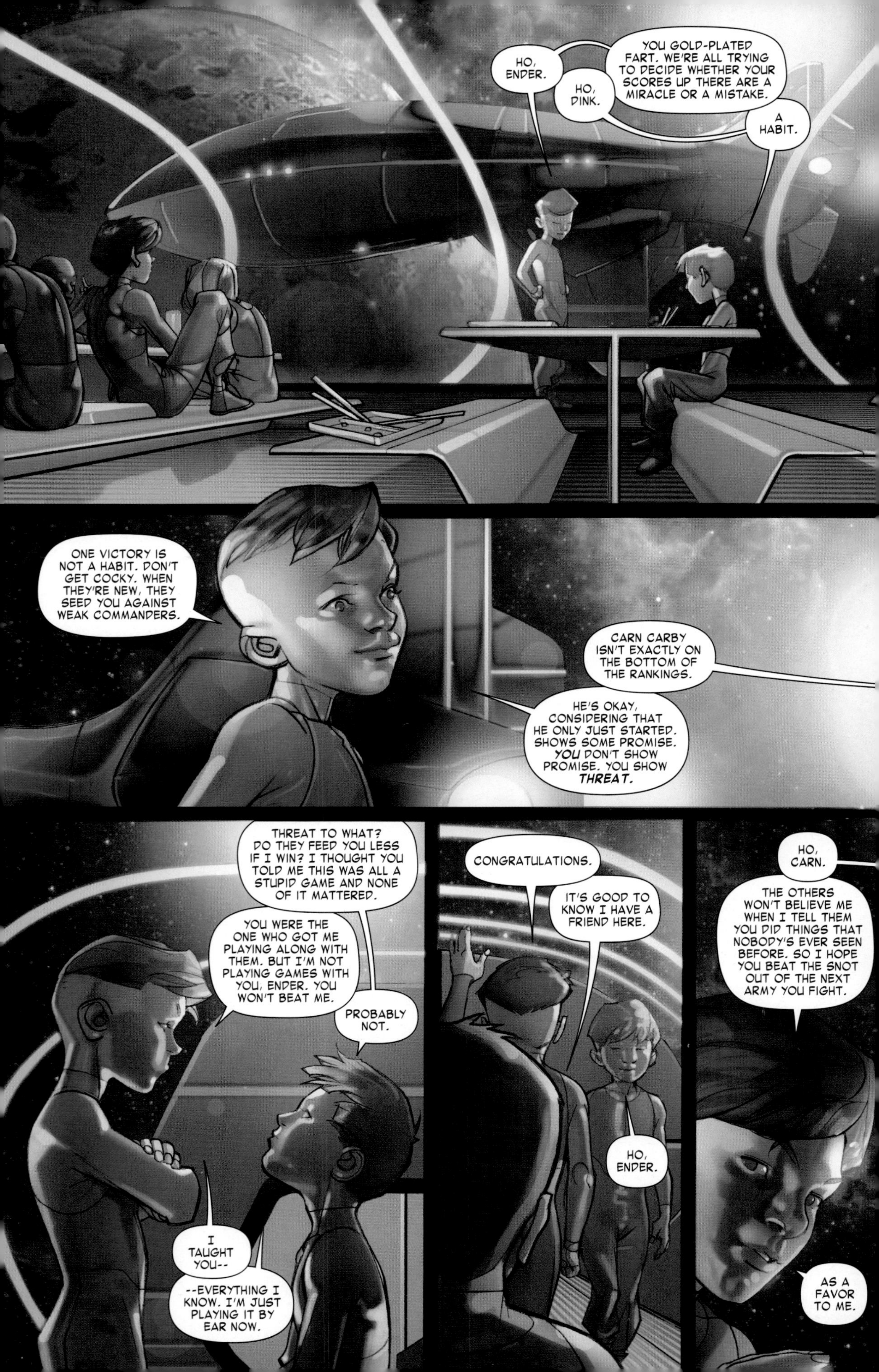
HO, ENDER.
HO, DINK.
YOU GOLD-PLATED FART. WE'RE ALL TRYING TO DECIDE WHETHER YOUR SCORES UP THERE ARE A MIRACLE OR A MISTAKE.
A HABIT.
ONE VICTORY IS NOT A HABIT. DON'T GET COCKY. WHEN THEY'RE NEW, THEY SEED YOU AGAINST WEAK COMMANDERS.
CARN CARBY ISN'T EXACTLY ON THE BOTTOM OF THE RANKINGS.
HE'S OKAY, CONSIDERING THAT HE ONLY JUST STARTED. SHOWS SOME PROMISE. YOU DON'T SHOW PROMISE. YOU SHOW THREAT.
THREAT TO WHAT? DO THEY FEED YOU LESS IF I WIN? I THOUGHT YOU TOLD ME THIS WAS ALL A STUPID GAME AND NONE OF IT MATTERED.
YOU WERE THE ONE WHO GOT ME PLAYING ALONG WITH THEM. BUT I'M NOT PLAYING GAMES WITH YOU, ENDER. YOU WON'T BEAT ME.
PROBABLY NOT.
I TAUGHT YOU--
--EVERYTHING I KNOW. I'M JUST PLAYING IT BY EAR NOW.
CONGRATULATIONS.
IT'S GOOD TO KNOW I HAVE A FRIEND HERE.
HO, ENDER.
HO, CARN.
THE OTHERS WON'T BELIEVE ME WHEN I TELL THEM YOU DID THINGS THAT NOBODY'S EVER SEEN BEFORE. SO I HOPE YOU BEAT THE SNOT OUT OF THE NEXT ARMY YOU FIGHT.
AS A FAVOR TO ME.

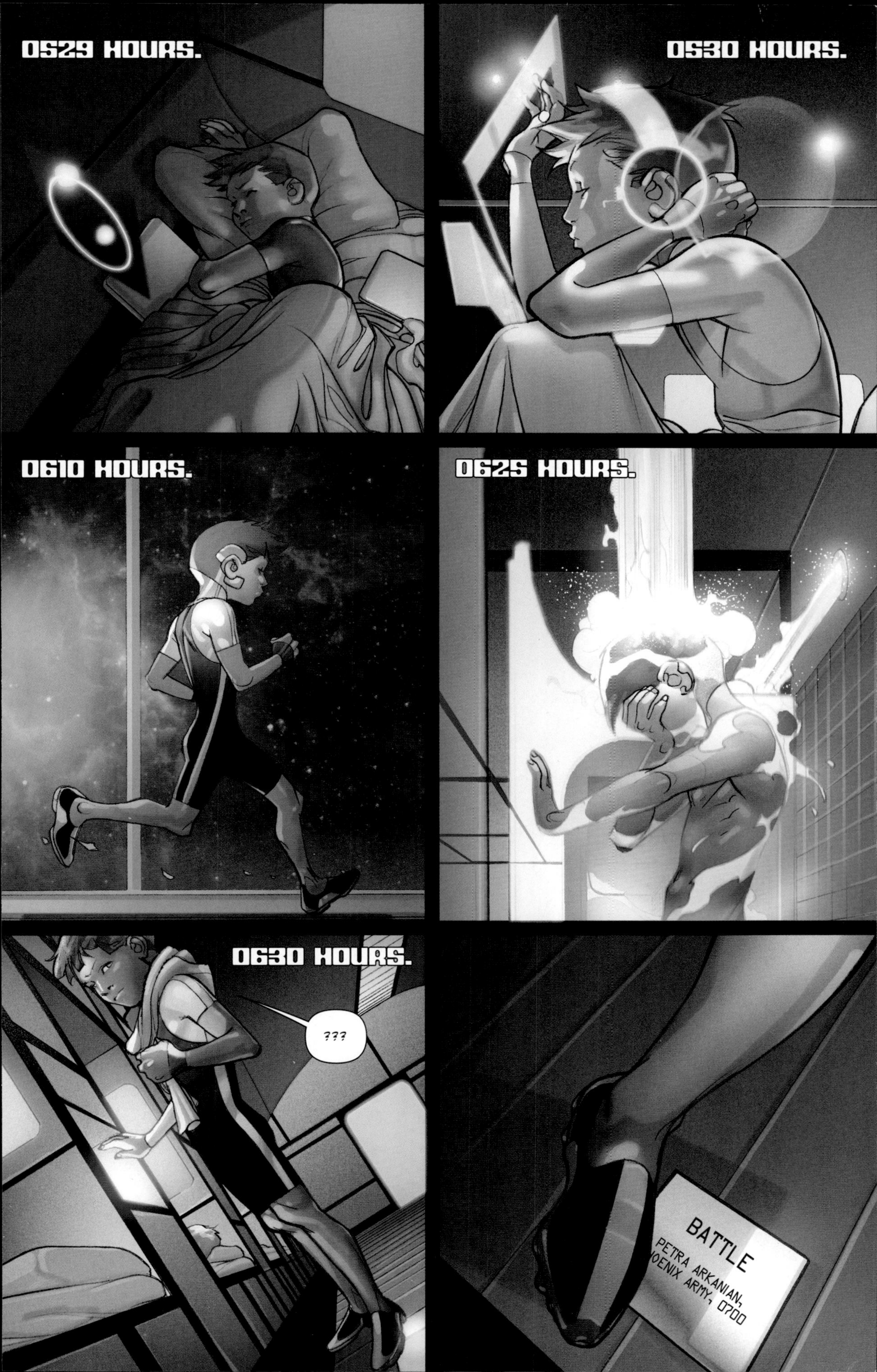
0529 HOURS.
0530 HOURS.
0610 HOURS.
0625 HOURS.
0630 HOURS.
???
BATTLE
PETRA ARKANIAN,
OENIX ARMY, 0700

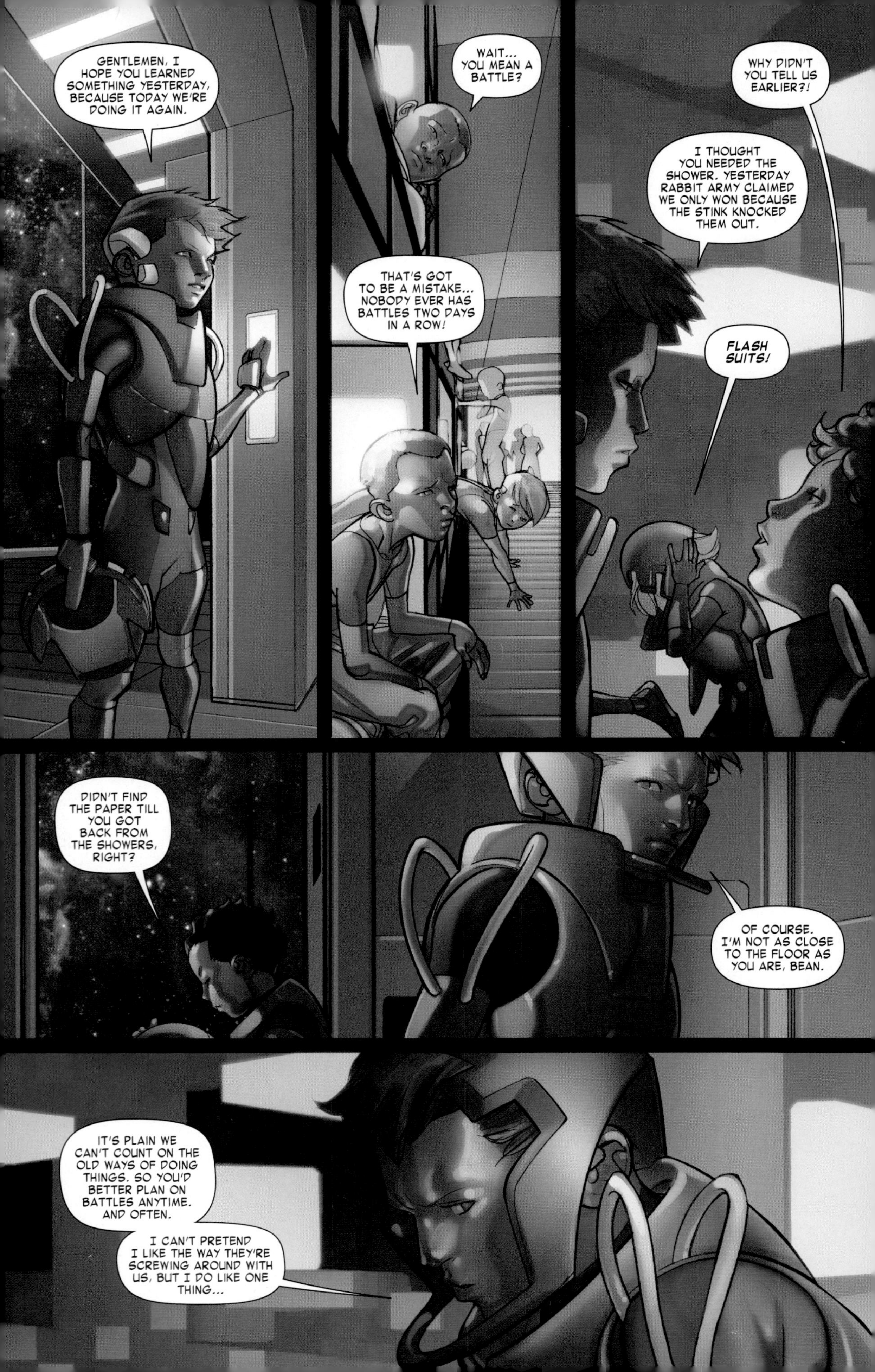
GENTLEMEN, I HOPE YOU LEARNED SOMETHING YESTERDAY, BECAUSE TODAY WE'RE DOING IT AGAIN.
WAIT... YOU MEAN A BATTLE?
THAT'S GOT TO BE A MISTAKE... NOBODY EVER HAS BATTLES TWO DAYS IN A ROW!
WHY DIDN'T YOU TELL US EARLIER?!
I THOUGHT YOU NEEDED THE SHOWER. YESTERDAY RABBIT ARMY CLAIMED WE ONLY WON BECAUSE THE STINK KNOCKED THEM OUT.
FLASH SUITS!
DIDN'T FIND THE PAPER TILL YOU GOT BACK FROM THE SHOWERS, RIGHT?
OF COURSE. I'M NOT AS CLOSE TO THE FLOOR AS YOU ARE, BEAN.
IT'S PLAIN WE CAN'T COUNT ON THE OLD WAYS OF DOING THINGS. SO YOU'D BETTER PLAN ON BATTLES ANYTIME. AND OFTEN.
I CAN'T PRETEND I LIKE THE WAY THEY'RE SCREWING AROUND WITH US, BUT I DO LIKE ONE THING...

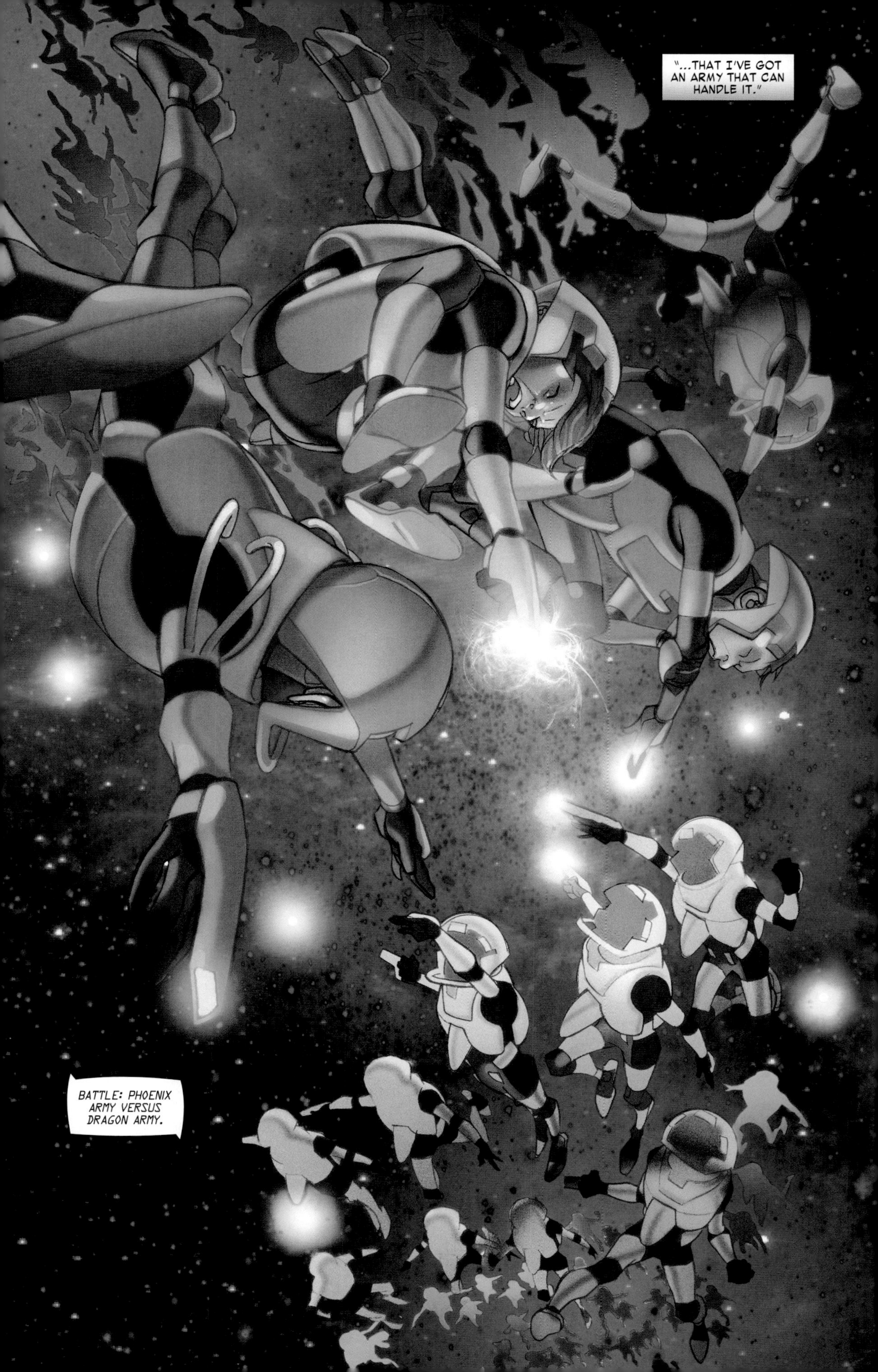
"...THAT I'VE GOT AN ARMY THAT CAN HANDLE IT."
BATTLE: PHOENIX ARMY VERSUS DRAGON ARMY.

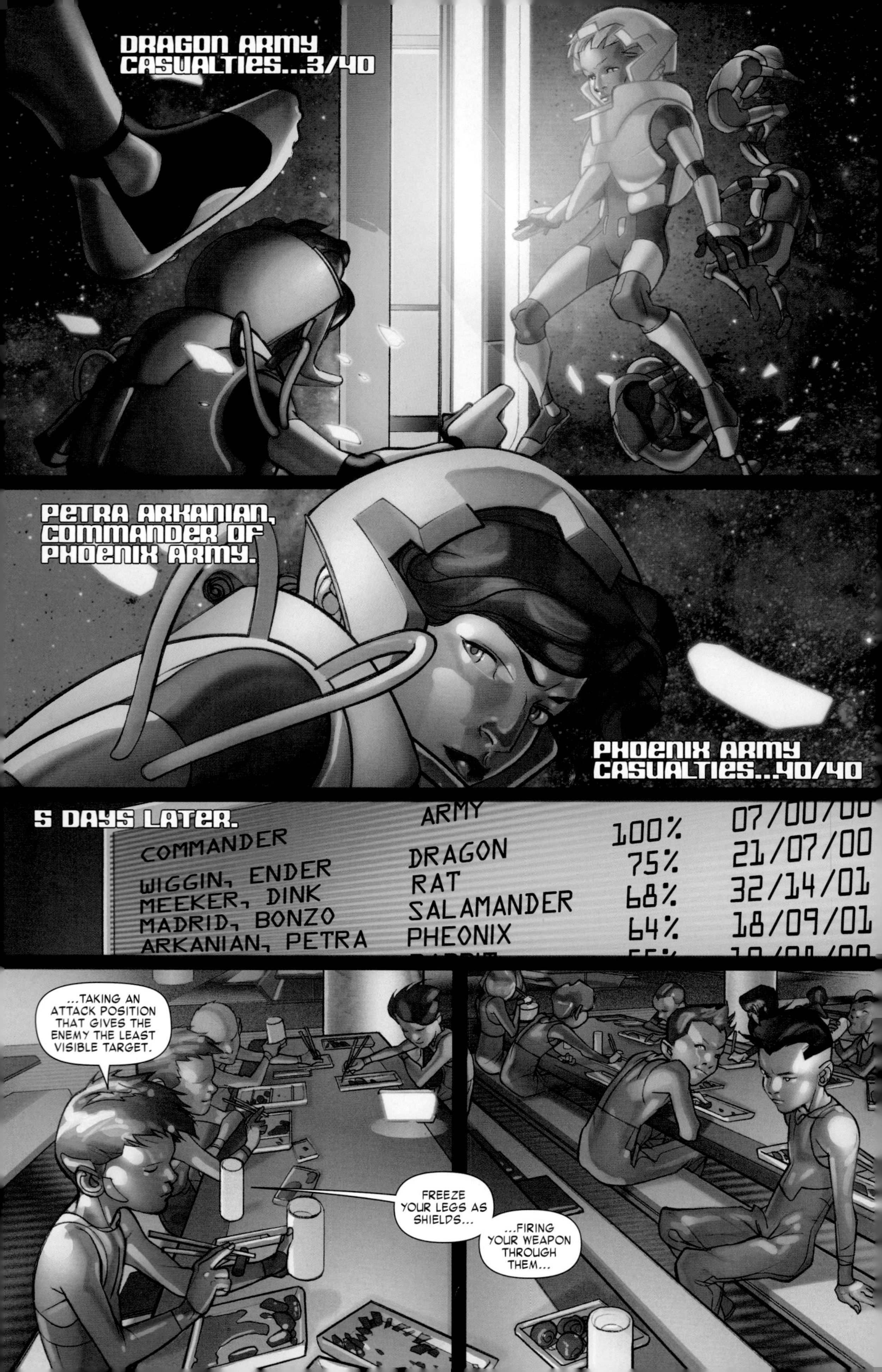
DRAGON ARMY CASUALTIES...3/40
PETRA ARKANIAN, COMMANDER OF PHOENIX ARMY.
PHOENIX ARMY CASUALTIES...40/40
5 DAYS LATER.
COMMANDER
ARMY
WIGGIN, ENDER DRAGON 100% 07/00/00
MEEKER, DINK RAT 75% 21/07/00
MADRID, BONZO SALAMANDER 68% 32/14/01
ARKANIAN, PETRA PHEONIX 64% 18/09/01
...TAKING AN ATTACK POSITION THAT GIVES THE ENEMY THE LEAST VISIBLE TARGET.
FREEZE YOUR LEGS AS SHIELDS...
...FIRING YOUR WEAPON THROUGH THEM...

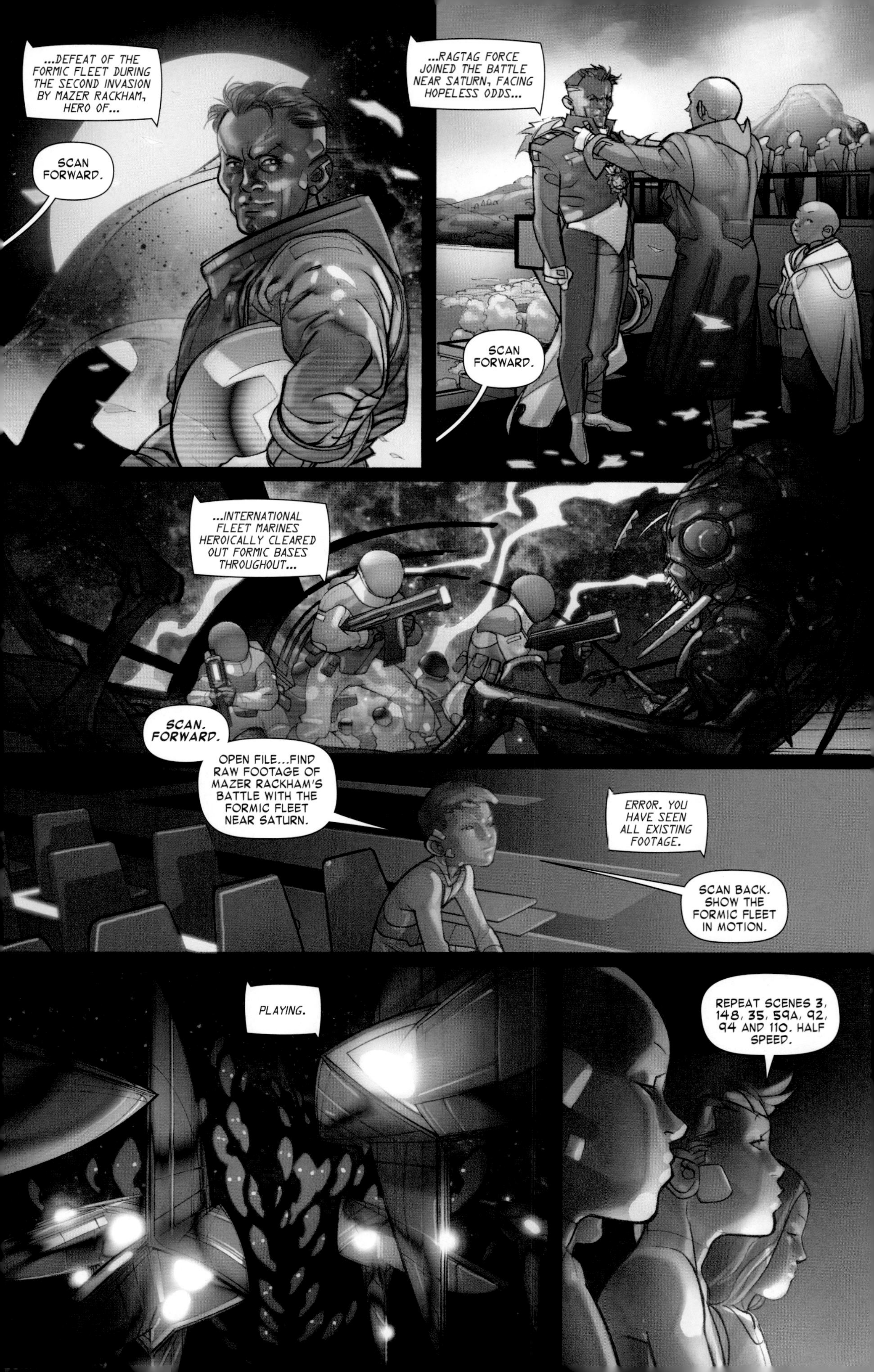
...DEFEAT OF THE FORMIC FLEET DURING THE SECOND INVASION BY MAZER RACKHAM, HERO OF...
SCAN FORWARD.
...RAGTAG FORCE JOINED THE BATTLE NEAR SATURN, FACING HOPELESS ODDS...
SCAN FORWARD.
...INTERNATIONAL FLEET MARINES HEROICALLY CLEARED OUT FORMIC BASES THROUGHOUT...
SCAN. FORWARD.
OPEN FILE...FIND RAW FOOTAGE OF MAZER RACKHAM'S BATTLE WITH THE FORMIC FLEET NEAR SATURN.
ERROR. YOU HAVE SEEN ALL EXISTING FOOTAGE.
SCAN BACK. SHOW THE FORMIC FLEET IN MOTION.
PLAYING.
REPEAT SCENES 3, 148, 35, 59A, 92, 94 AND 110. HALF SPEED.

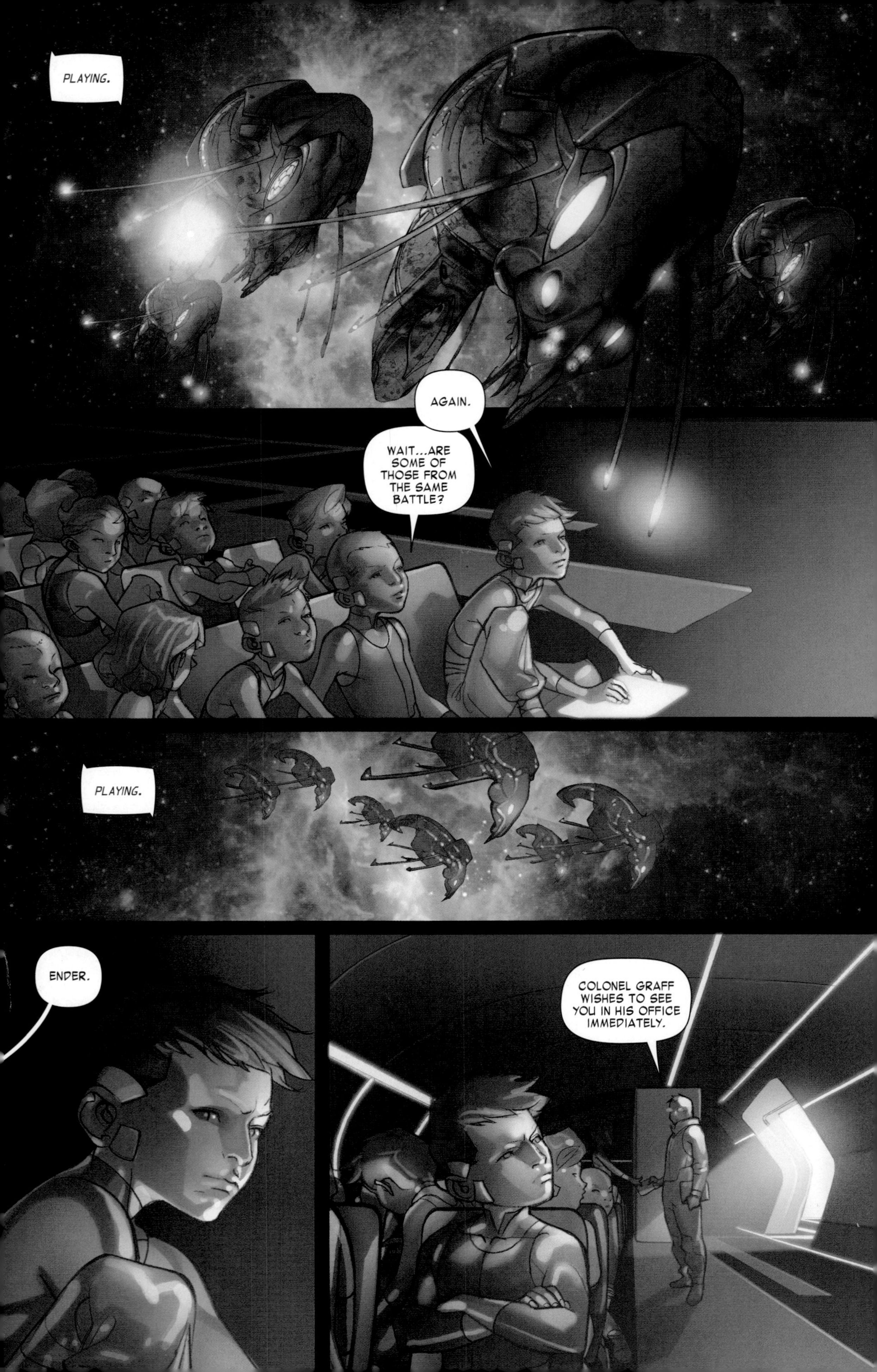
PLAYING.
AGAIN.
WAIT...ARE SOME OF THOSE FROM THE SAME BATTLE?
PLAYING.
ENDER.
COLONEL GRAFF WISHES TO SEE YOU IN HIS OFFICE IMMEDIATELY.

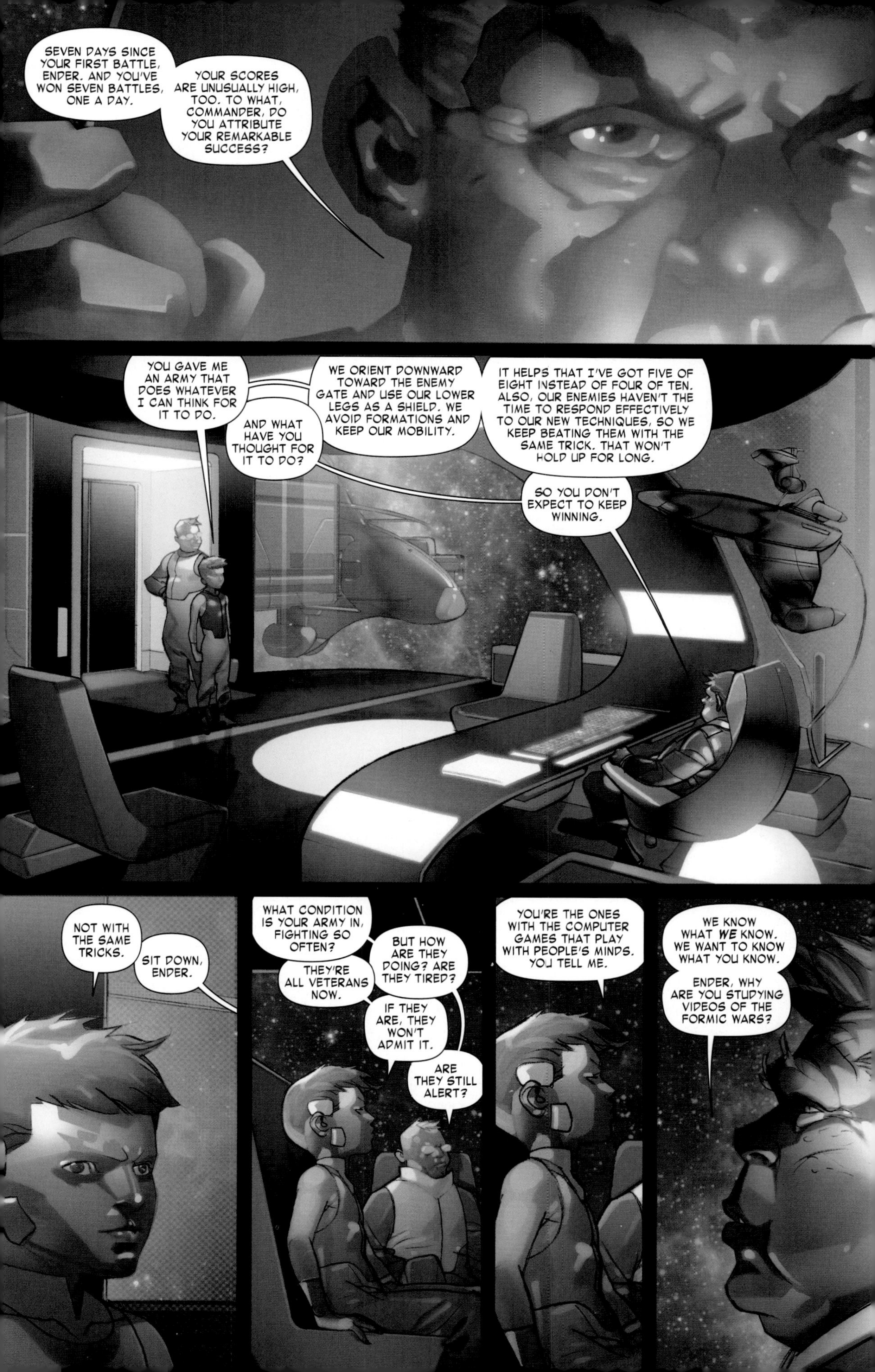
SEVEN DAYS SINCE YOUR FIRST BATTLE, ENDER. AND YOU'VE WON SEVEN BATTLES, ONE A DAY.
YOUR SCORES ARE UNUSUALLY HIGH, TOO. TO WHAT, COMMANDER, DO YOU ATTRIBUTE YOUR REMARKABLE SUCCESS?
YOU GAVE ME AN ARMY THAT DOES WHATEVER I CAN THINK FOR IT TO DO.
AND WHAT HAVE YOU THOUGHT FOR IT TO DO?
WE ORIENT DOWNWARD TOWARD THE ENEMY GATE AND USE OUR LOWER LEGS AS A SHIELD. WE AVOID FORMATIONS AND KEEP OUR MOBILITY.
IT HELPS THAT I'VE GOT FIVE OF EIGHT INSTEAD OF FOUR OF TEN. ALSO, OUR ENEMIES HAVEN'T THE TIME TO RESPOND EFFECTIVELY TO OUR NEW TECHNIQUES, SO WE KEEP BEATING THEM WITH THE SAME TRICK. THAT WON'T HOLD UP FOR LONG.
SO YOU DON'T EXPECT TO KEEP WINNING.
NOT WITH THE SAME TRICKS.
SIT DOWN, ENDER.
WHAT CONDITION IS YOUR ARMY IN, FIGHTING SO OFTEN?
THEY'RE ALL VETERANS NOW.
BUT HOW ARE THEY DOING? ARE THEY TIRED?
IF THEY ARE, THEY WON'T ADMIT IT.
ARE THEY STILL ALERT?
YOU'RE THE ONES WITH THE COMPUTER GAMES THAT PLAY WITH PEOPLE'S MINDS. YOU TELL ME.
WE KNOW WHAT WE KNOW. WE WANT TO KNOW WHAT YOU KNOW.
ENDER, WHY ARE YOU STUDYING VIDEOS OF THE FORMIC WARS?

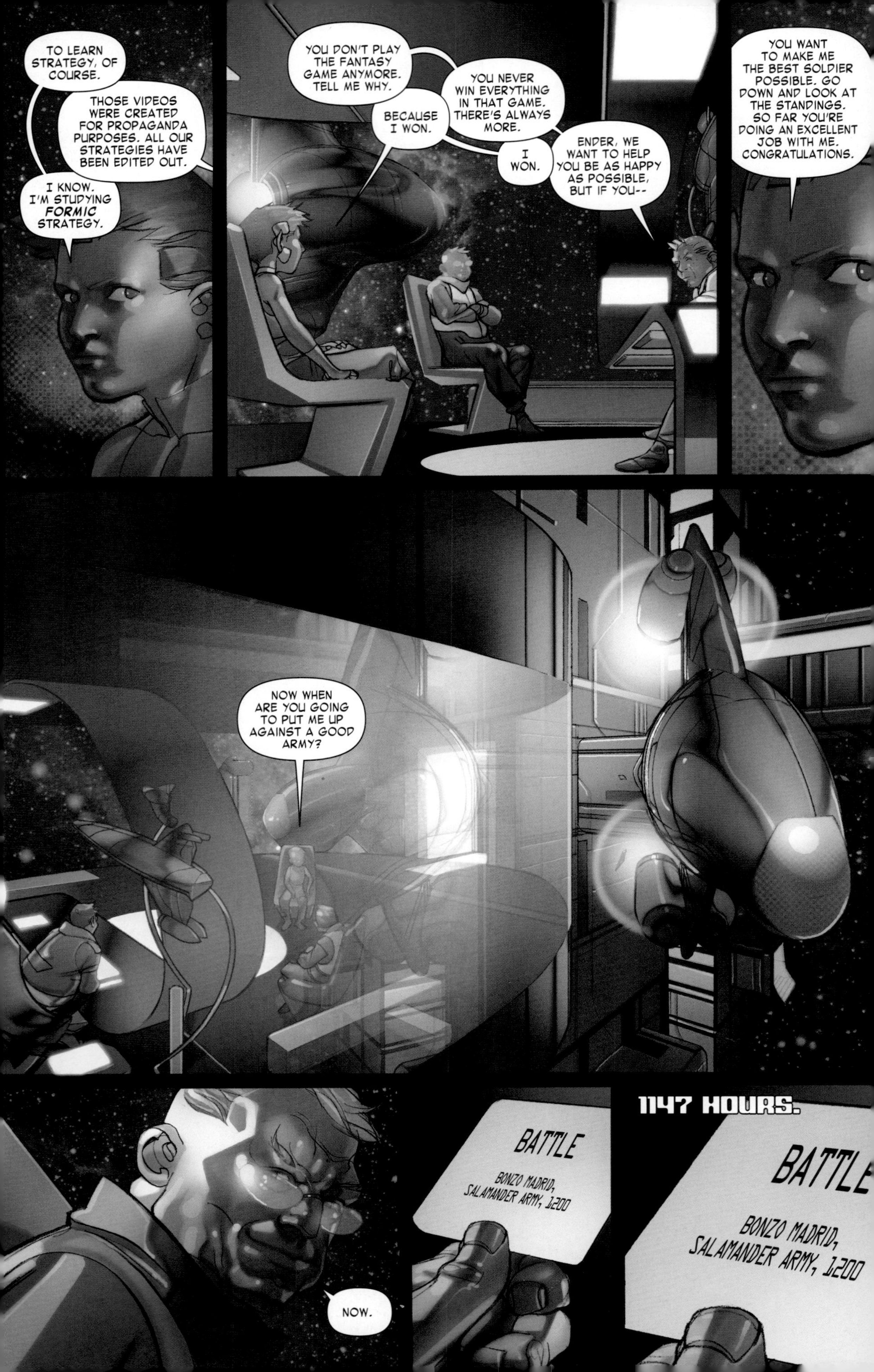
TO LEARN STRATEGY, OF COURSE.
THOSE VIDEOS WERE CREATED FOR PROPAGANDA PURPOSES. ALL OUR STRATEGIES HAVE BEEN EDITED OUT.
I KNOW. I'M STUDYING FORMIC STRATEGY.
YOU DON'T PLAY THE FANTASY GAME ANYMORE. TELL ME WHY.
BECAUSE I WON.
YOU NEVER WIN EVERYTHING IN THAT GAME. THERE'S ALWAYS MORE.
I WON.
ENDER, WE WANT TO HELP YOU BE AS HAPPY AS POSSIBLE, BUT IF YOU--
YOU WANT TO MAKE ME THE BEST SOLDIER POSSIBLE. GO DOWN AND LOOK AT THE STANDINGS. SO FAR YOU'RE DOING AN EXCELLENT JOB WITH ME. CONGRATULATIONS.
NOW WHEN ARE YOU GOING TO PUT ME UP AGAINST A GOOD ARMY?
NOW.
BATTLE
BONZO MADRID, SALAMANDER ARMY, 1200
1147 HOURS.
BATTLE
BONZO MADRID, SALAMANDER ARMY, 1200

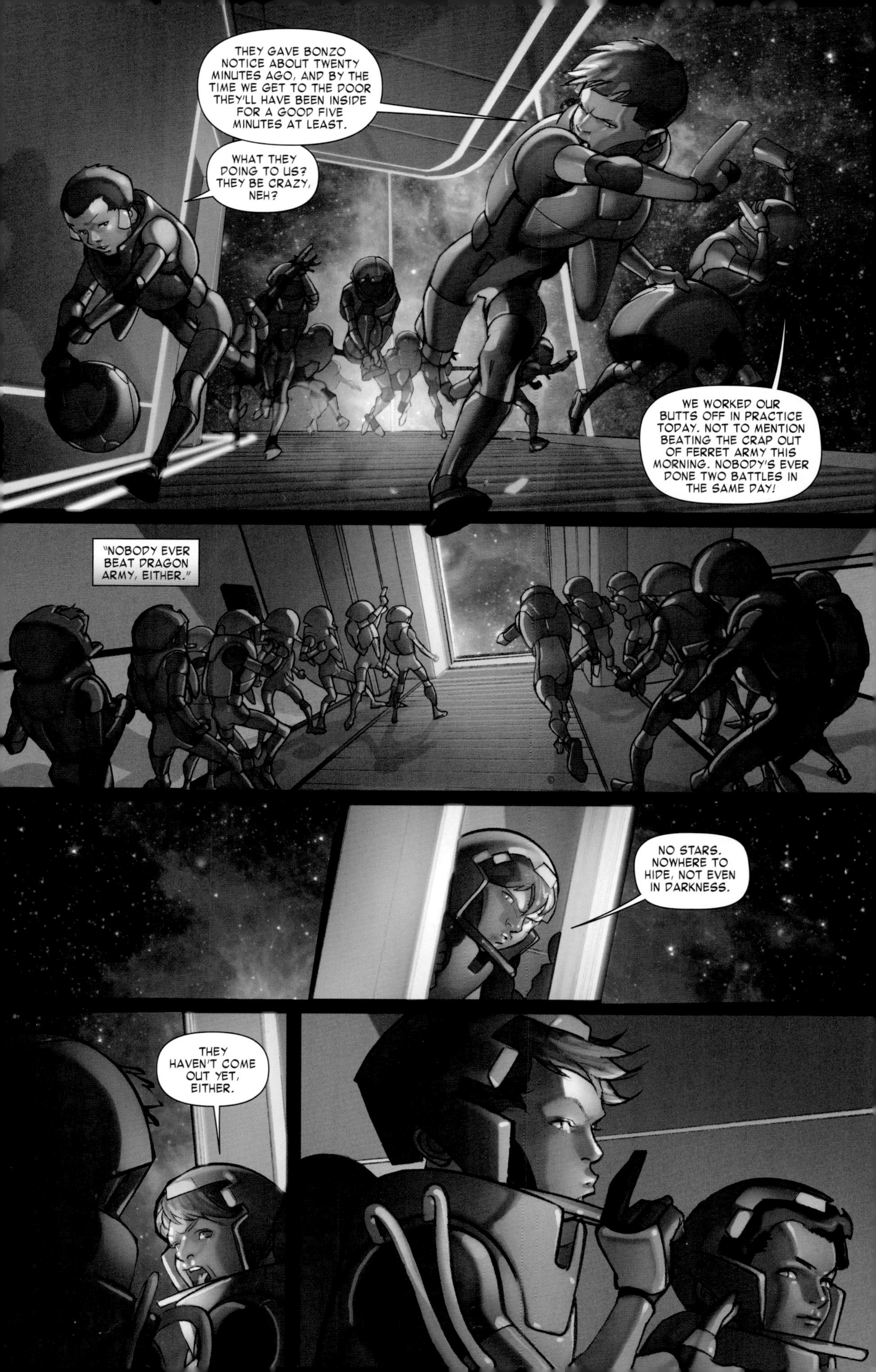
THEY GAVE BONZO NOTICE ABOUT TWENTY MINUTES AGO, AND BY THE TIME WE GET TO THE DOOR THEY'LL HAVE BEEN INSIDE FOR A GOOD FIVE MINUTES AT LEAST.
WHAT THEY DOING TO US? THEY BE CRAZY, NEH?
WE WORKED OUR BUTTS OFF IN PRACTICE TODAY. NOT TO MENTION BEATING THE CRAP OUT OF FERRET ARMY THIS MORNING. NOBODY'S EVER DONE TWO BATTLES IN THE SAME DAY!
"NOBODY EVER BEAT DRAGON ARMY, EITHER."
NO STARS. NOWHERE TO HIDE, NOT EVEN IN DARKNESS.
THEY HAVEN'T COME OUT YET, EITHER.

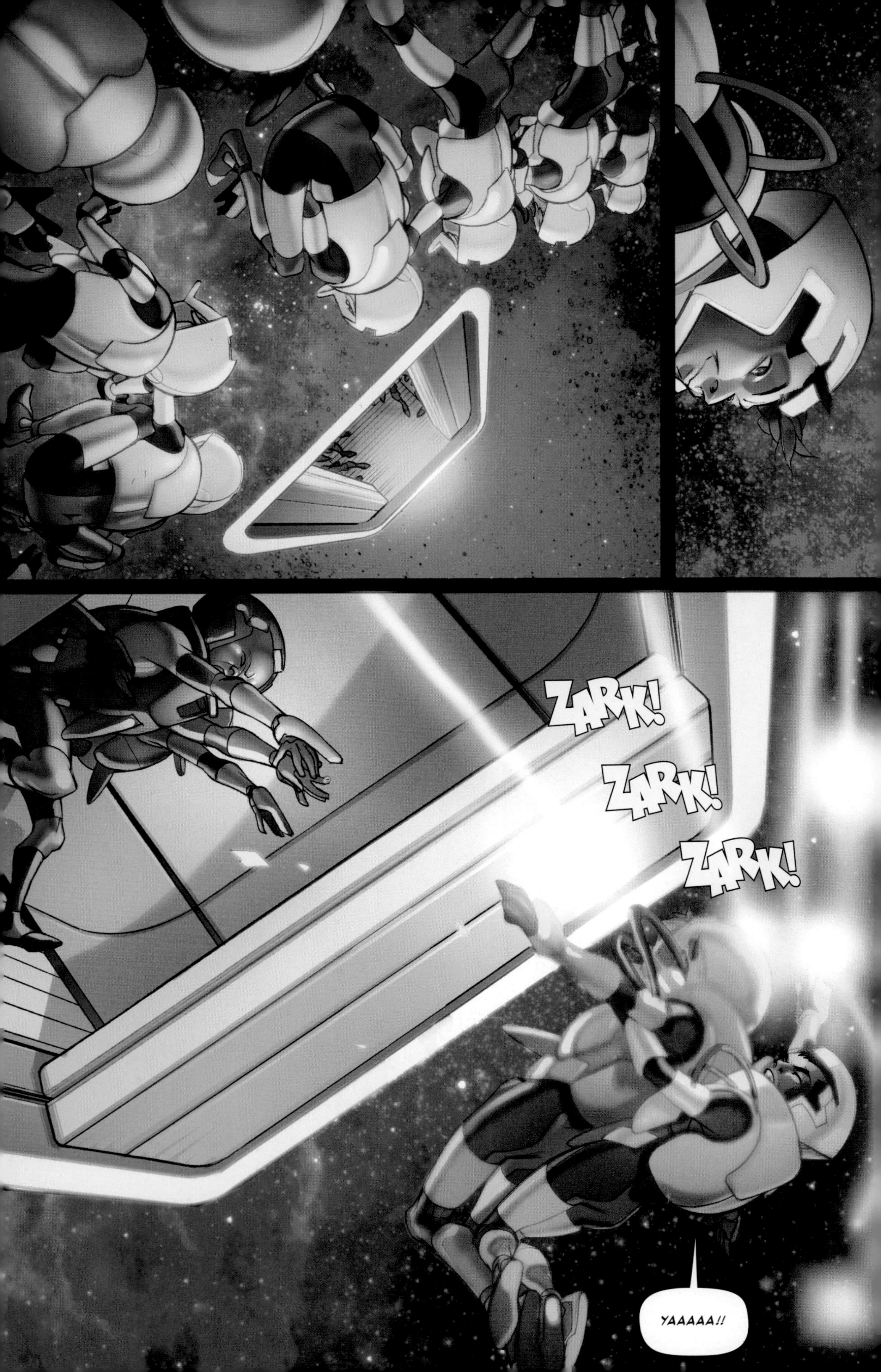
ZARK!
ZARK!
ZARK!
YAAAAA!!

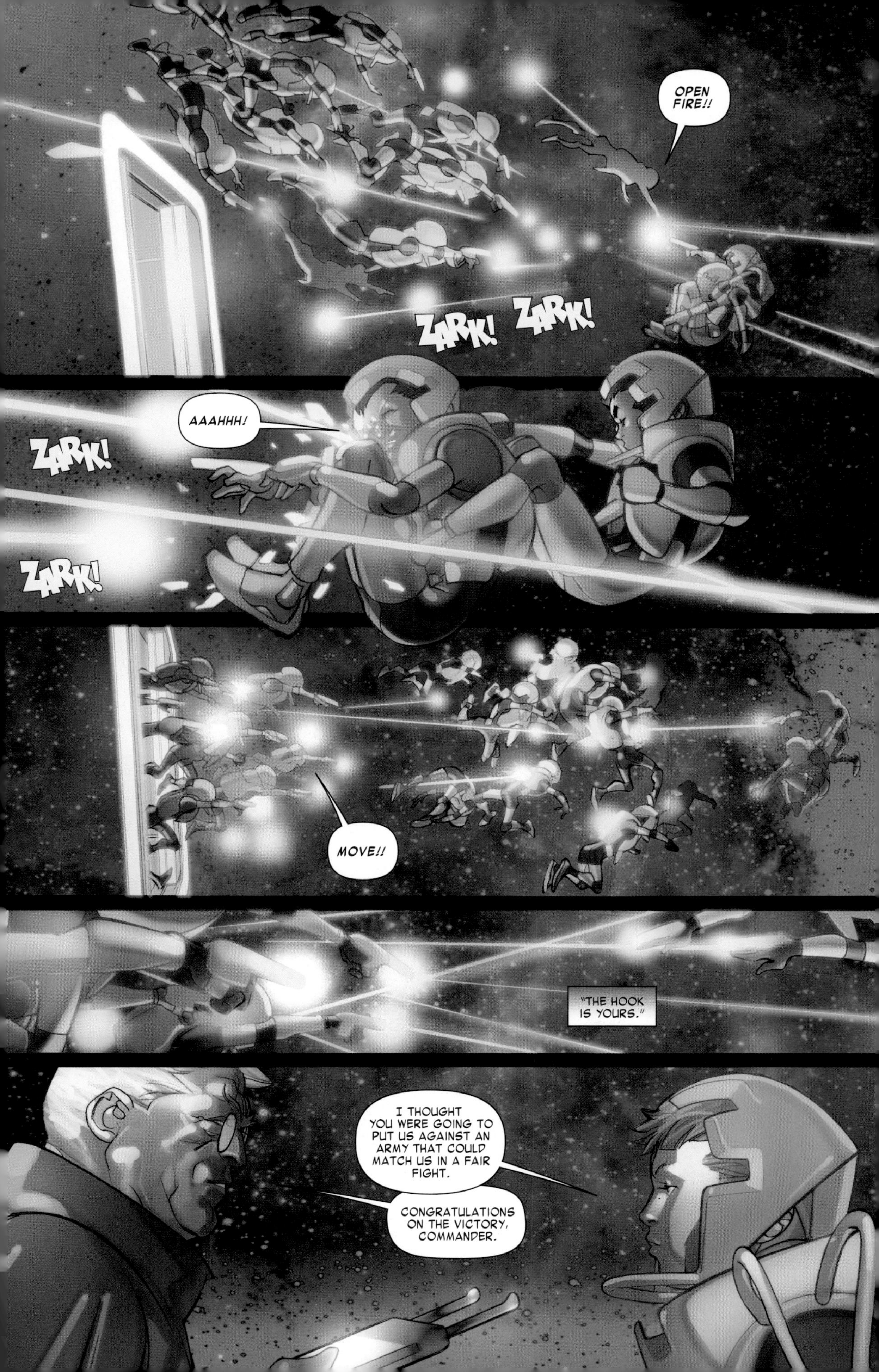
OPEN FIRE!!
ZARK! ZARK!
AAAHHH!
ZARK!
ZARK!
MOVE!!
"THE HOOK IS YOURS."
I THOUGHT YOU WERE GOING TO PUT US AGAINST AN ARMY THAT COULD MATCH US IN A FAIR FIGHT.
CONGRATULATIONS ON THE VICTORY, COMMANDER.

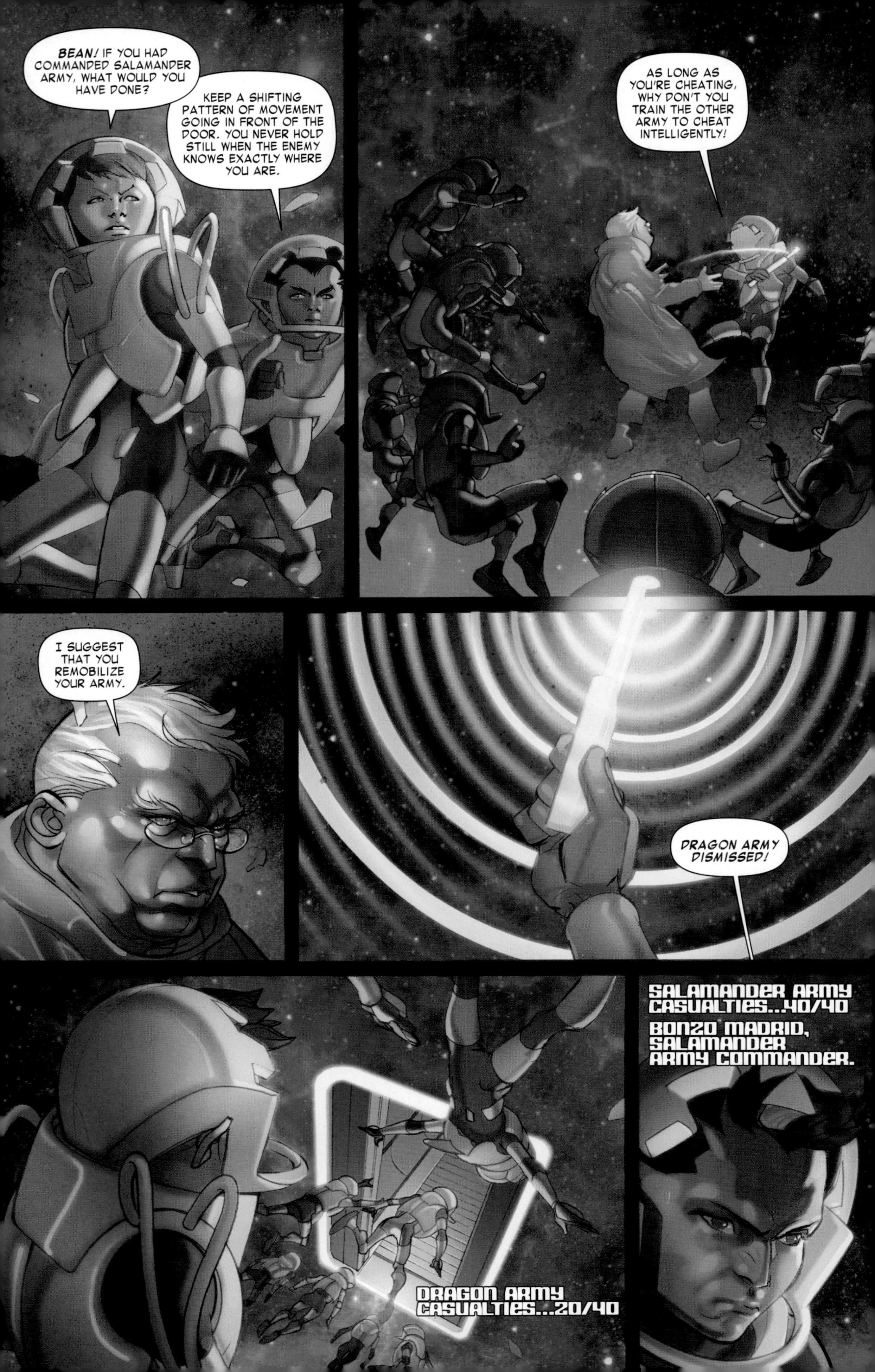
BEAN! IF YOU HAD COMMANDED SALAMANDER ARMY, WHAT WOULD YOU HAVE DONE?
KEEP A SHIFTING PATTERN OF MOVEMENT GOING IN FRONT OF THE DOOR. YOU NEVER HOLD STILL WHEN THE ENEMY KNOWS EXACTLY WHERE YOU ARE.
AS LONG AS YOU'RE CHEATING, WHY DON'T YOU TRAIN THE OTHER ARMY TO CHEAT INTELLIGENTLY!
I SUGGEST THAT YOU REMOBILIZE YOUR ARMY.
DRAGON ARMY DISMISSED!
DRAGON ARMY CASUALTIES...20/40
SALAMANDER ARMY CASUALTIES...40/40
BONZO MADRID, SALAMANDER ARMY COMMANDER.

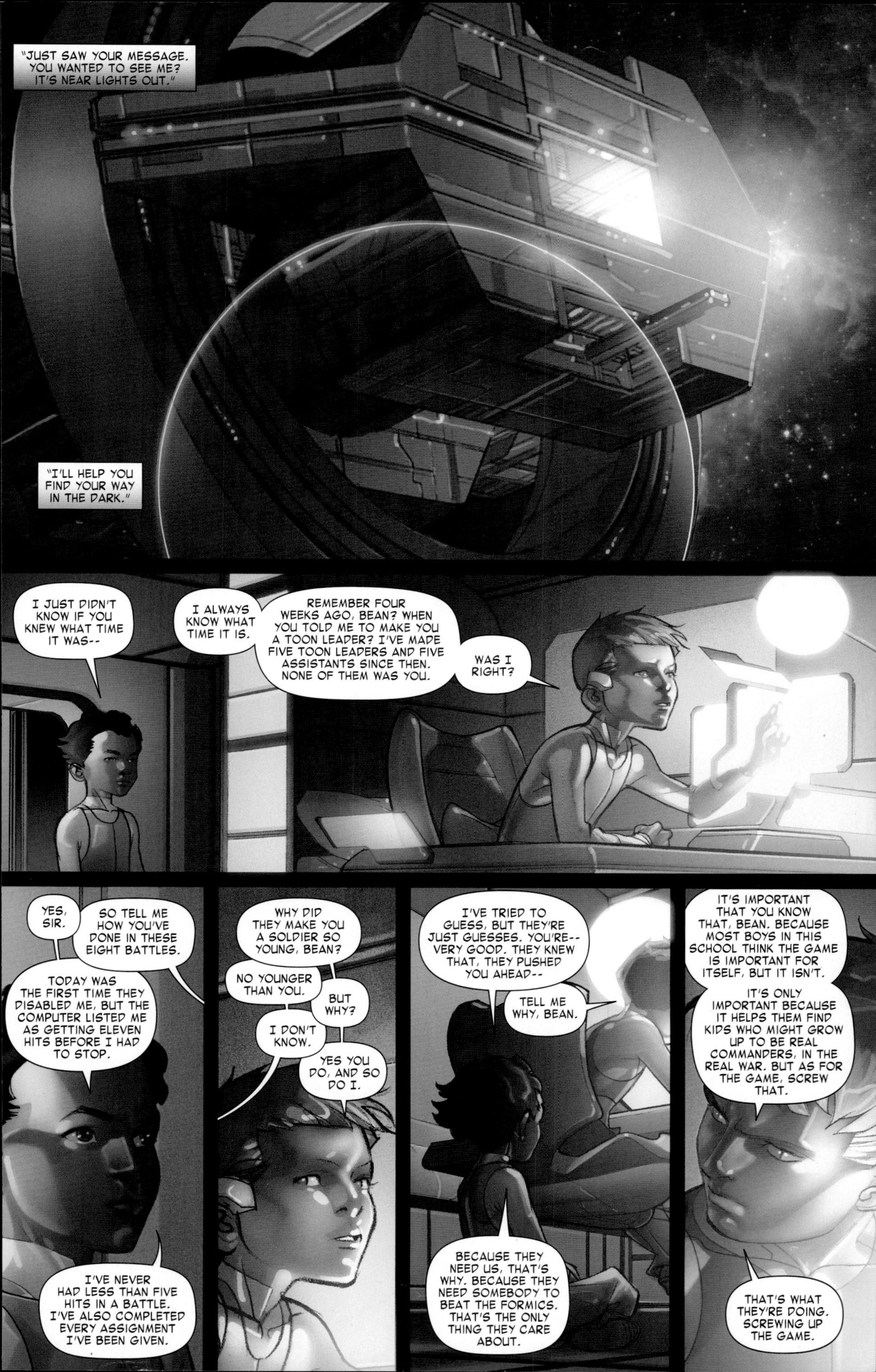
"JUST SAW YOUR MESSAGE. YOU WANTED TO SEE ME? IT'S NEAR LIGHTS OUT."
"I'LL HELP YOU FIND YOUR WAY IN THE DARK."
I JUST DIDN'T KNOW IF YOU KNEW WHAT TIME IT WAS--
I ALWAYS KNOW WHAT TIME IT IS.
REMEMBER FOUR WEEKS AGO, BEAN? WHEN YOU TOLD ME TO MAKE YOU A TOON LEADER? I'VE MADE FIVE TOON LEADERS AND FIVE ASSISTANTS SINCE THEN. NONE OF THEM WAS YOU.
WAS I RIGHT?
YES, SIR.
SO TELL ME HOW YOU'VE DONE IN THESE EIGHT BATTLES.
TODAY WAS THE FIRST TIME THEY DISABLED ME, BUT THE COMPUTER LISTED ME AS GETTING ELEVEN HITS BEFORE I HAD TO STOP.
I'VE NEVER HAD LESS THAN FIVE HITS IN A BATTLE. I'VE ALSO COMPLETED EVERY ASSIGNMENT I'VE BEEN GIVEN.
WHY DID THEY MAKE YOU A SOLDIER SO YOUNG, BEAN?
NO YOUNGER THAN YOU.
BUT WHY?
I DON'T KNOW.
YES YOU DO, AND SO DO I.
I'VE TRIED TO GUESS, BUT THEY'RE JUST GUESSES. YOU'RE--VERY GOOD. THEY KNEW THAT, THEY PUSHED YOU AHEAD--
TELL ME WHY, BEAN.
BECAUSE THEY NEED US, THAT'S WHY. BECAUSE THEY NEED SOMEBODY TO BEAT THE FORMICS. THAT'S THE ONLY THING THEY CARE ABOUT.
IT'S IMPORTANT THAT YOU KNOW THAT, BEAN. BECAUSE MOST BOYS IN THIS SCHOOL THINK THE GAME IS IMPORTANT FOR ITSELF, BUT IT ISN'T.
IT'S ONLY IMPORTANT BECAUSE IT HELPS THEM FIND KIDS WHO MIGHT GROW UP TO BE REAL COMMANDERS, IN THE REAL WAR. BUT AS FOR THE GAME, SCREW THAT.
THAT'S WHAT THEY'RE DOING. SCREWING UP THE GAME.

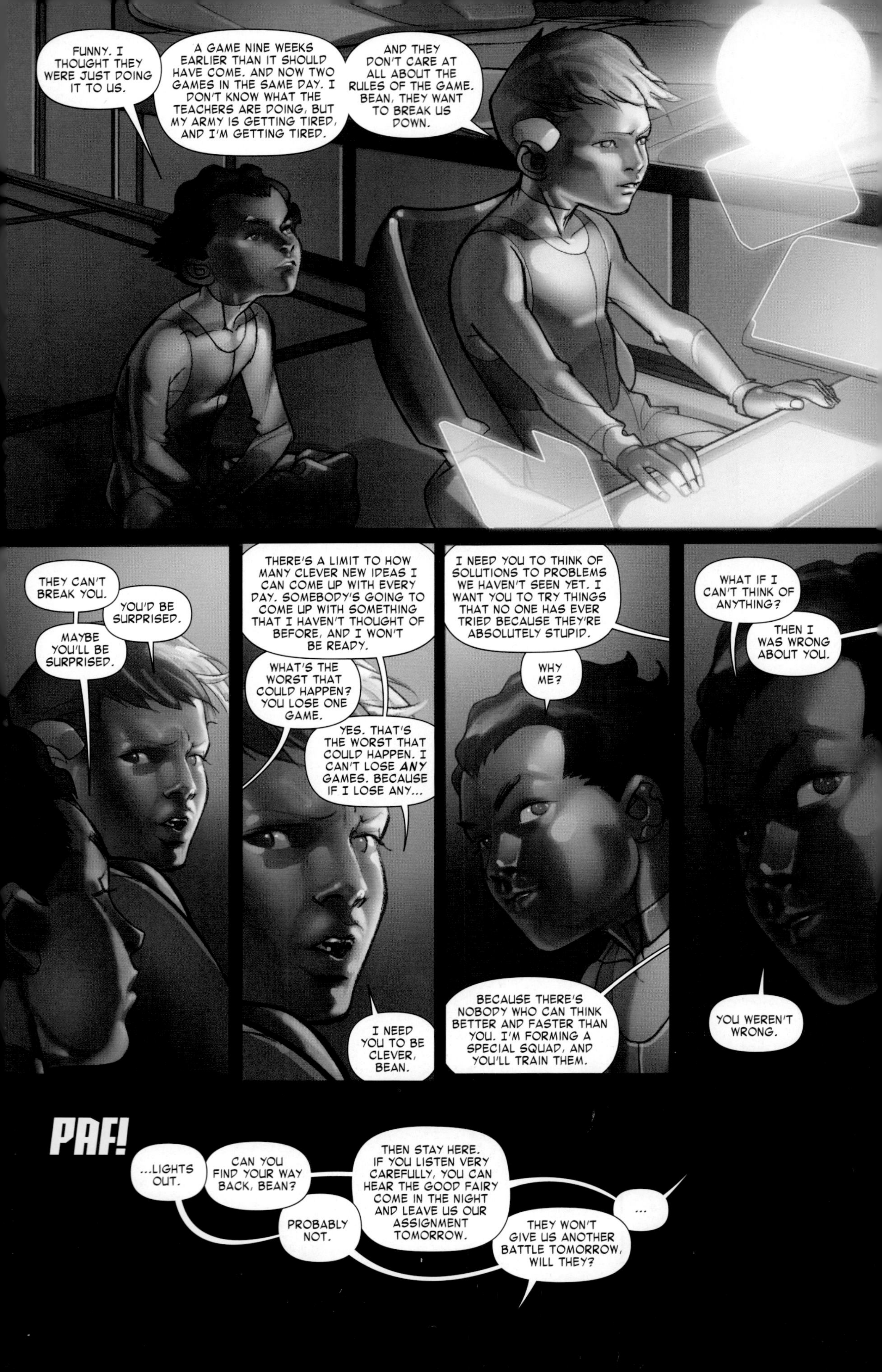
FUNNY. I THOUGHT THEY WERE JUST DOING IT TO US.
A GAME NINE WEEKS EARLIER THAN IT SHOULD HAVE COME. AND NOW TWO GAMES IN THE SAME DAY. I DON'T KNOW WHAT THE TEACHERS ARE DOING, BUT MY ARMY IS GETTING TIRED, AND I'M GETTING TIRED.
AND THEY DON'T CARE AT ALL ABOUT THE RULES OF THE GAME. BEAN, THEY WANT TO BREAK US DOWN.
THEY CAN'T BREAK YOU.
YOU'D BE SURPRISED.
MAYBE YOU'LL BE SURPRISED.
THERE'S A LIMIT TO HOW MANY CLEVER NEW IDEAS I CAN COME UP WITH EVERY DAY. SOMEBODY'S GOING TO COME UP WITH SOMETHING THAT I HAVEN'T THOUGHT OF BEFORE, AND I WON'T BE READY.
WHAT'S THE WORST THAT COULD HAPPEN? YOU LOSE ONE GAME.
YES. THAT'S THE WORST THAT COULD HAPPEN. I CAN'T LOSE ANY GAMES. BECAUSE IF I LOSE ANY...
I NEED YOU TO BE CLEVER, BEAN.
I NEED YOU TO THINK OF SOLUTIONS TO PROBLEMS WE HAVEN'T SEEN YET. I WANT YOU TO TRY THINGS THAT NO ONE HAS EVER TRIED BECAUSE THEY'RE ABSOLUTELY STUPID.
WHY ME?
BECAUSE THERE'S NOBODY WHO CAN THINK BETTER AND FASTER THAN YOU. I'M FORMING A SPECIAL SQUAD, AND YOU'LL TRAIN THEM.
WHAT IF I CAN'T THINK OF ANYTHING?
THEN I WAS WRONG ABOUT YOU.
YOU WEREN'T WRONG.
PAF!
...LIGHTS OUT.
CAN YOU FIND YOUR WAY BACK, BEAN?
PROBABLY NOT.
THEN STAY HERE. IF YOU LISTEN VERY CAREFULLY, YOU CAN HEAR THE GOOD FAIRY COME IN THE NIGHT AND LEAVE US OUR ASSIGNMENT TOMORROW.
...
THEY WON'T GIVE US ANOTHER BATTLE TOMORROW, WILL THEY?

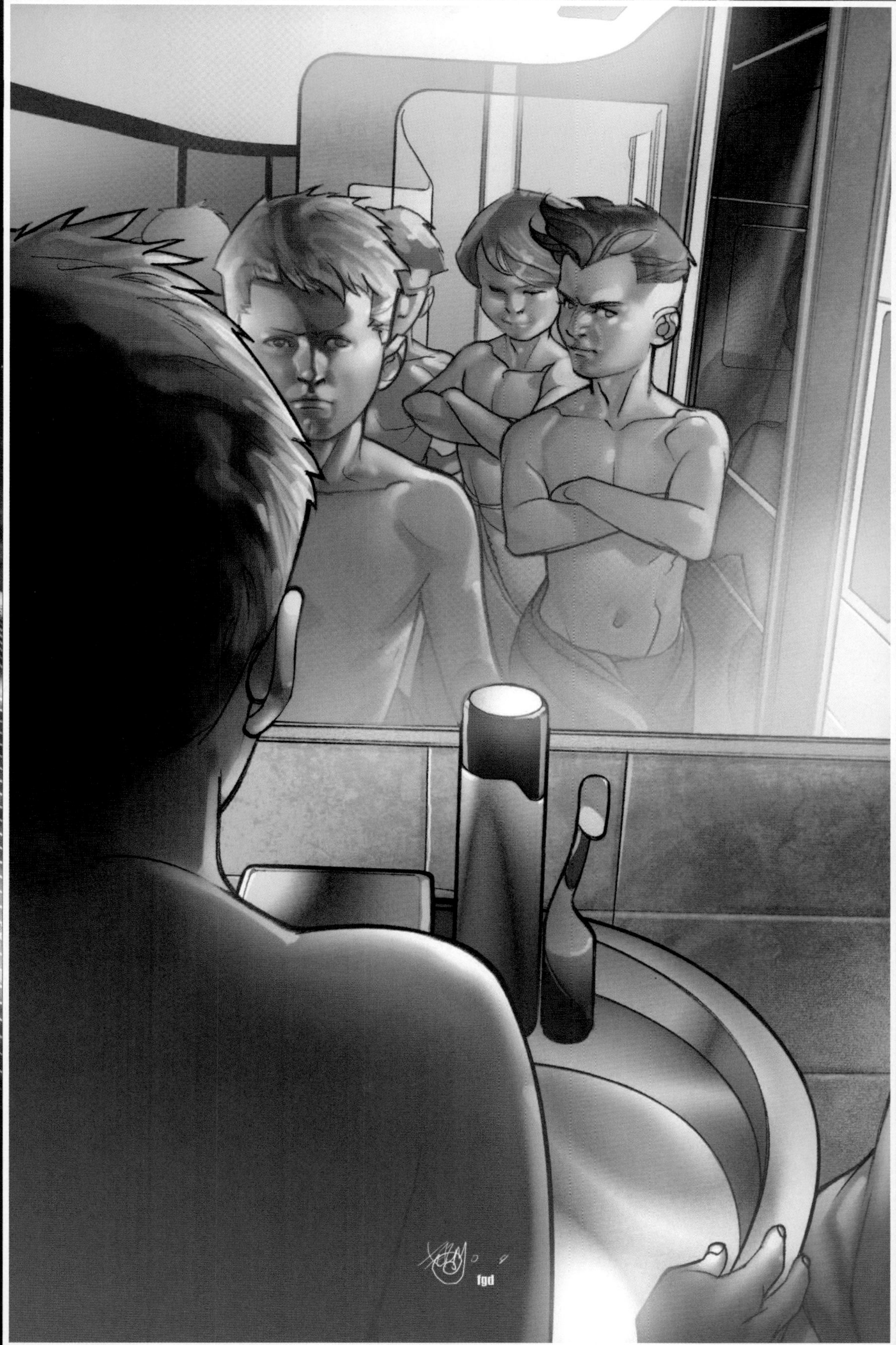

T H R E E

<<<THIS IS A TRANSCRIPT FROM AN EMERGENCY MEETING CALLED BY GENERAL PACE OF INTERNATIONAL FLEET MILITARY POLICE, MAXIMUM SECURITY CLEARANCE>>>

GRAFF: Ah. I guess this means Dap filed a report.

PACE: Colonel Graff, you have known for eight days that there is a conspiracy among some of the more vicious of these "children" to cause the beating of Ender Wiggin, if they can. And that some members of this conspiracy, notably the boy commonly called Bonzo Madrid, are quite likely to exhibit no self-restraint when this punishment takes place, so that Ender Wiggin, an inestimably important international resource, will be placed in serious danger of having his brains pasted on the walls of your orbiting schoolhouse. And you, fully warned of this danger, propose to do exactly...

G: Nothing.

P: Ender Wiggin has provoked Bonzo Madrid beyond human endurance. And you have no military police standing by to break up disturbances. It is unconscionable.

G: General Pace, when Ender Wiggin holds our fleets in his control, when he must make the decisions that bring us victory or destruction, will there be military police to come save him if things get out of hand?

P: I fail to see the connection.

G: Obviously. But the connection is there. Ender Wiggin must believe that no matter what happens, no adult will ever, ever step in to help him in any way. He must believe, to the core of his soul, that he can only do what he and the other children work out for themselves. If he does not believe that, then he will never reach the peak of his abilities.

P: He will also not reach the peak of his abilities if he is dead or permanently crippled.

G: He won't be.

P: God help you if you're wrong.

G: God help us all if I'm wrong.

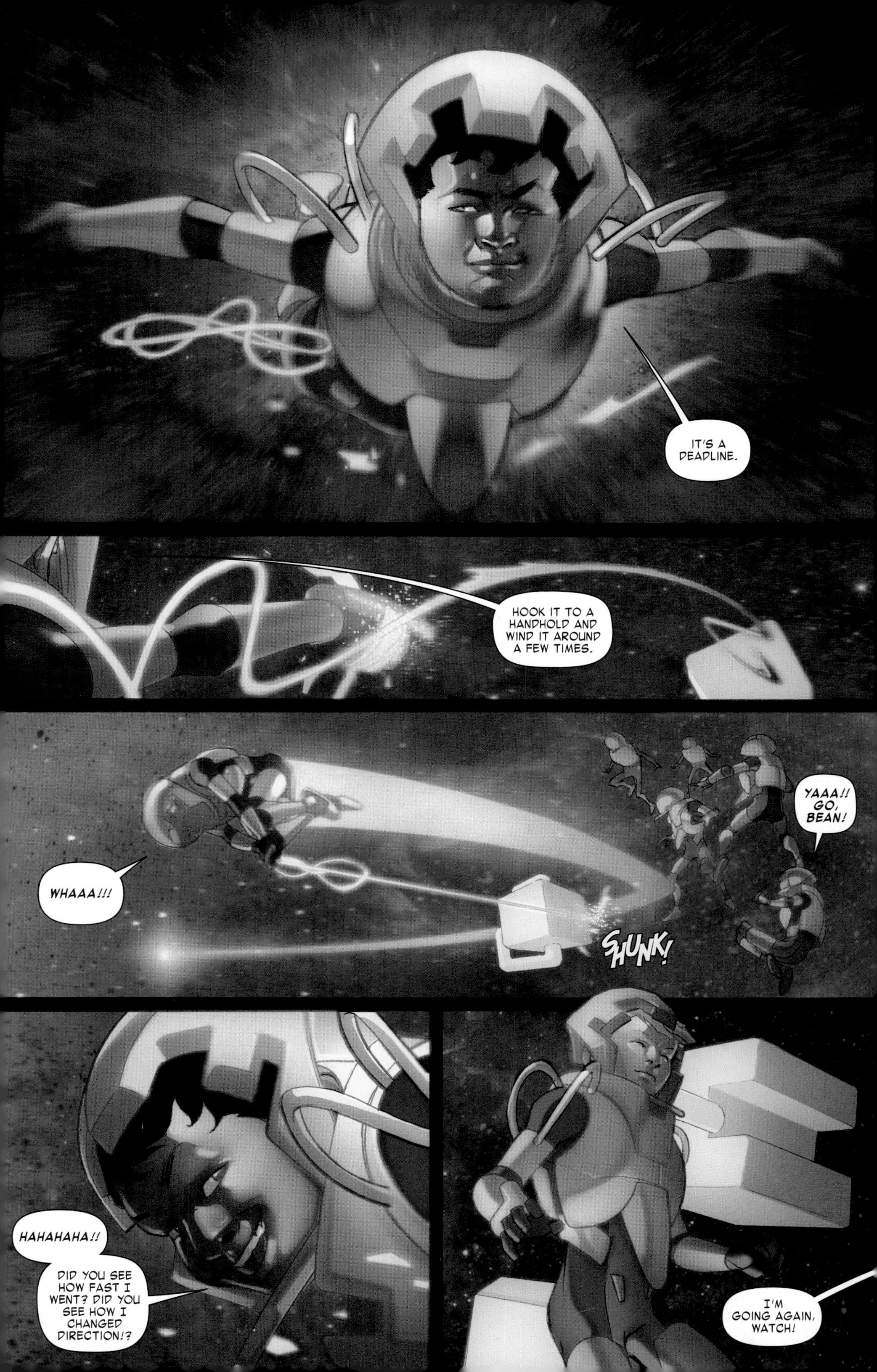
IT'S A DEADLINE.
HOOK IT TO A HANDHOLD AND WIND IT AROUND A FEW TIMES.
WHAAA!!!
YAAA!! GO, BEAN!
SHUNK!
HAHAHAHA!!
DID YOU SEE HOW FAST I WENT? DID YOU SEE HOW I CHANGED DIRECTION!?
I'M GOING AGAIN, WATCH!

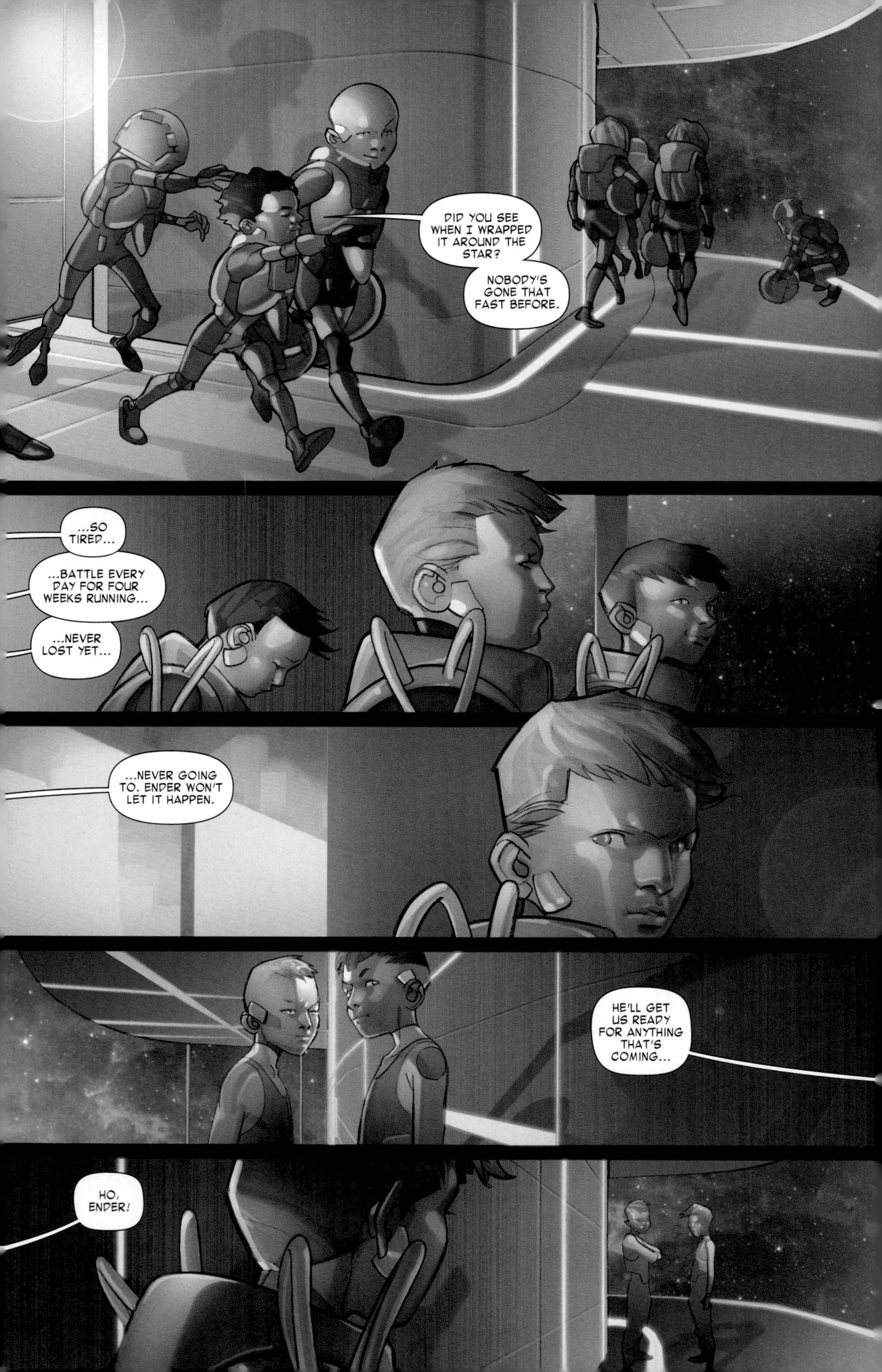
DID YOU SEE WHEN I WRAPPED IT AROUND THE STAR?
NOBODY'S GONE THAT FAST BEFORE.
...SO TIRED...
...BATTLE EVERY DAY FOR FOUR WEEKS RUNNING...
...NEVER LOST YET...
...NEVER GOING TO. ENDER WON'T LET IT HAPPEN.
HE'LL GET US READY FOR ANYTHING THAT'S COMING...
HO, ENDER!

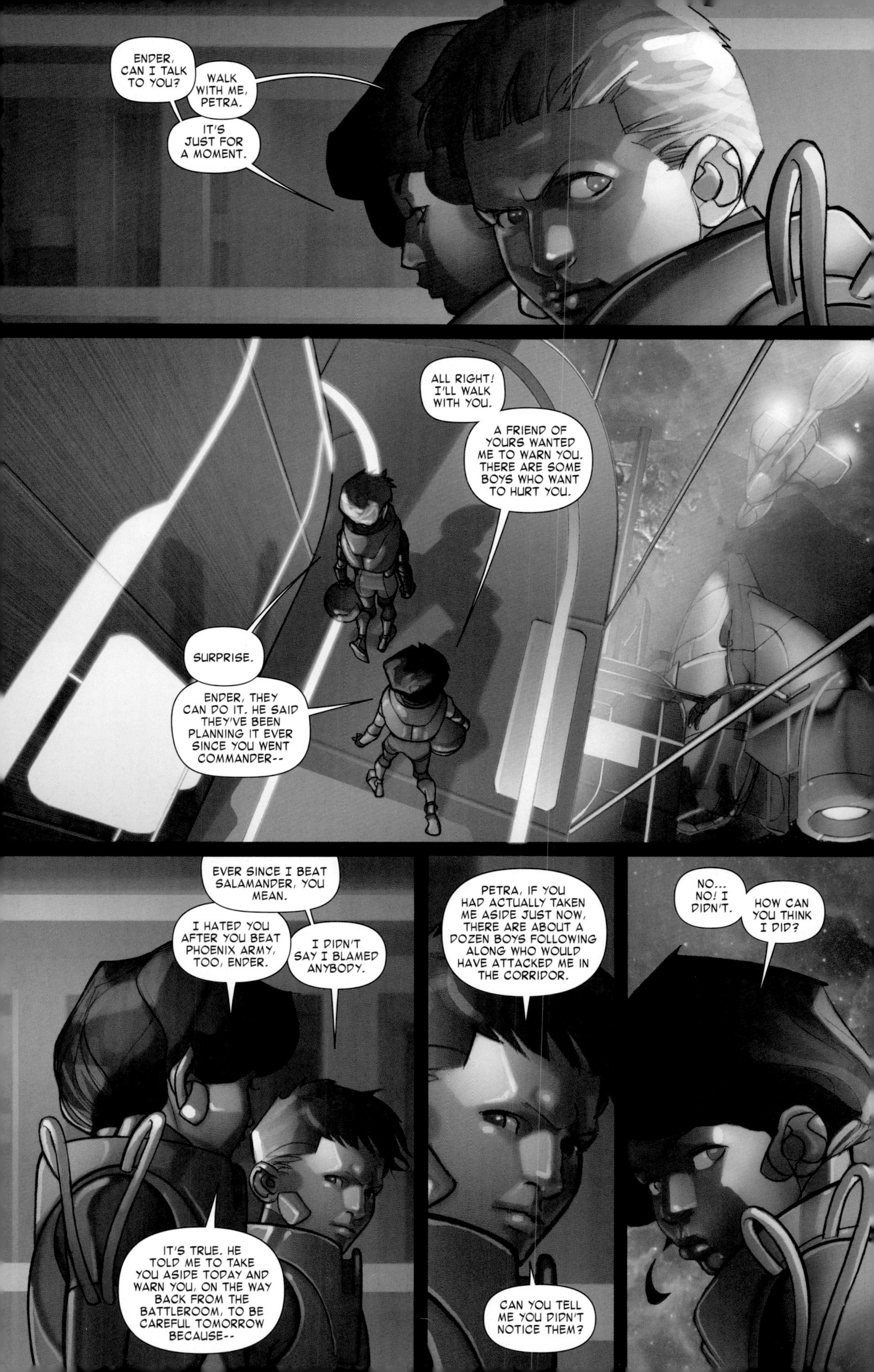
ENDER, CAN I TALK TO YOU?
WALK WITH ME, PETRA.
IT'S JUST FOR A MOMENT.
ALL RIGHT! I'LL WALK WITH YOU.
A FRIEND OF YOURS WANTED ME TO WARN YOU. THERE ARE SOME BOYS WHO WANT TO HURT YOU.
SURPRISE.
ENDER, THEY CAN DO IT. HE SAID THEY'VE BEEN PLANNING IT EVER SINCE YOU WENT COMMANDER--
EVER SINCE I BEAT SALAMANDER, YOU MEAN.
I HATED YOU AFTER YOU BEAT PHOENIX ARMY, TOO, ENDER.
I DIDN'T SAY I BLAMED ANYBODY.
IT'S TRUE. HE TOLD ME TO TAKE YOU ASIDE TODAY AND WARN YOU, ON THE WAY BACK FROM THE BATTLEROOM, TO BE CAREFUL TOMORROW BECAUSE--
PETRA, IF YOU HAD ACTUALLY TAKEN ME ASIDE JUST NOW, THERE ARE ABOUT A DOZEN BOYS FOLLOWING ALONG WHO WOULD HAVE ATTACKED ME IN THE CORRIDOR.
CAN YOU TELL ME YOU DIDN'T NOTICE THEM?
NO... NO! I DIDN'T.
HOW CAN YOU THINK I DID?

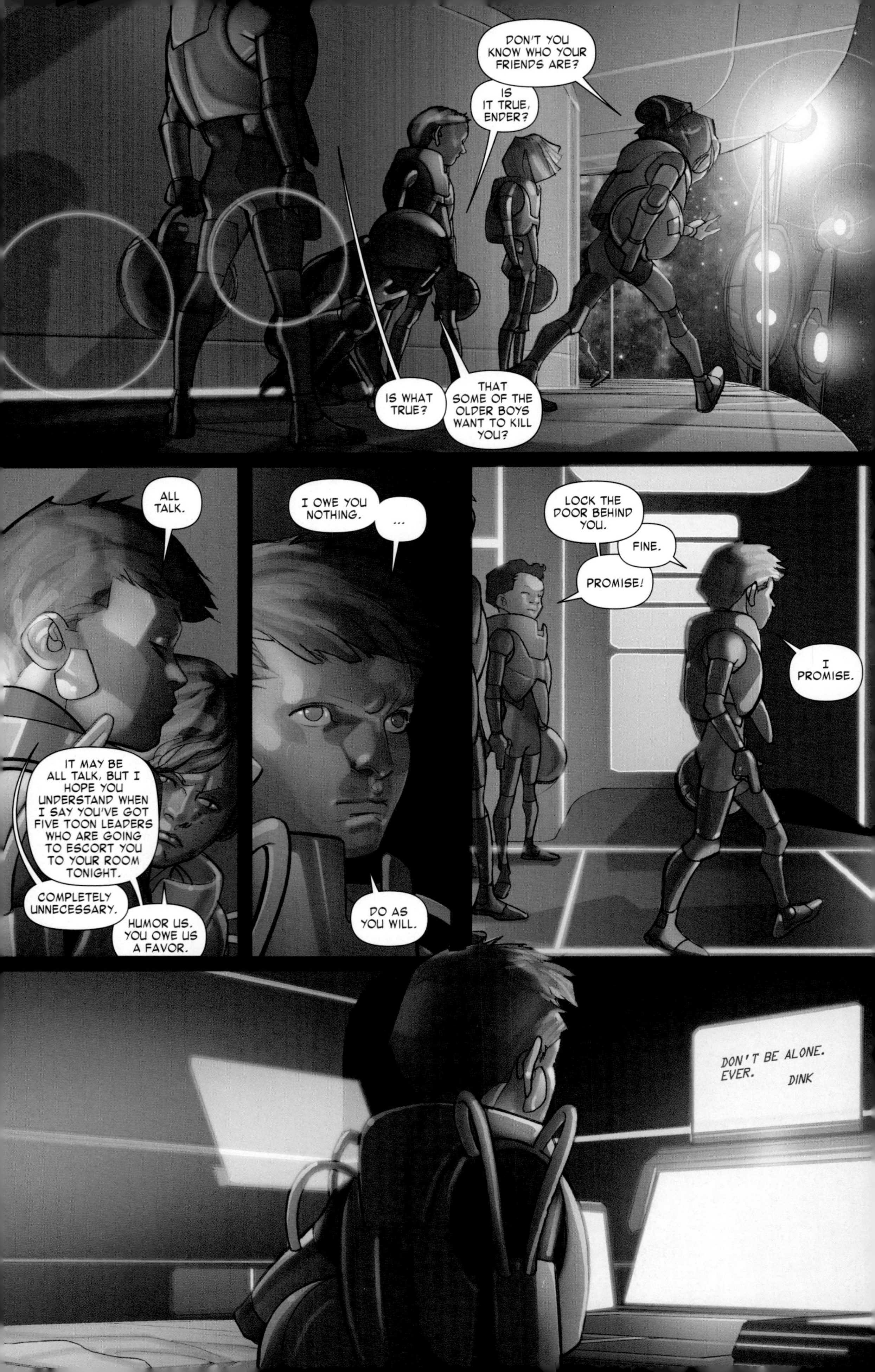
DON'T YOU KNOW WHO YOUR FRIENDS ARE?
IS IT TRUE, ENDER?
IS WHAT TRUE?
THAT SOME OF THE OLDER BOYS WANT TO KILL YOU?
ALL TALK.
IT MAY BE ALL TALK, BUT I HOPE YOU UNDERSTAND WHEN I SAY YOU'VE GOT FIVE TOON LEADERS WHO ARE GOING TO ESCORT YOU TO YOUR ROOM TONIGHT.
COMPLETELY UNNECESSARY.
HUMOR US. YOU OWE US A FAVOR.
I OWE YOU NOTHING.
...
DO AS YOU WILL.
LOCK THE DOOR BEHIND YOU.
FINE.
PROMISE!
I PROMISE.
DON'T BE ALONE. EVER. DINK

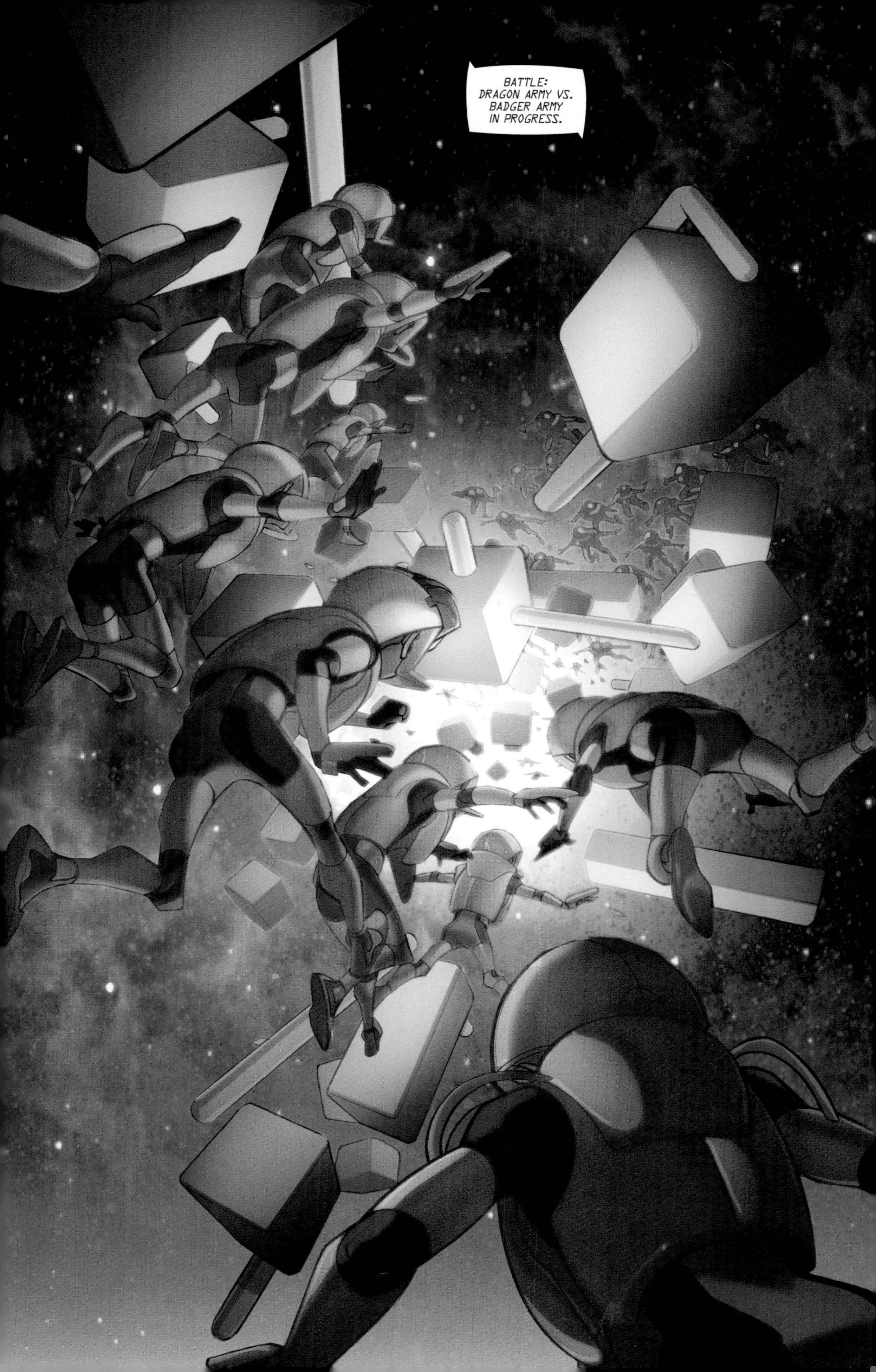
BATTLE:
DRAGON ARMY VS.
BADGER ARMY
IN PROGRESS.

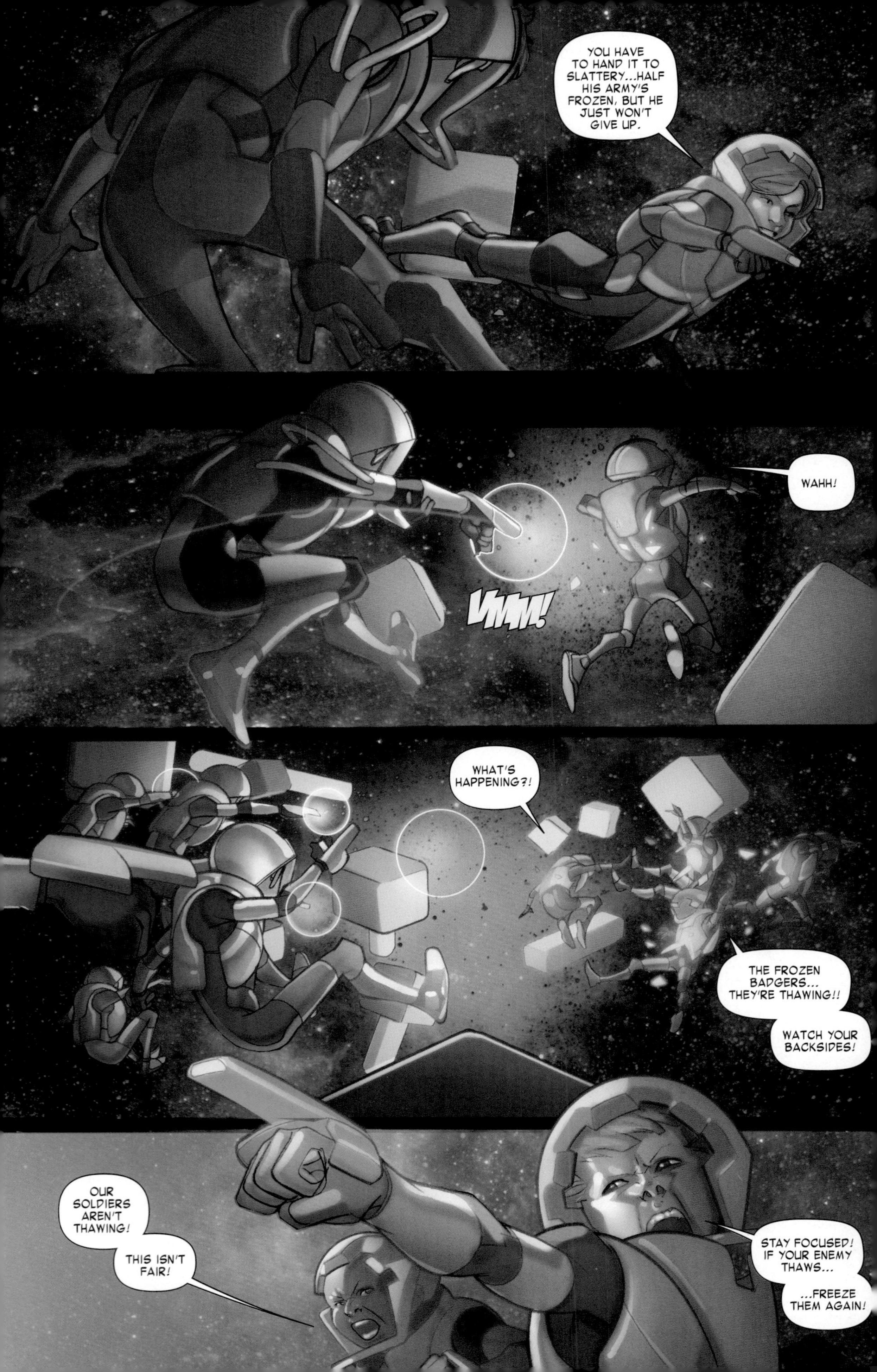
YOU HAVE TO HAND IT TO SLATTERY...HALF HIS ARMY'S FROZEN, BUT HE JUST WON'T GIVE UP.
WAHH!
VMMM!
WHAT'S HAPPENING?!
THE FROZEN BADGERS... THEY'RE THAWING!!
WATCH YOUR BACKSIDES!
OUR SOLDIERS AREN'T THAWING!
THIS ISN'T FAIR!
STAY FOCUSED! IF YOUR ENEMY THAWS...
...FREEZE THEM AGAIN!

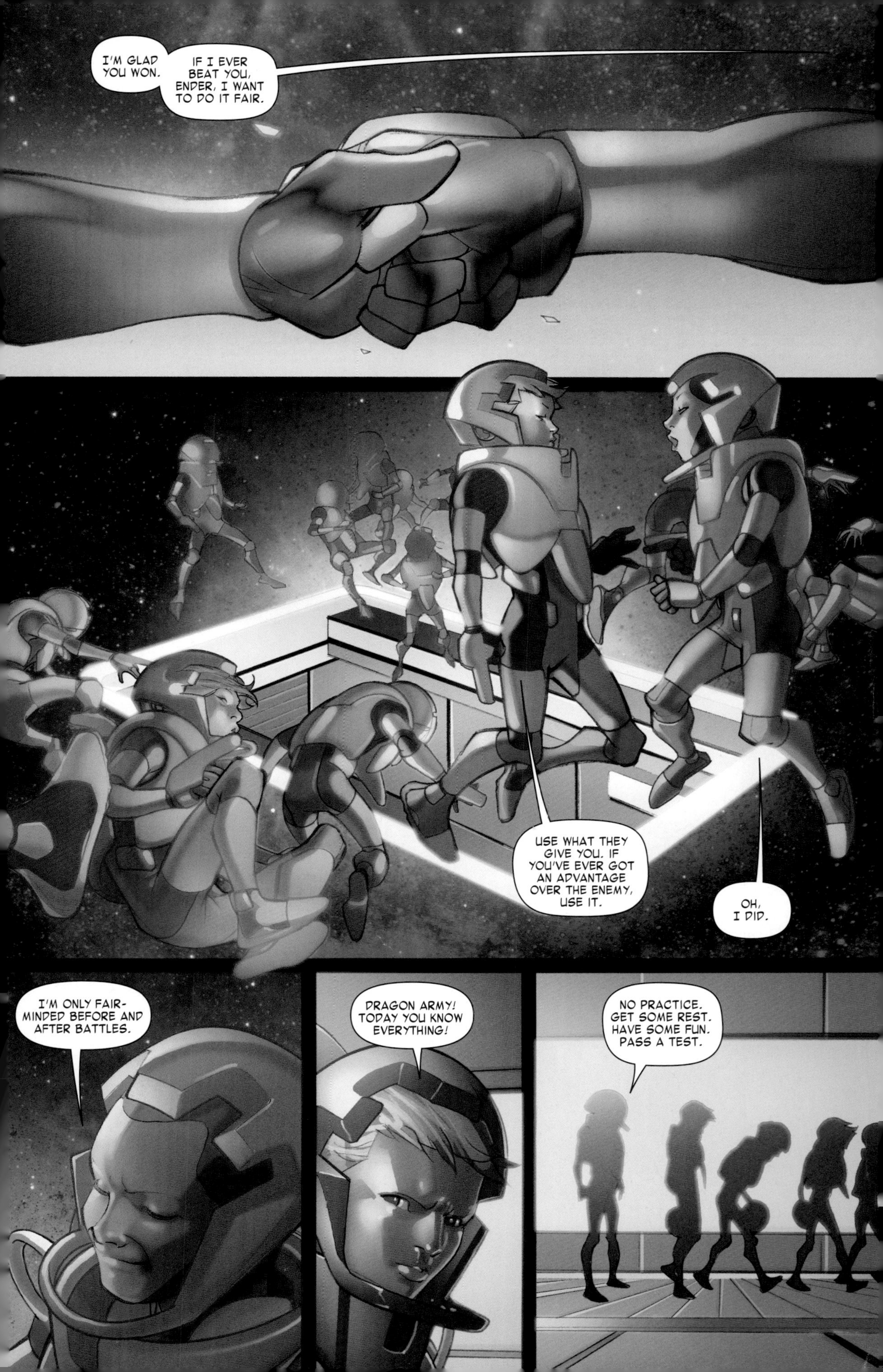
I'M GLAD YOU WON.
IF I EVER BEAT YOU, ENDER, I WANT TO DO IT FAIR.
USE WHAT THEY GIVE YOU. IF YOU'VE EVER GOT AN ADVANTAGE OVER THE ENEMY, USE IT.
OH, I DID.
I'M ONLY FAIR-MINDED BEFORE AND AFTER BATTLES.
DRAGON ARMY! TODAY YOU KNOW EVERYTHING!
NO PRACTICE. GET SOME REST. HAVE SOME FUN. PASS A TEST.

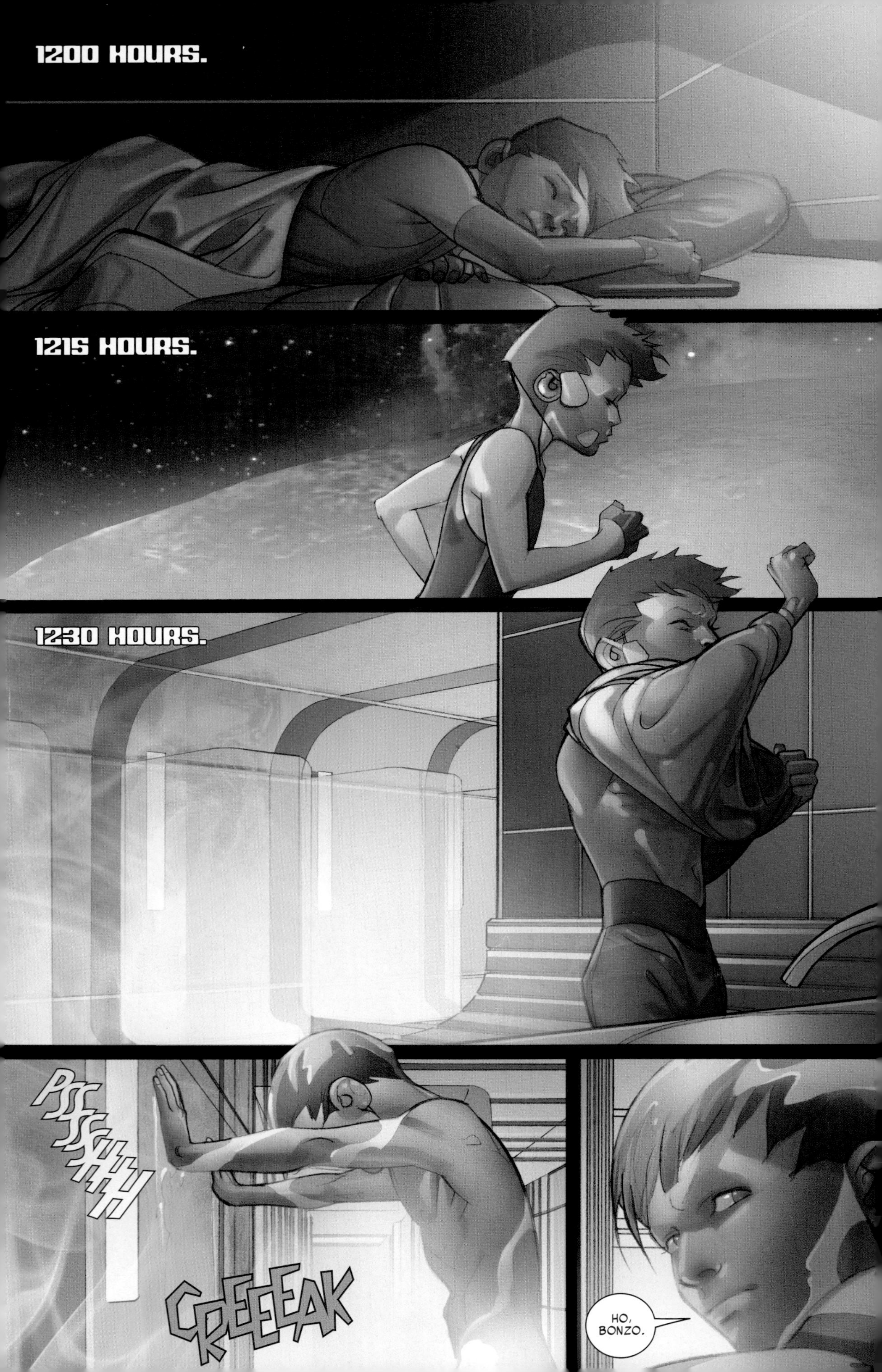

1200 HOURS.
1215 HOURS.
1230 HOURS.
PSSSSHHHH
CREEEAK
HO, BONZO.

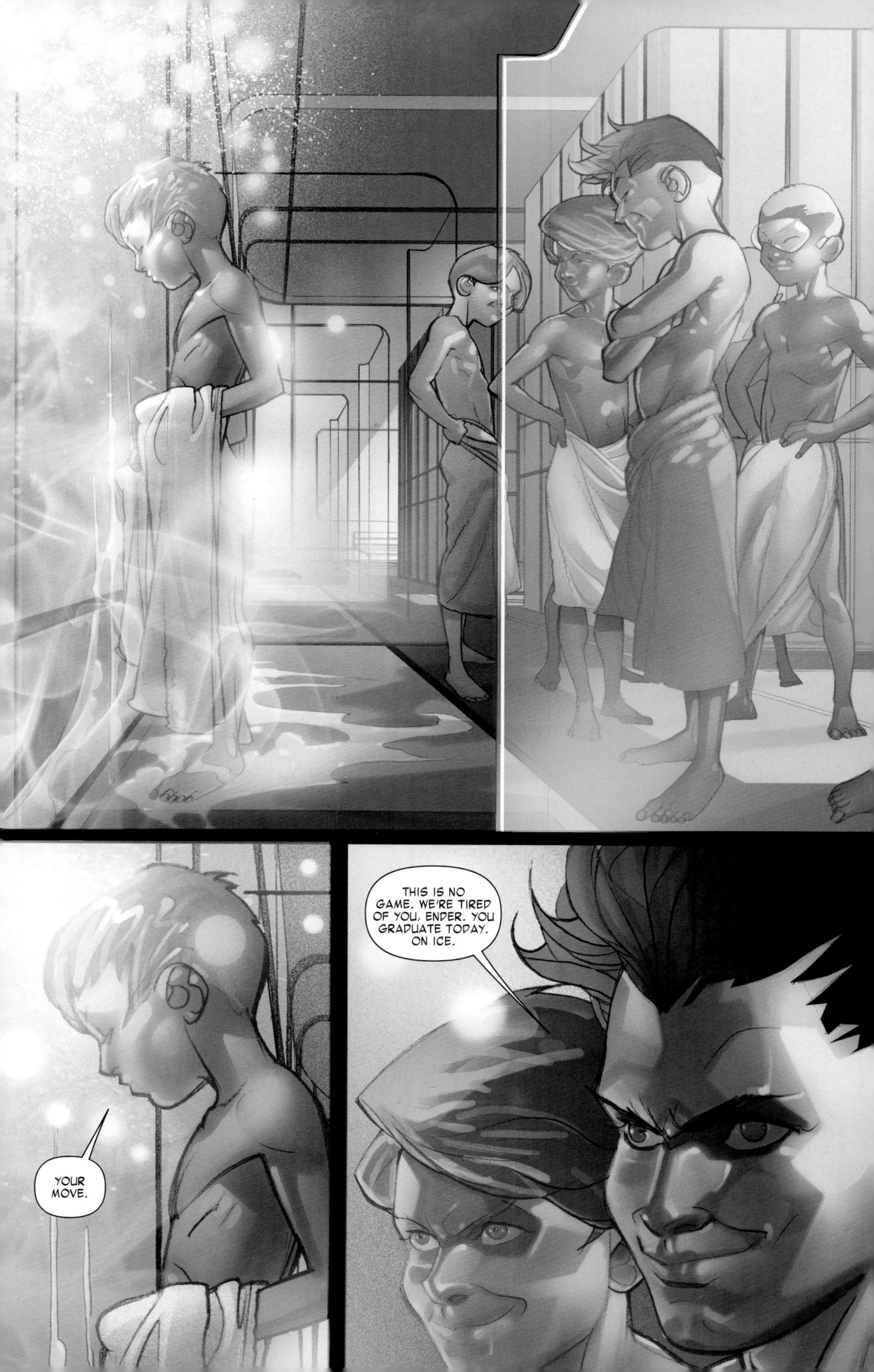
THIS IS NO GAME. WE'RE TIRED OF YOU, ENDER. YOU GRADUATE TODAY. ON ICE.
YOUR MOVE.

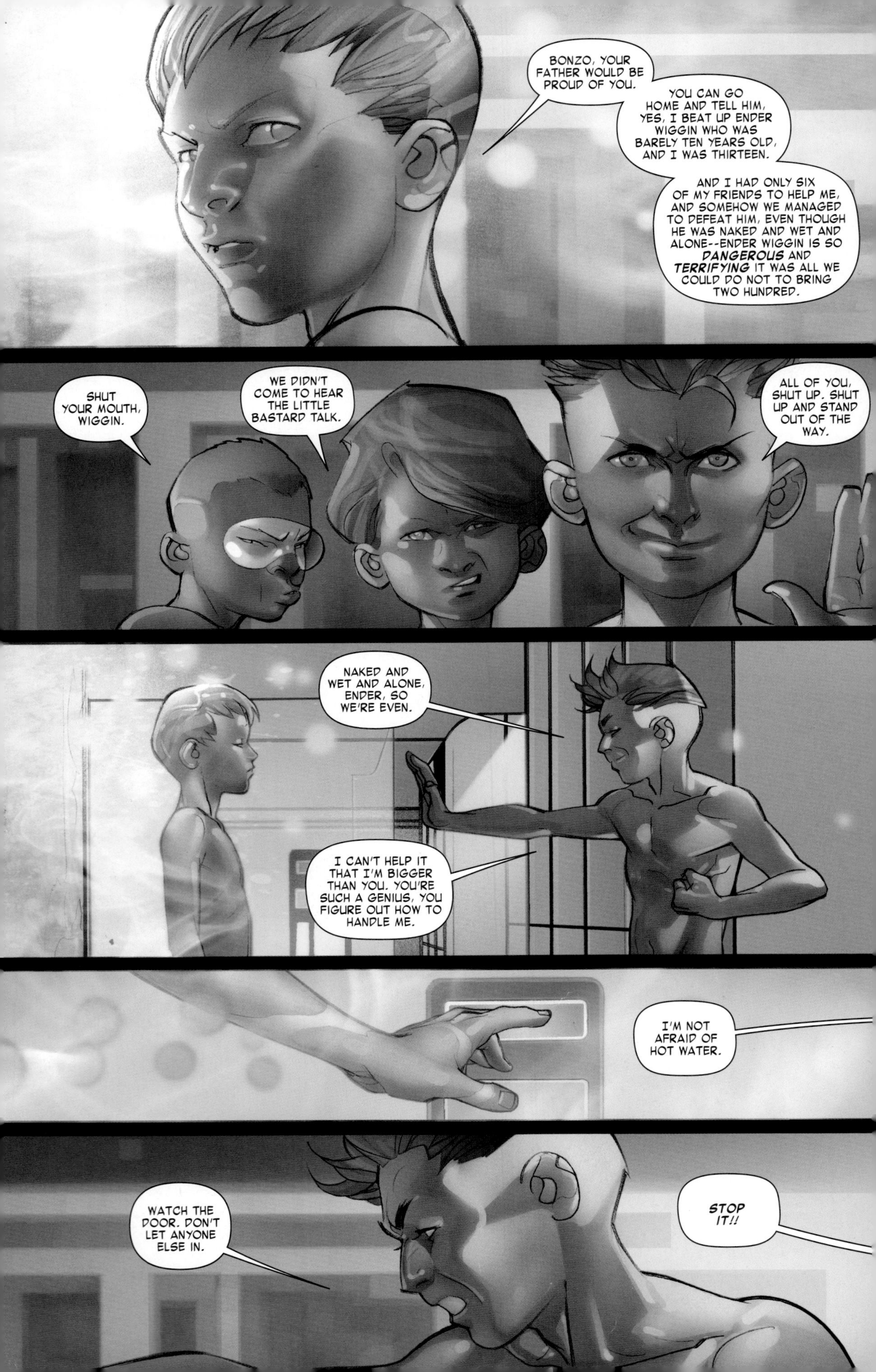
BONZO, YOUR FATHER WOULD BE PROUD OF YOU.
YOU CAN GO HOME AND TELL HIM, YES, I BEAT UP ENDER WIGGIN WHO WAS BARELY TEN YEARS OLD, AND I WAS THIRTEEN.
AND I HAD ONLY SIX OF MY FRIENDS TO HELP ME, AND SOMEHOW WE MANAGED TO DEFEAT HIM, EVEN THOUGH HE WAS NAKED AND WET AND ALONE--ENDER WIGGIN IS SO DANGEROUS AND TERRIFYING IT WAS ALL WE COULD DO NOT TO BRING TWO HUNDRED.
SHUT YOUR MOUTH, WIGGIN.
WE DIDN'T COME TO HEAR THE LITTLE BASTARD TALK.
ALL OF YOU, SHUT UP. SHUT UP AND STAND OUT OF THE WAY.
NAKED AND WET AND ALONE, ENDER, SO WE'RE EVEN.
I CAN'T HELP IT THAT I'M BIGGER THAN YOU. YOU'RE SUCH A GENIUS, YOU FIGURE OUT HOW TO HANDLE ME.
I'M NOT AFRAID OF HOT WATER.
WATCH THE DOOR. DON'T LET ANYONE ELSE IN.
STOP IT!!

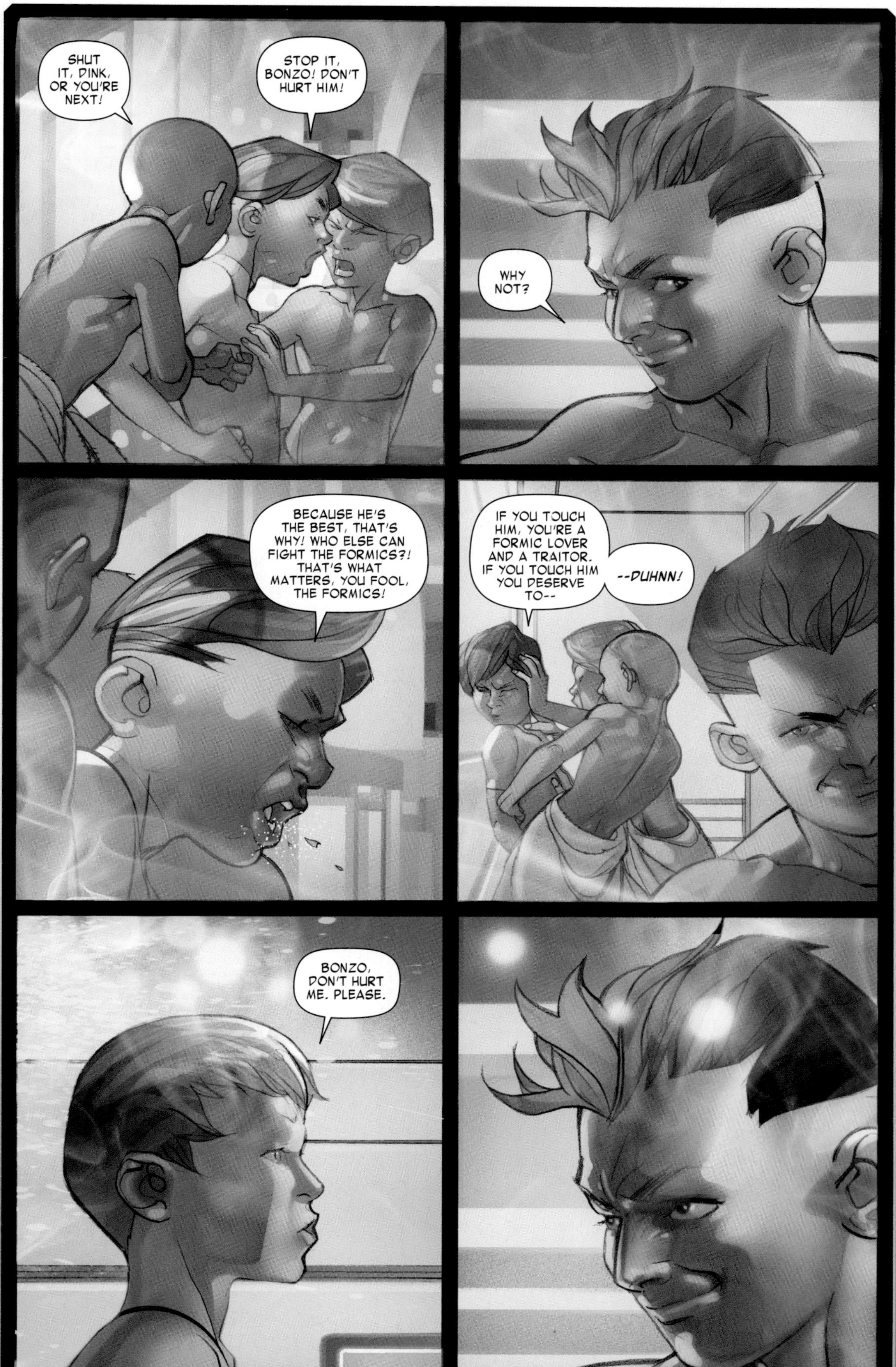
SHUT IT, DINK, OR YOU'RE NEXT!
STOP IT, BONZO! DON'T HURT HIM!
WHY NOT?
BECAUSE HE'S THE BEST, THAT'S WHY! WHO ELSE CAN FIGHT THE FORMICS?! THAT'S WHAT MATTERS, YOU FOOL, THE FORMICS!
IF YOU TOUCH HIM, YOU'RE A FORMIC LOVER AND A TRAITOR. IF YOU TOUCH HIM YOU DESERVE TO--
--DUHNN!
BONZO, DON'T HURT ME. PLEASE.

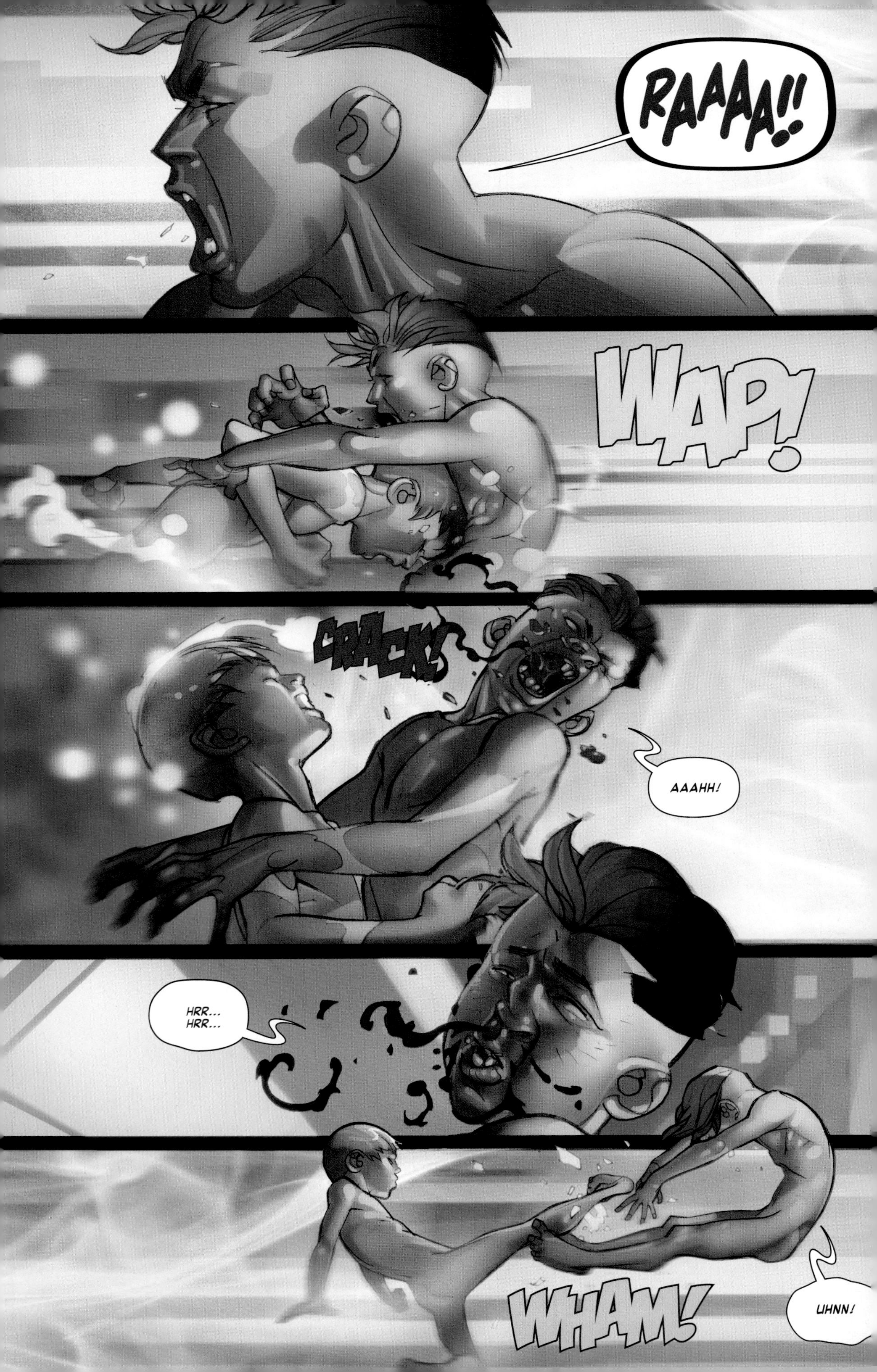
RAAAA!!
WAP!
CRACK!
AAAHH!
HRR... HRR...
WHAM!
UHNN!

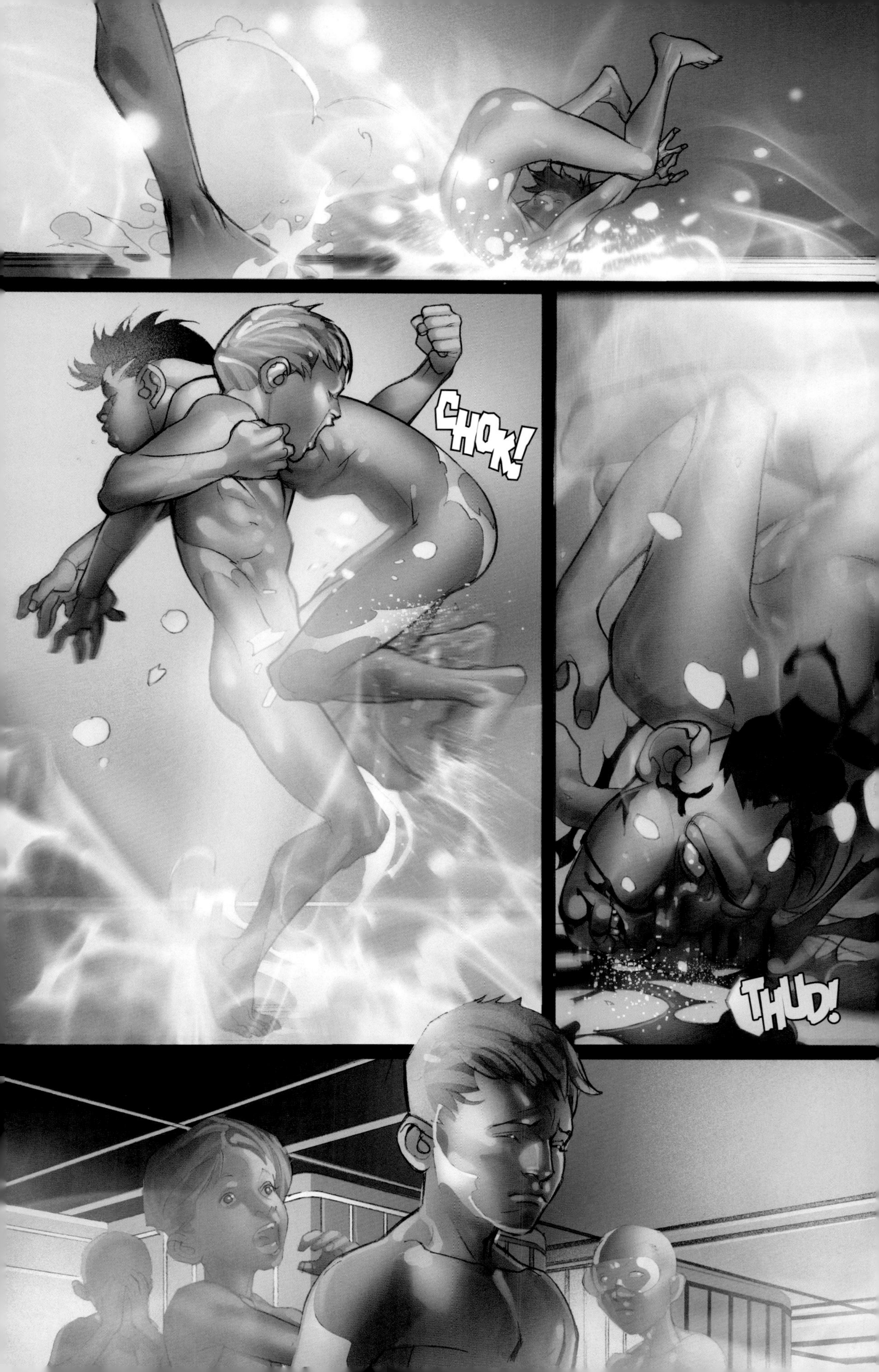
CHOK!
THUD!

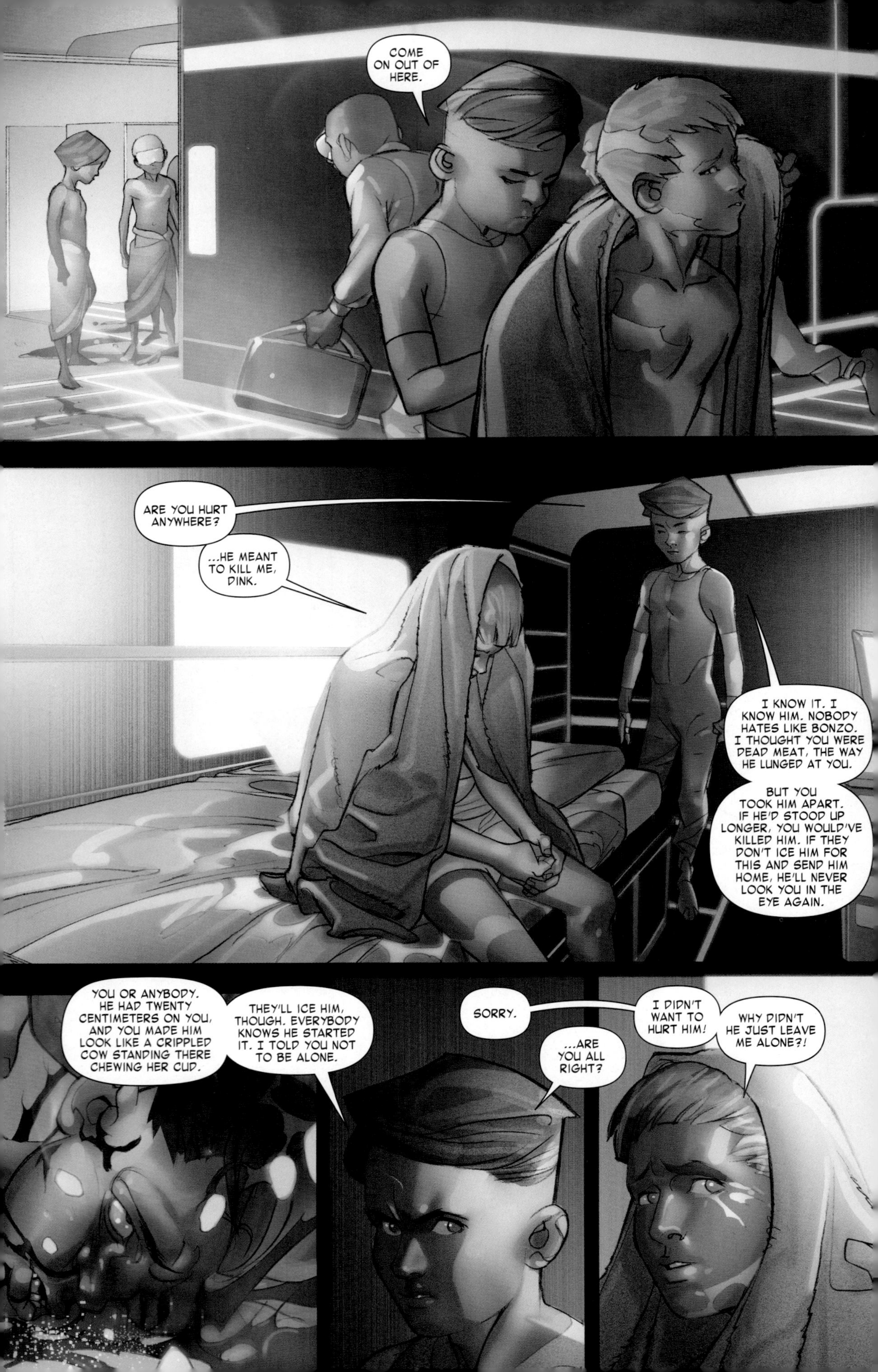

COME ON OUT OF HERE.
ARE YOU HURT ANYWHERE?
...HE MEANT TO KILL ME, DINK.
I KNOW IT. I KNOW HIM. NOBODY HATES LIKE BONZO. I THOUGHT YOU WERE DEAD MEAT, THE WAY HE LUNGED AT YOU.
BUT YOU TOOK HIM APART. IF HE'D STOOD UP LONGER, YOU WOULD'VE KILLED HIM. IF THEY DON'T ICE HIM FOR THIS AND SEND HIM HOME, HE'LL NEVER LOOK YOU IN THE EYE AGAIN.
YOU OR ANYBODY. HE HAD TWENTY CENTIMETERS ON YOU, AND YOU MADE HIM LOOK LIKE A CRIPPLED COW STANDING THERE CHEWING HER CUD.
THEY'LL ICE HIM, THOUGH. EVERYBODY KNOWS HE STARTED IT. I TOLD YOU NOT TO BE ALONE.
SORRY.
...ARE YOU ALL RIGHT?
I DIDN'T WANT TO HURT HIM!
WHY DIDN'T HE JUST LEAVE ME ALONE?!

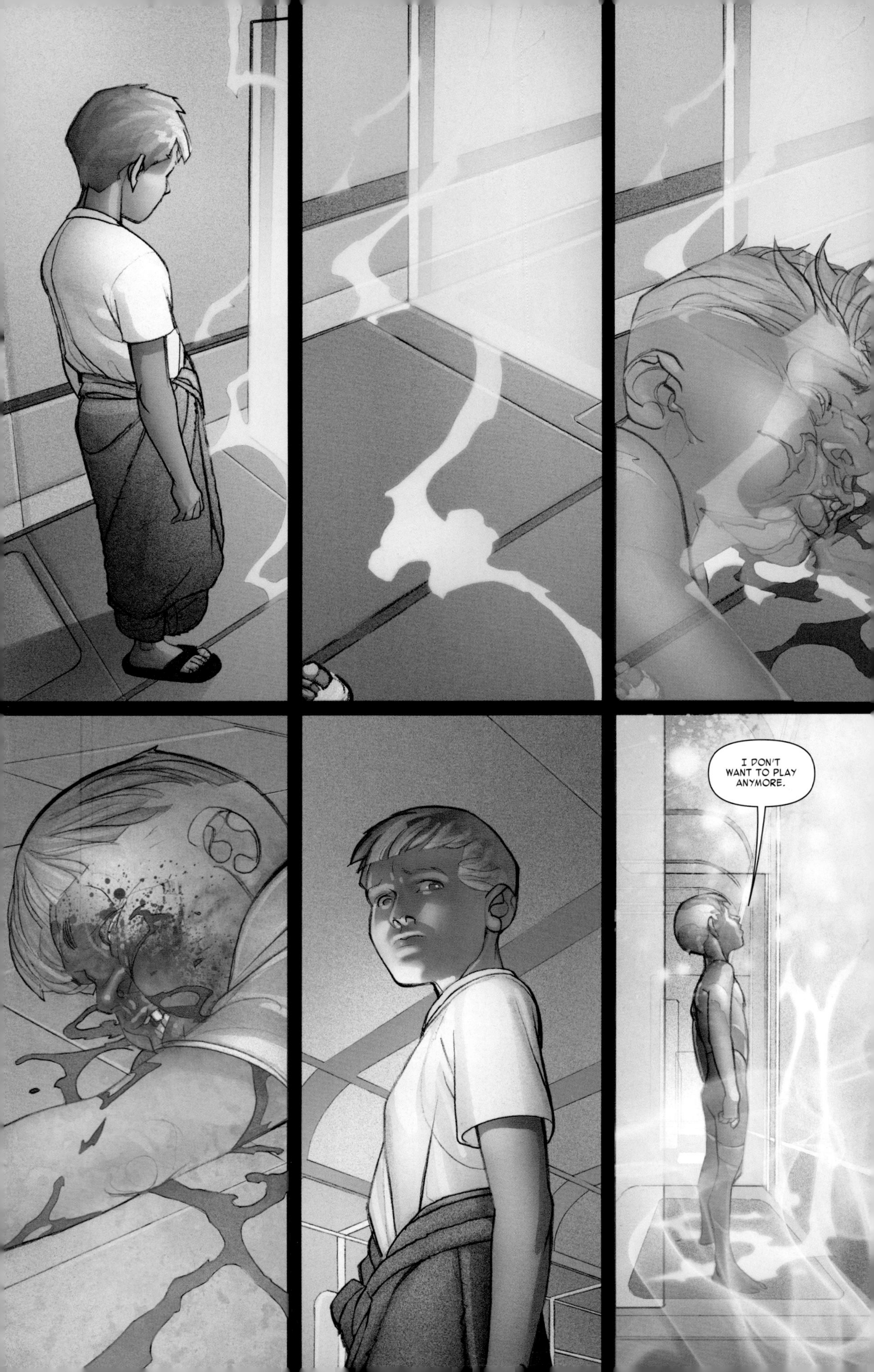
I DON'T WANT TO PLAY ANYMORE.

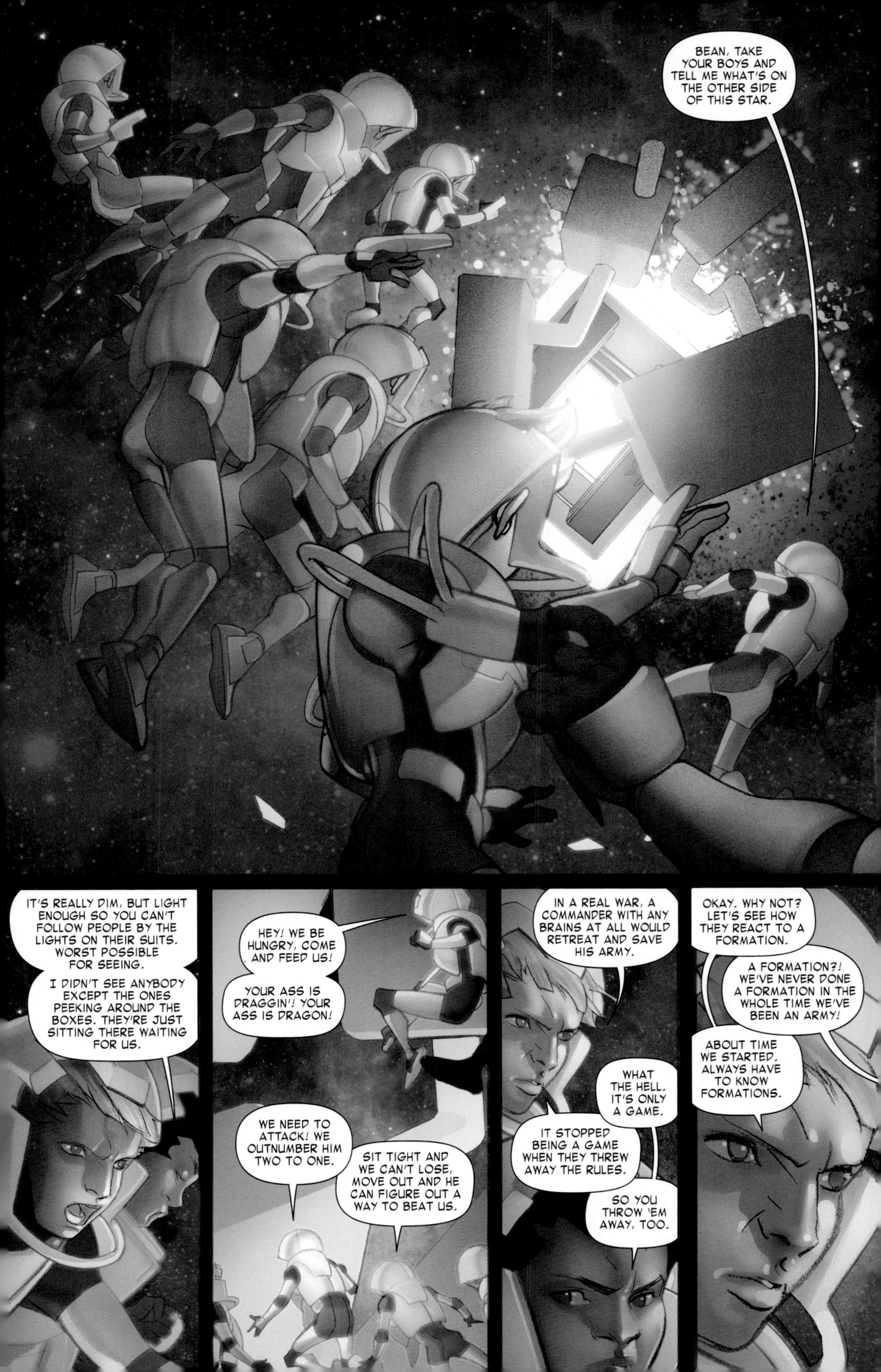
BEAN, TAKE YOUR BOYS AND TELL ME WHAT'S ON THE OTHER SIDE OF THIS STAR.
IT'S REALLY DIM, BUT LIGHT ENOUGH SO YOU CAN'T FOLLOW PEOPLE BY THE LIGHTS ON THEIR SUITS. WORST POSSIBLE FOR SEEING.
I DIDN'T SEE ANYBODY EXCEPT THE ONES PEEKING AROUND THE BOXES. THEY'RE JUST SITTING THERE WAITING FOR US.
HEY! WE BE HUNGRY, COME AND FEED US!
YOUR ASS IS DRAGGIN'! YOUR ASS IS DRAGON!
WE NEED TO ATTACK! WE OUTNUMBER HIM TWO TO ONE.
SIT TIGHT AND WE CAN'T LOSE, MOVE OUT AND HE CAN FIGURE OUT A WAY TO BEAT US.
IN A REAL WAR, A COMMANDER WITH ANY BRAINS AT ALL WOULD RETREAT AND SAVE HIS ARMY.
WHAT THE HELL. IT'S ONLY A GAME.
IT STOPPED BEING A GAME WHEN THEY THREW AWAY THE RULES.
SO YOU THROW 'EM AWAY, TOO.
OKAY. WHY NOT? LET'S SEE HOW THEY REACT TO A FORMATION.
A FORMATION?! WE'VE NEVER DONE A FORMATION IN THE WHOLE TIME WE'VE BEEN AN ARMY!
ABOUT TIME WE STARTED. ALWAYS HAVE TO KNOW FORMATIONS.

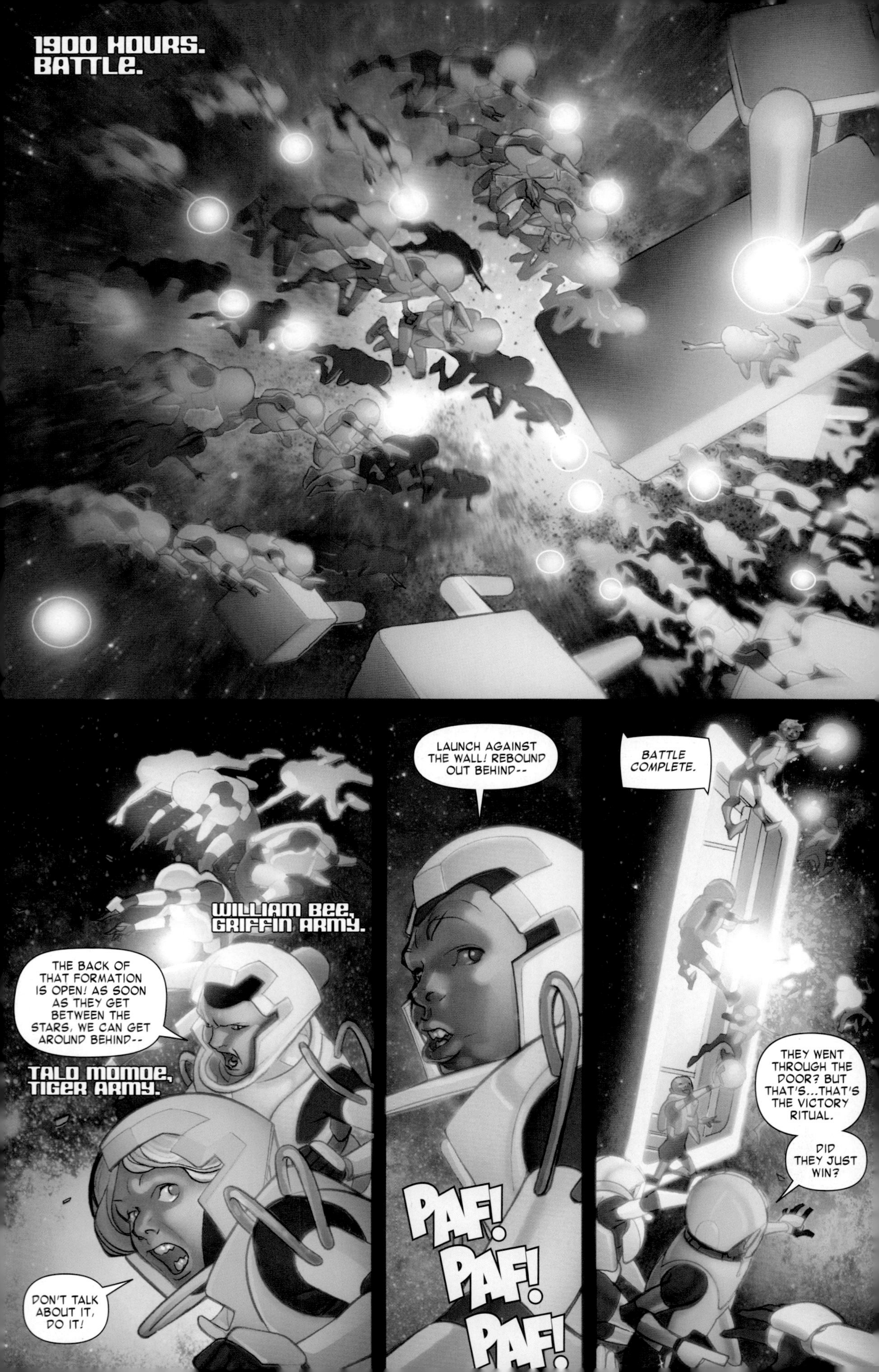

1900 HOURS. BATTLE.
WILLIAM BEE, GRIFFIN ARMY.
THE BACK OF THAT FORMATION IS OPEN! AS SOON AS THEY GET BETWEEN THE STARS, WE CAN GET AROUND BEHIND--
TALO MOMOE, TIGER ARMY.
DON'T TALK ABOUT IT, DO IT!
LAUNCH AGAINST THE WALL! REBOUND OUT BEHIND--
PAF! PAF! PAF!
BATTLE COMPLETE.
THEY WENT THROUGH THE DOOR? BUT THAT'S...THAT'S THE VICTORY RITUAL.
DID THEY JUST WIN?

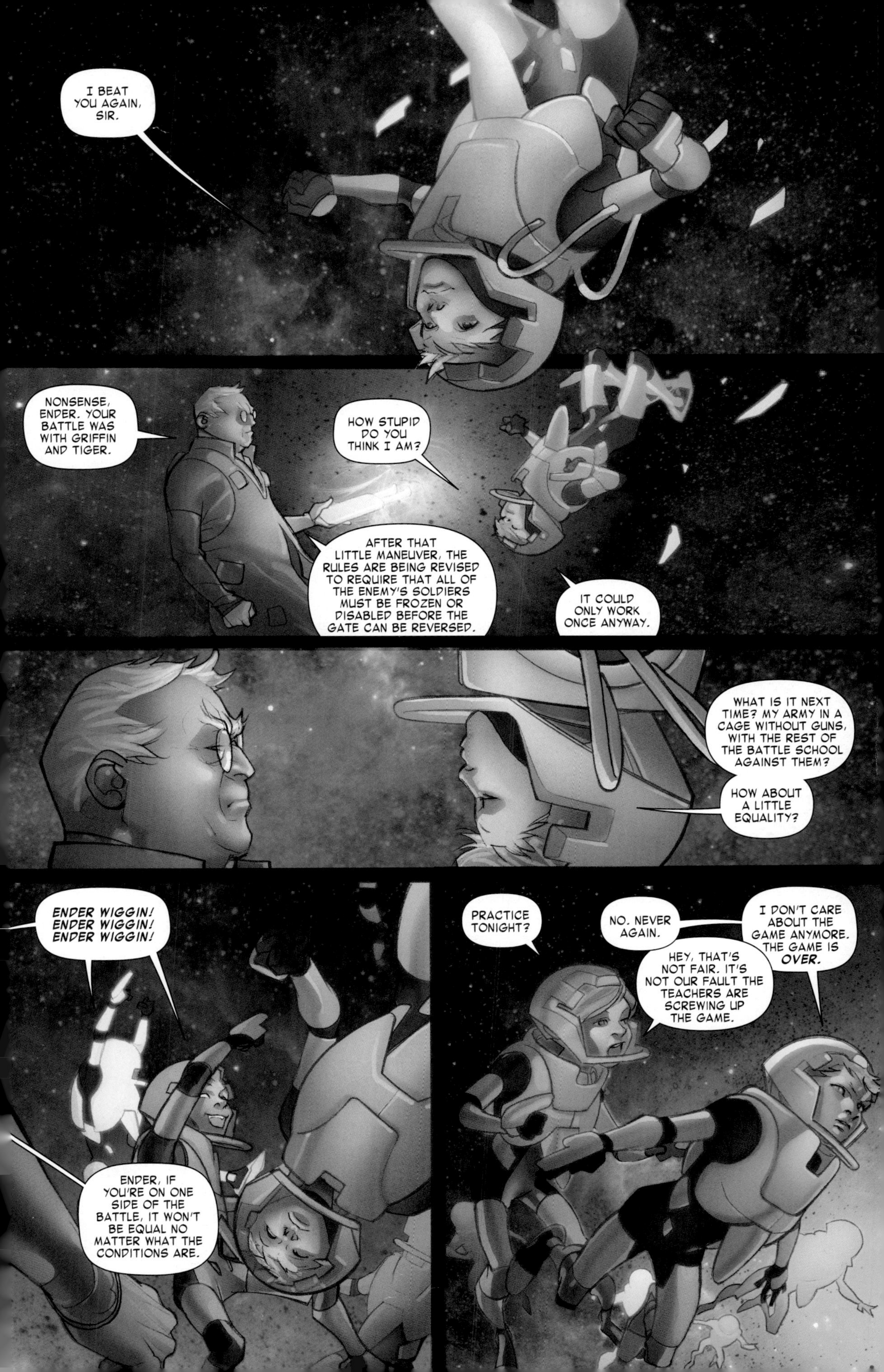
I BEAT YOU AGAIN, SIR.
NONSENSE, ENDER. YOUR BATTLE WAS WITH GRIFFIN AND TIGER.
HOW STUPID DO YOU THINK I AM?
AFTER THAT LITTLE MANEUVER, THE RULES ARE BEING REVISED TO REQUIRE THAT ALL OF THE ENEMY'S SOLDIERS MUST BE FROZEN OR DISABLED BEFORE THE GATE CAN BE REVERSED.
IT COULD ONLY WORK ONCE ANYWAY.
WHAT IS IT NEXT TIME? MY ARMY IN A CAGE WITHOUT GUNS, WITH THE REST OF THE BATTLE SCHOOL AGAINST THEM?
HOW ABOUT A LITTLE EQUALITY?
ENDER, IF YOU'RE ON ONE SIDE OF THE BATTLE, IT WON'T BE EQUAL NO MATTER WHAT THE CONDITIONS ARE.
ENDER WIGGIN! ENDER WIGGIN! ENDER WIGGIN!
PRACTICE TONIGHT?
NO. NEVER AGAIN.
HEY, THAT'S NOT FAIR. IT'S NOT OUR FAULT THE TEACHERS ARE SCREWING UP THE GAME.
I DON'T CARE ABOUT THE GAME ANYMORE. THE GAME IS ***OVER.***

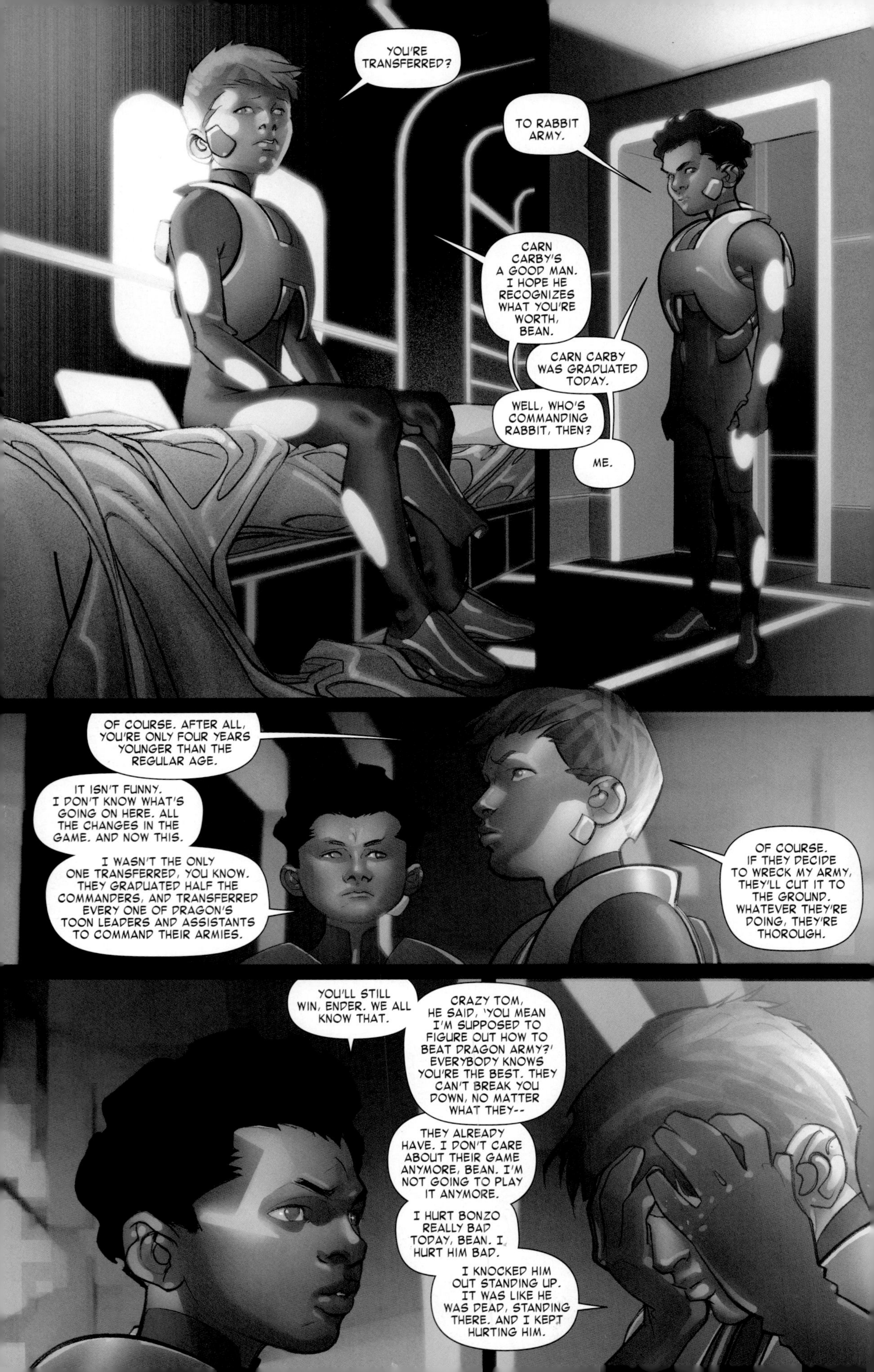
YOU'RE TRANSFERRED?
TO RABBIT ARMY.
CARN CARBY'S A GOOD MAN. I HOPE HE RECOGNIZES WHAT YOU'RE WORTH, BEAN.
CARN CARBY WAS GRADUATED TODAY.
WELL, WHO'S COMMANDING RABBIT, THEN?
ME.
OF COURSE. AFTER ALL, YOU'RE ONLY FOUR YEARS YOUNGER THAN THE REGULAR AGE.
IT ISN'T FUNNY. I DON'T KNOW WHAT'S GOING ON HERE. ALL THE CHANGES IN THE GAME. AND NOW THIS.
I WASN'T THE ONLY ONE TRANSFERRED, YOU KNOW. THEY GRADUATED HALF THE COMMANDERS, AND TRANSFERRED EVERY ONE OF DRAGON'S TOON LEADERS AND ASSISTANTS TO COMMAND THEIR ARMIES.
OF COURSE. IF THEY DECIDE TO WRECK MY ARMY, THEY'LL CUT IT TO THE GROUND. WHATEVER THEY'RE DOING, THEY'RE THOROUGH.
YOU'LL STILL WIN, ENDER. WE ALL KNOW THAT.
CRAZY TOM, HE SAID, 'YOU MEAN I'M SUPPOSED TO FIGURE OUT HOW TO BEAT DRAGON ARMY?' EVERYBODY KNOWS YOU'RE THE BEST. THEY CAN'T BREAK YOU DOWN, NO MATTER WHAT THEY--
THEY ALREADY HAVE. I DON'T CARE ABOUT THEIR GAME ANYMORE, BEAN. I'M NOT GOING TO PLAY IT ANYMORE.
I HURT BONZO REALLY BAD TODAY, BEAN. I HURT HIM BAD.
I KNOCKED HIM OUT STANDING UP. IT WAS LIKE HE WAS DEAD, STANDING THERE. AND I KEPT HURTING HIM.

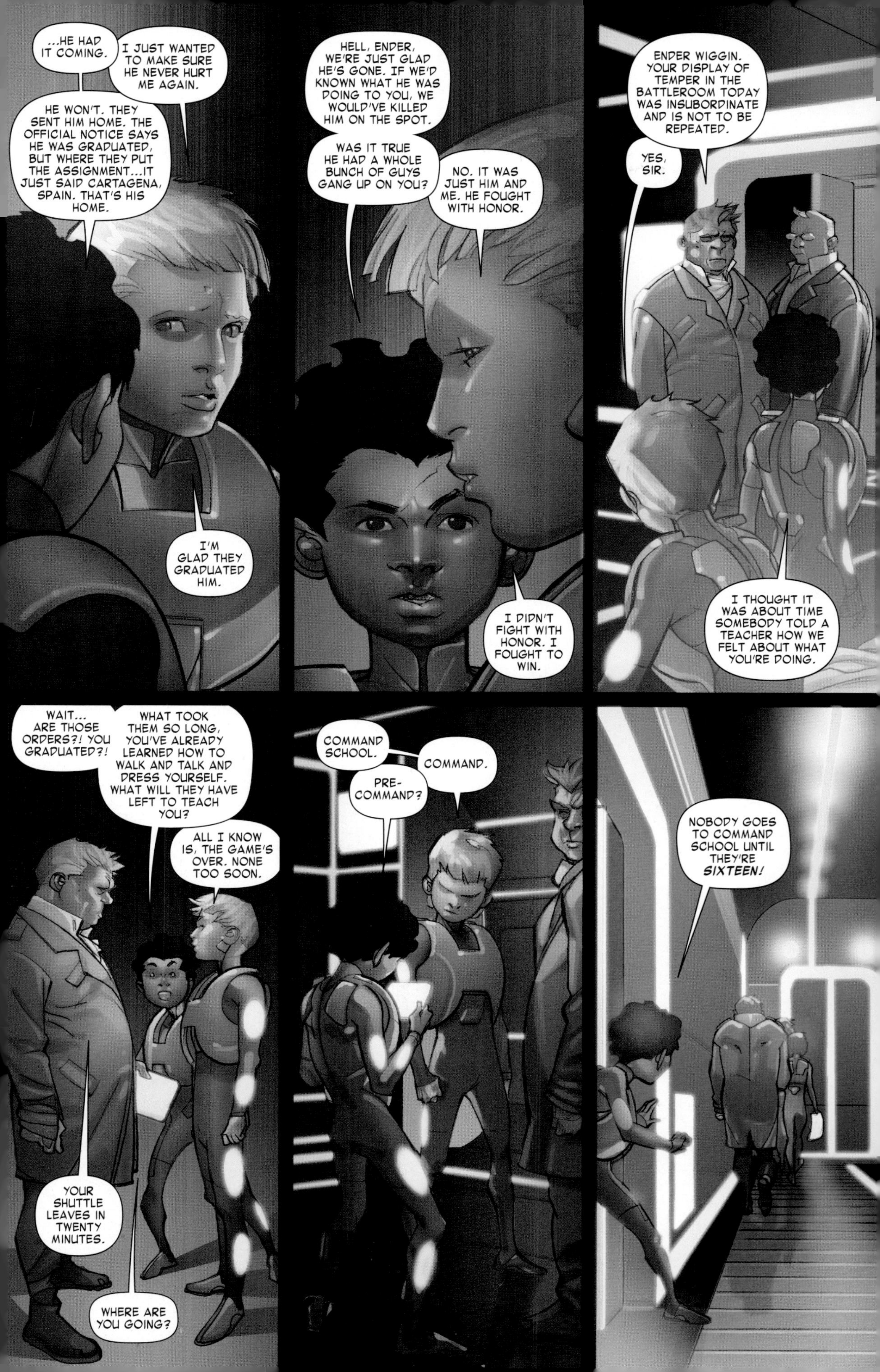
...HE HAD IT COMING.
I JUST WANTED TO MAKE SURE HE NEVER HURT ME AGAIN.
HE WON'T. THEY SENT HIM HOME. THE OFFICIAL NOTICE SAYS HE WAS GRADUATED, BUT WHERE THEY PUT THE ASSIGNMENT...IT JUST SAID CARTAGENA, SPAIN. THAT'S HIS HOME.
I'M GLAD THEY GRADUATED HIM.
HELL, ENDER, WE'RE JUST GLAD HE'S GONE. IF WE'D KNOWN WHAT HE WAS DOING TO YOU, WE WOULD'VE KILLED HIM ON THE SPOT.
WAS IT TRUE HE HAD A WHOLE BUNCH OF GUYS GANG UP ON YOU?
NO. IT WAS JUST HIM AND ME. HE FOUGHT WITH HONOR.
I DIDN'T FIGHT WITH HONOR. I FOUGHT TO WIN.
ENDER WIGGIN. YOUR DISPLAY OF TEMPER IN THE BATTLEROOM TODAY WAS INSUBORDINATE AND IS NOT TO BE REPEATED.
YES, SIR.
I THOUGHT IT WAS ABOUT TIME SOMEBODY TOLD A TEACHER HOW WE FELT ABOUT WHAT YOU'RE DOING.
WAIT... ARE THOSE ORDERS?! YOU GRADUATED?!
WHAT TOOK THEM SO LONG, YOU'VE ALREADY LEARNED HOW TO WALK AND TALK AND DRESS YOURSELF. WHAT WILL THEY HAVE LEFT TO TEACH YOU?
ALL I KNOW IS, THE GAME'S OVER. NONE TOO SOON.
YOUR SHUTTLE LEAVES IN TWENTY MINUTES.
WHERE ARE YOU GOING?
COMMAND SCHOOL.
PRE-COMMAND?
COMMAND.
NOBODY GOES TO COMMAND SCHOOL UNTIL THEY'RE *SIXTEEN!*

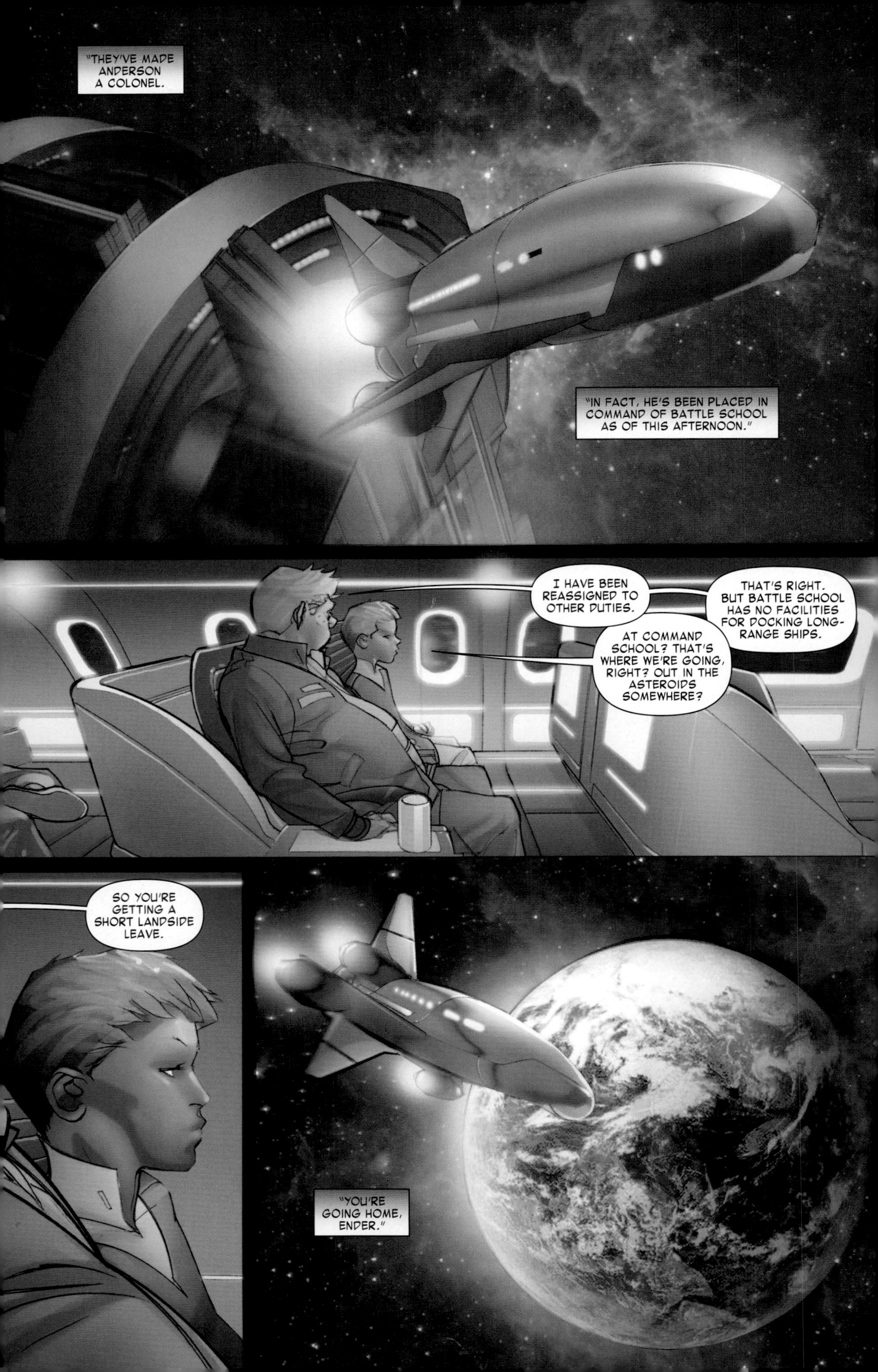
"THEY'VE MADE ANDERSON A COLONEL.
"IN FACT, HE'S BEEN PLACED IN COMMAND OF BATTLE SCHOOL AS OF THIS AFTERNOON."
I HAVE BEEN REASSIGNED TO OTHER DUTIES.
AT COMMAND SCHOOL? THAT'S WHERE WE'RE GOING, RIGHT? OUT IN THE ASTEROIDS SOMEWHERE?
THAT'S RIGHT. BUT BATTLE SCHOOL HAS NO FACILITIES FOR DOCKING LONG-RANGE SHIPS.
SO YOU'RE GETTING A SHORT LANDSIDE LEAVE.
"YOU'RE GOING HOME, ENDER."

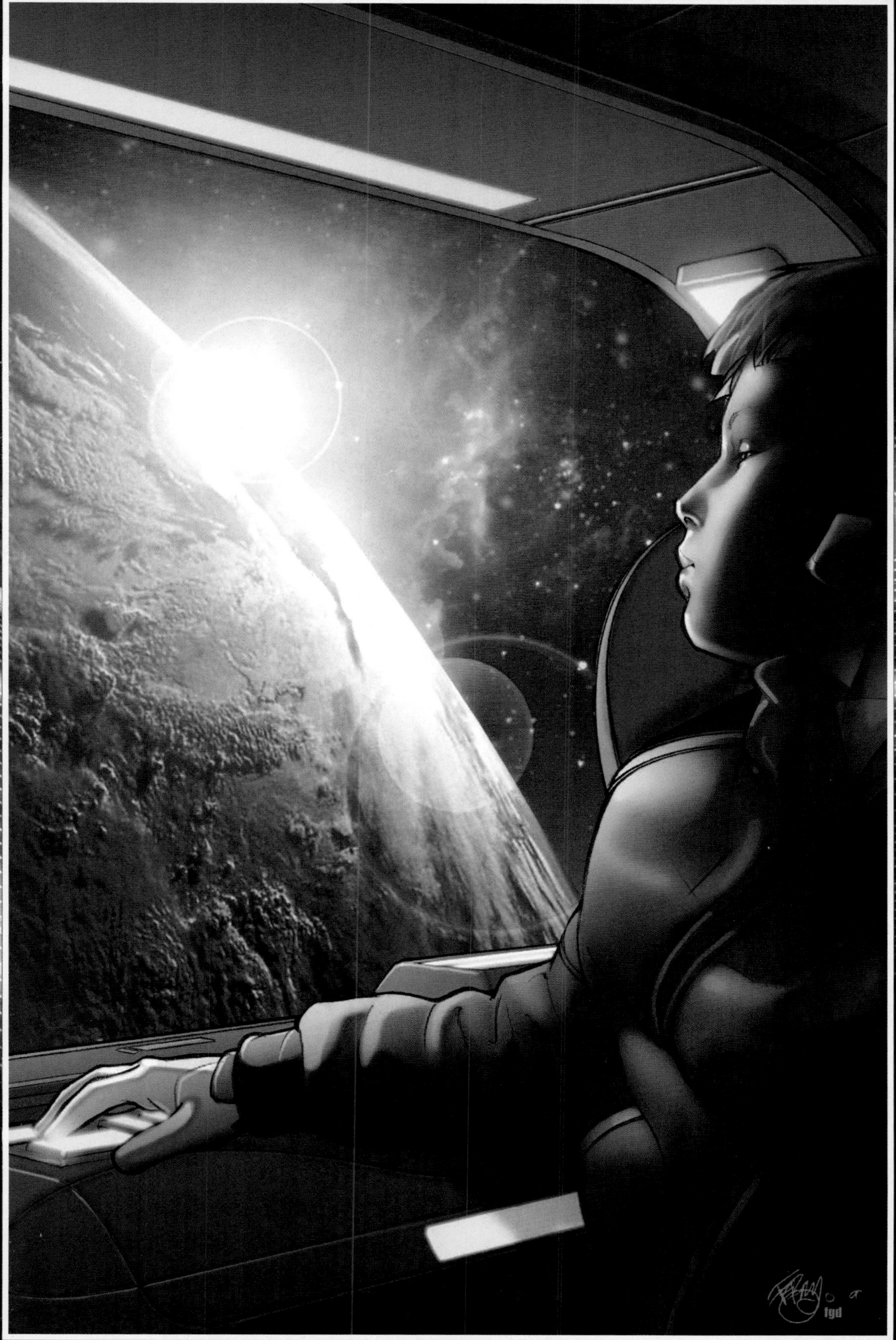

F O U R

INTERNATIONAL FLEET MONITORED COMMUNICATIONS
PARTICIPANTS: COLONEL ANDERSON, MAJOR IMBU
REF ID # 23504-22-991, KEYWORD SEARCH: 'GRAFF'

<<<TRANSCRIPT OF A CONVERSATION HELD AT BATTLE SCHOOL AFTER
THE DEPARTURE OF COL. GRAFF AND ENDER WIGGIN>>>

ANDERSON: They didn't tell me whether Colonel Graff was being
promoted or court-martialed. Just transferred.

IMBU: Is that a good or bad sign?

A: Who knows? On the one hand, Ender Wiggin not only survived, he
passed a threshold, he graduated in dazzlingly good shape, you have
to give old Graff credit for that. On the other hand, there's the fourth
passenger on the shuttle. The one travelling in a bag.

I: Only the second death in the history of the school. At least it wasn't a
suicide this time.

A: How is murder better, Major Imbu?

I: It wasn't murder, Colonel. We have it on video from two angles. No one
can blame Ender.

A: But they might blame Graff. At least they had the good sense not to
tell Ender that the boy died.

I: It's the second time, too.

A: They didn't tell him about Stilson, either.

I: The kid is scary.

A: Ender Wiggin isn't a killer. He just wins—thoroughly. If anybody's
going to be scared, let it be the Formics.

I: Makes you almost feel sorry for them, knowing Ender's going to be
coming after them.

A: The only one I feel sorry for is Ender. But not sorry enough to suggest
they ought to let up on him. I just got access to the material that Graff's
been getting all this time. About fleet movements, that sort of thing. I
used to sleep easy at night.

I: Time's getting short?

A: Leave it at this–they didn't graduate him to Command School a day too
soon. And maybe a couple of years too late.

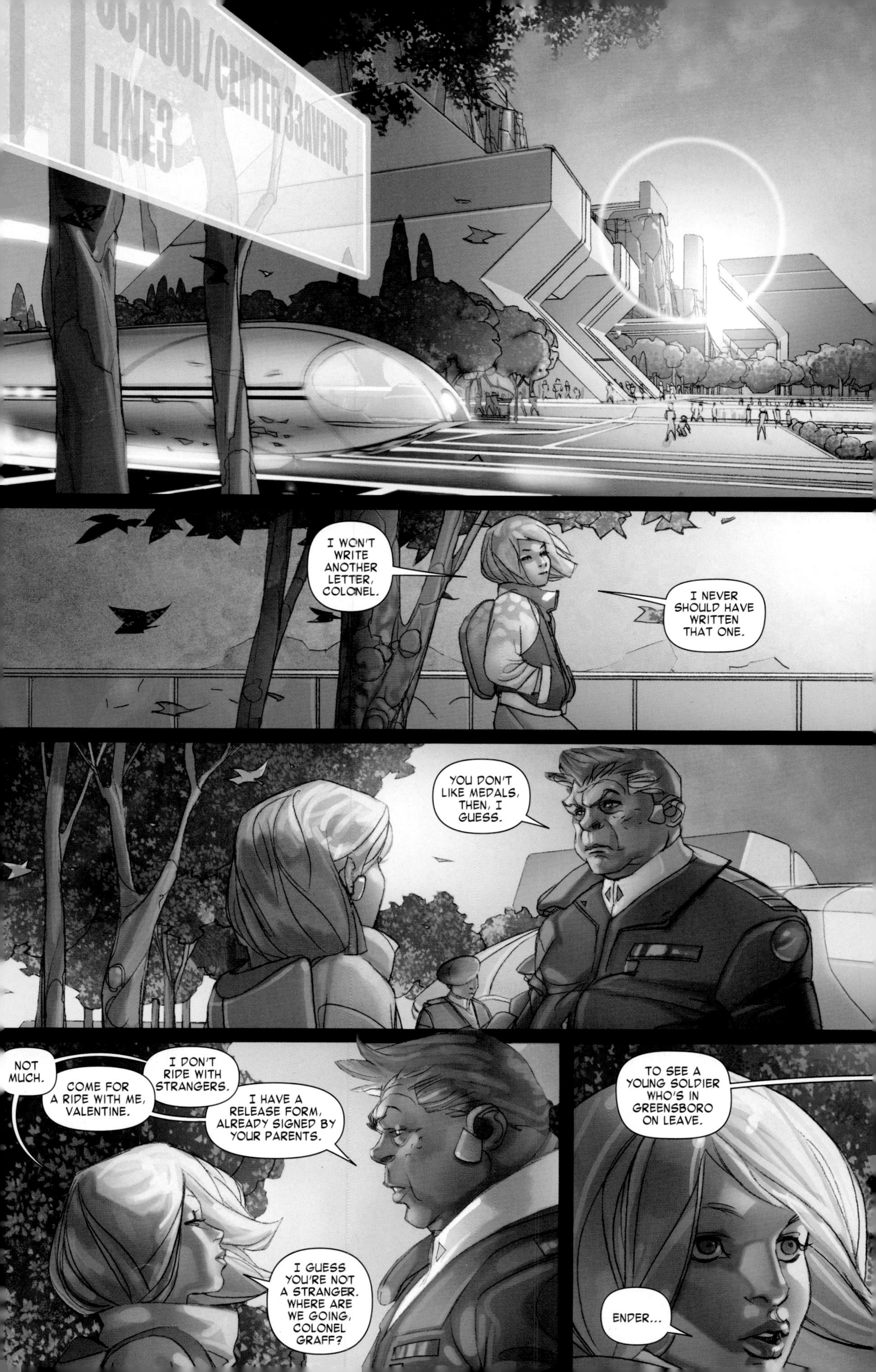
SCHOOL/CENTER 33AVENUE
LINE3
I WON'T WRITE ANOTHER LETTER, COLONEL.
I NEVER SHOULD HAVE WRITTEN THAT ONE.
YOU DON'T LIKE MEDALS, THEN, I GUESS.
NOT MUCH.
COME FOR A RIDE WITH ME, VALENTINE.
I DON'T RIDE WITH STRANGERS.
I HAVE A RELEASE FORM, ALREADY SIGNED BY YOUR PARENTS.
I GUESS YOU'RE NOT A STRANGER. WHERE ARE WE GOING, COLONEL GRAFF?
TO SEE A YOUNG SOLDIER WHO'S IN GREENSBORO ON LEAVE.
ENDER...

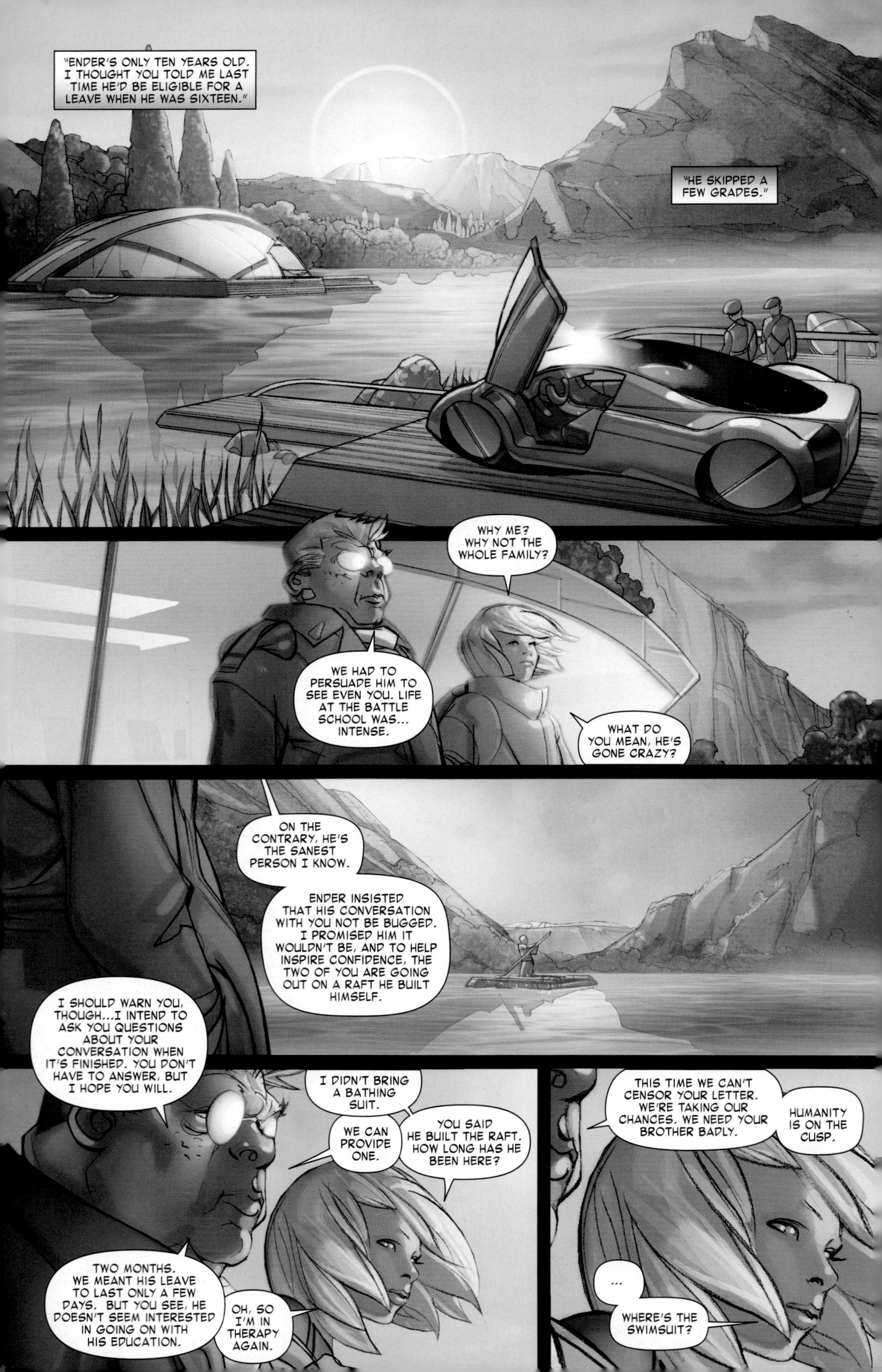
"ENDER'S ONLY TEN YEARS OLD. I THOUGHT YOU TOLD ME LAST TIME HE'D BE ELIGIBLE FOR A LEAVE WHEN HE WAS SIXTEEN."
"HE SKIPPED A FEW GRADES."
WHY ME? WHY NOT THE WHOLE FAMILY?
WE HAD TO PERSUADE HIM TO SEE EVEN YOU. LIFE AT THE BATTLE SCHOOL WAS... INTENSE.
WHAT DO YOU MEAN, HE'S GONE CRAZY?
ON THE CONTRARY, HE'S THE SANEST PERSON I KNOW.
ENDER INSISTED THAT HIS CONVERSATION WITH YOU NOT BE BUGGED. I PROMISED HIM IT WOULDN'T BE, AND TO HELP INSPIRE CONFIDENCE, THE TWO OF YOU ARE GOING OUT ON A RAFT HE BUILT HIMSELF.
I SHOULD WARN YOU, THOUGH...I INTEND TO ASK YOU QUESTIONS ABOUT YOUR CONVERSATION WHEN IT'S FINISHED. YOU DON'T HAVE TO ANSWER, BUT I HOPE YOU WILL.
I DIDN'T BRING A BATHING SUIT.
WE CAN PROVIDE ONE.
YOU SAID HE BUILT THE RAFT. HOW LONG HAS HE BEEN HERE?
TWO MONTHS. WE MEANT HIS LEAVE TO LAST ONLY A FEW DAYS. BUT YOU SEE, HE DOESN'T SEEM INTERESTED IN GOING ON WITH HIS EDUCATION.
OH, SO I'M IN THERAPY AGAIN.
THIS TIME WE CAN'T CENSOR YOUR LETTER. WE'RE TAKING OUR CHANCES. WE NEED YOUR BROTHER BADLY.
HUMANITY IS ON THE CUSP.
...
WHERE'S THE SWIMSUIT?

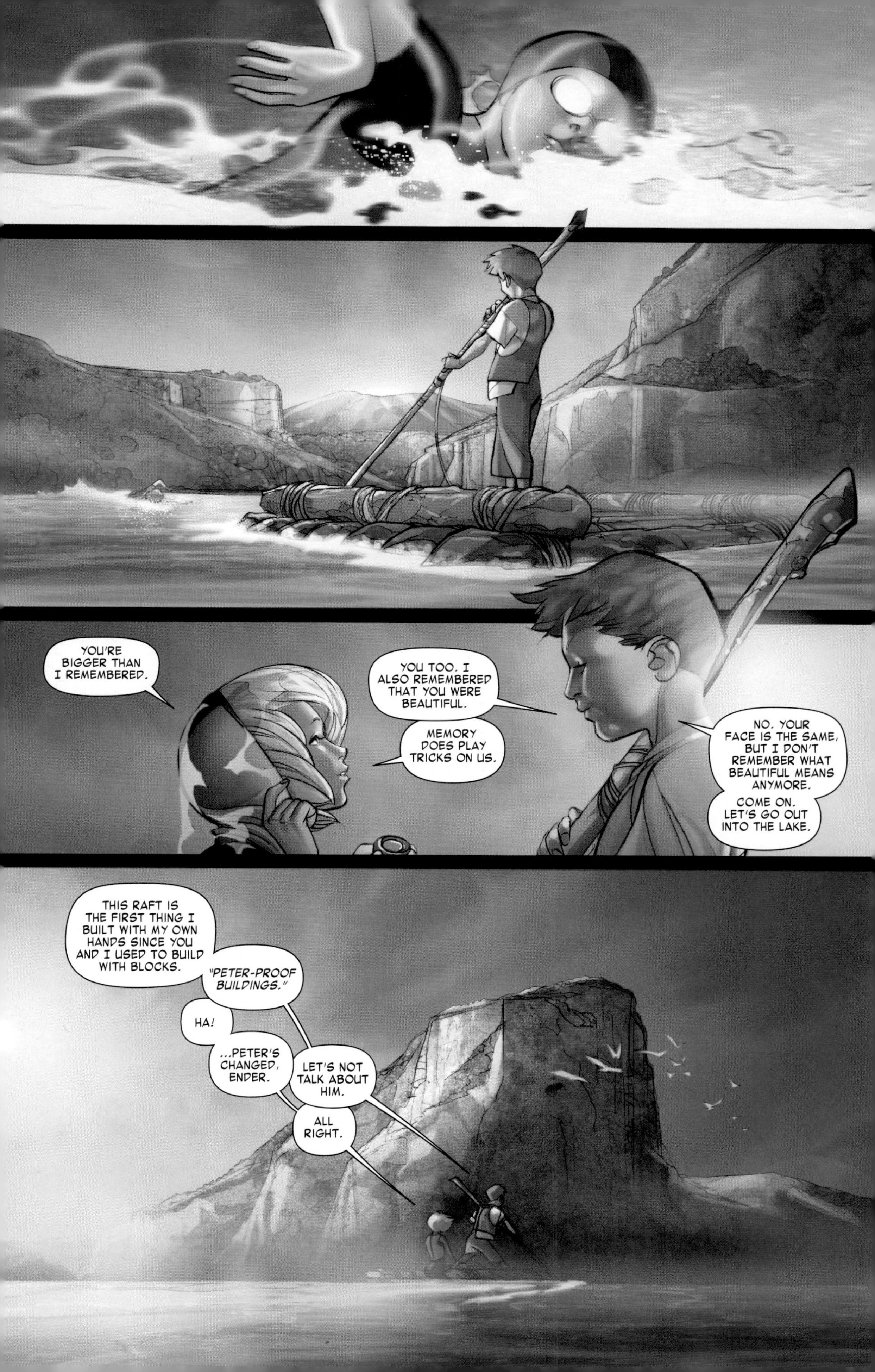
YOU'RE BIGGER THAN I REMEMBERED.
YOU TOO. I ALSO REMEMBERED THAT YOU WERE BEAUTIFUL.
MEMORY DOES PLAY TRICKS ON US.
NO. YOUR FACE IS THE SAME, BUT I DON'T REMEMBER WHAT BEAUTIFUL MEANS ANYMORE.
COME ON. LET'S GO OUT INTO THE LAKE.
THIS RAFT IS THE FIRST THING I BUILT WITH MY OWN HANDS SINCE YOU AND I USED TO BUILD WITH BLOCKS.
"PETER-PROOF BUILDINGS."
HA!
...PETER'S CHANGED, ENDER.
LET'S NOT TALK ABOUT HIM.
ALL RIGHT.

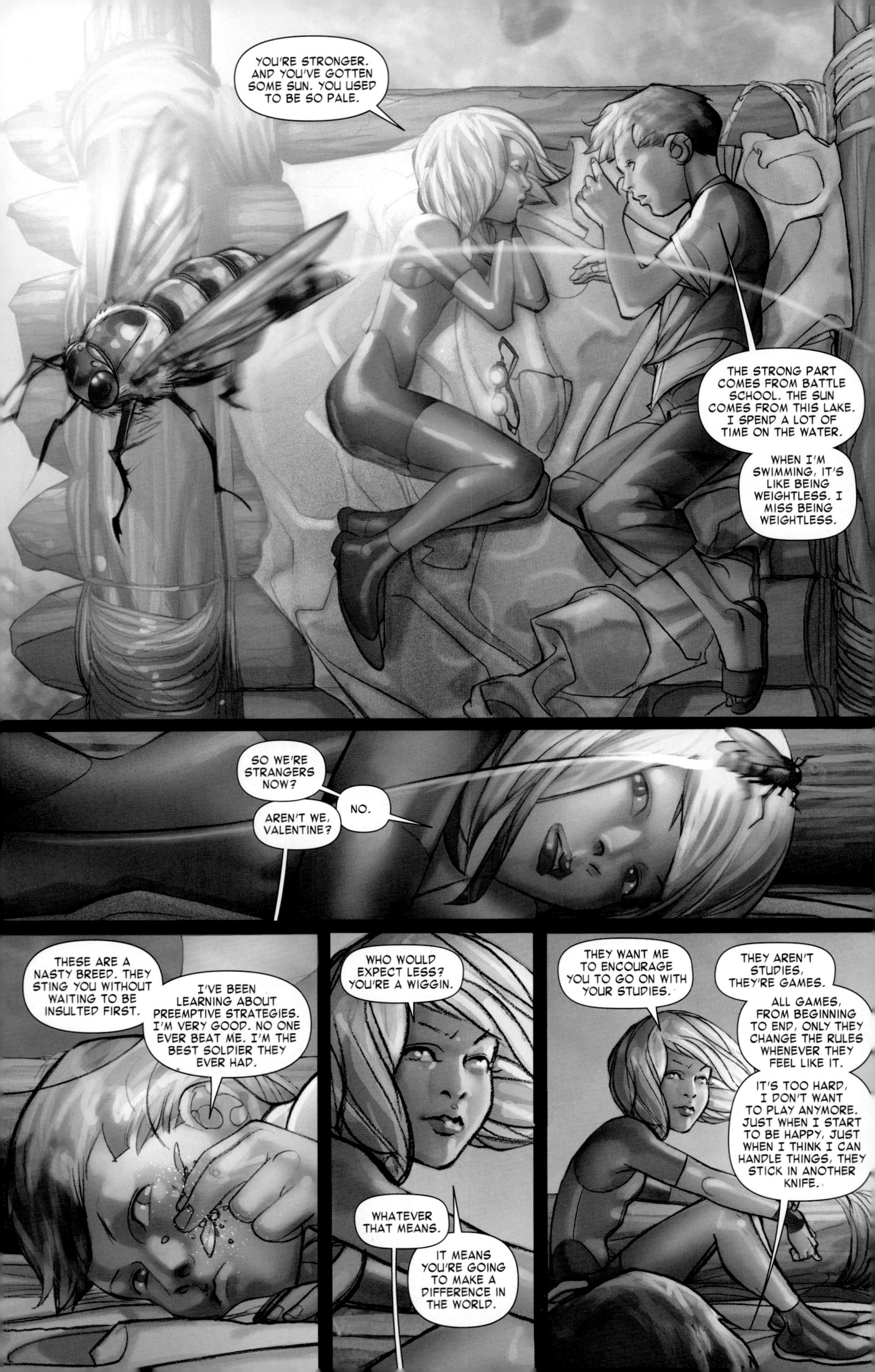
YOU'RE STRONGER. AND YOU'VE GOTTEN SOME SUN. YOU USED TO BE SO PALE.
THE STRONG PART COMES FROM BATTLE SCHOOL. THE SUN COMES FROM THIS LAKE. I SPEND A LOT OF TIME ON THE WATER.
WHEN I'M SWIMMING, IT'S LIKE BEING WEIGHTLESS. I MISS BEING WEIGHTLESS.
SO WE'RE STRANGERS NOW?
NO.
AREN'T WE, VALENTINE?
THESE ARE A NASTY BREED. THEY STING YOU WITHOUT WAITING TO BE INSULTED FIRST.
I'VE BEEN LEARNING ABOUT PREEMPTIVE STRATEGIES. I'M VERY GOOD. NO ONE EVER BEAT ME. I'M THE BEST SOLDIER THEY EVER HAD.
WHO WOULD EXPECT LESS? YOU'RE A WIGGIN.
WHATEVER THAT MEANS.
IT MEANS YOU'RE GOING TO MAKE A DIFFERENCE IN THE WORLD.
THEY WANT ME TO ENCOURAGE YOU TO GO ON WITH YOUR STUDIES.
THEY AREN'T STUDIES, THEY'RE GAMES.
ALL GAMES, FROM BEGINNING TO END, ONLY THEY CHANGE THE RULES WHENEVER THEY FEEL LIKE IT.
IT'S TOO HARD, I DON'T WANT TO PLAY ANYMORE. JUST WHEN I START TO BE HAPPY, JUST WHEN I THINK I CAN HANDLE THINGS, THEY STICK IN ANOTHER KNIFE.

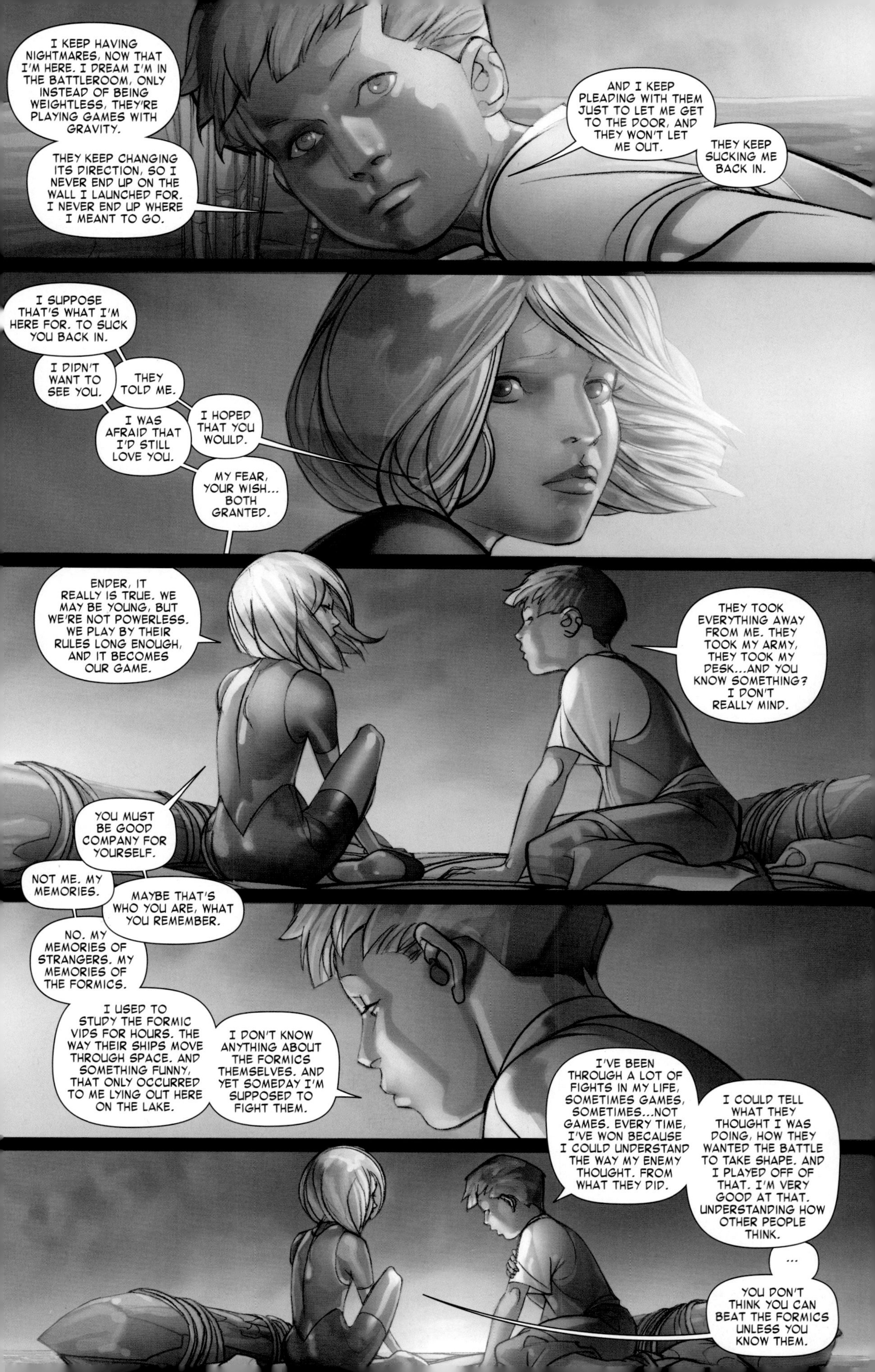
I KEEP HAVING NIGHTMARES, NOW THAT I'M HERE. I DREAM I'M IN THE BATTLEROOM, ONLY INSTEAD OF BEING WEIGHTLESS, THEY'RE PLAYING GAMES WITH GRAVITY.
THEY KEEP CHANGING ITS DIRECTION, SO I NEVER END UP ON THE WALL I LAUNCHED FOR. I NEVER END UP WHERE I MEANT TO GO.
AND I KEEP PLEADING WITH THEM JUST TO LET ME GET TO THE DOOR, AND THEY WON'T LET ME OUT.
THEY KEEP SUCKING ME BACK IN.
I SUPPOSE THAT'S WHAT I'M HERE FOR. TO SUCK YOU BACK IN.
I DIDN'T WANT TO SEE YOU.
THEY TOLD ME.
I WAS AFRAID THAT I'D STILL LOVE YOU.
I HOPED THAT YOU WOULD.
MY FEAR, YOUR WISH... BOTH GRANTED.
ENDER, IT REALLY IS TRUE. WE MAY BE YOUNG, BUT WE'RE NOT POWERLESS. WE PLAY BY THEIR RULES LONG ENOUGH, AND IT BECOMES OUR GAME.
THEY TOOK EVERYTHING AWAY FROM ME. THEY TOOK MY ARMY, THEY TOOK MY DESK...AND YOU KNOW SOMETHING? I DON'T REALLY MIND.
YOU MUST BE GOOD COMPANY FOR YOURSELF.
NOT ME. MY MEMORIES.
MAYBE THAT'S WHO YOU ARE, WHAT YOU REMEMBER.
NO. MY MEMORIES OF STRANGERS. MY MEMORIES OF THE FORMICS.
I USED TO STUDY THE FORMIC VIDS FOR HOURS. THE WAY THEIR SHIPS MOVE THROUGH SPACE. AND SOMETHING FUNNY, THAT ONLY OCCURRED TO ME LYING OUT HERE ON THE LAKE.
I DON'T KNOW ANYTHING ABOUT THE FORMICS THEMSELVES. AND YET SOMEDAY I'M SUPPOSED TO FIGHT THEM.
I'VE BEEN THROUGH A LOT OF FIGHTS IN MY LIFE, SOMETIMES GAMES, SOMETIMES...NOT GAMES. EVERY TIME, I'VE WON BECAUSE I COULD UNDERSTAND THE WAY MY ENEMY THOUGHT. FROM WHAT THEY DID.
I COULD TELL WHAT THEY THOUGHT I WAS DOING, HOW THEY WANTED THE BATTLE TO TAKE SHAPE. AND I PLAYED OFF OF THAT. I'M VERY GOOD AT THAT. UNDERSTANDING HOW OTHER PEOPLE THINK.
...
YOU DON'T THINK YOU CAN BEAT THE FORMICS UNLESS YOU KNOW THEM.

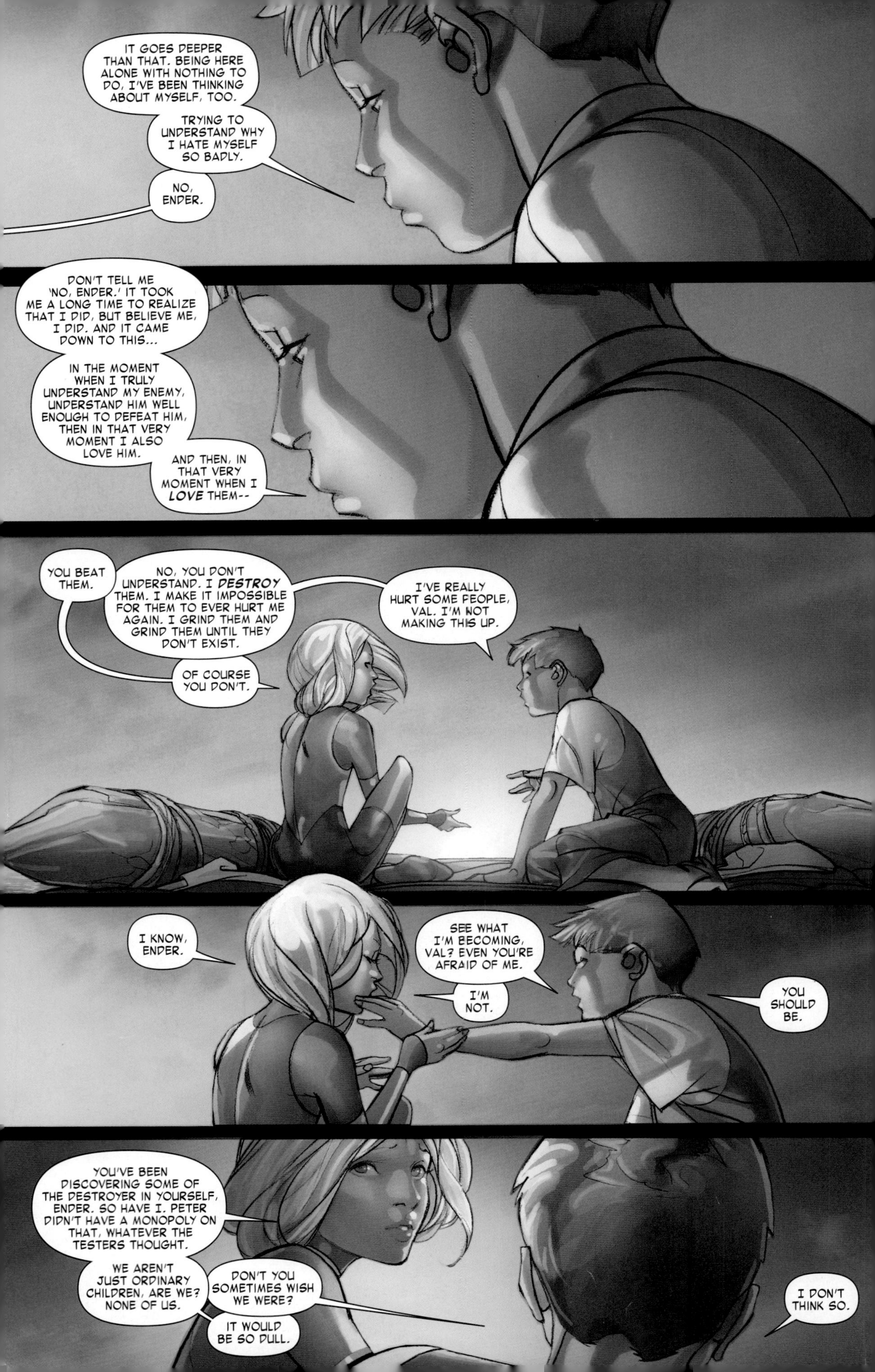
IT GOES DEEPER THAN THAT. BEING HERE ALONE WITH NOTHING TO DO, I'VE BEEN THINKING ABOUT MYSELF, TOO.
TRYING TO UNDERSTAND WHY I HATE MYSELF SO BADLY.
NO, ENDER.
DON'T TELL ME 'NO, ENDER.' IT TOOK ME A LONG TIME TO REALIZE THAT I DID, BUT BELIEVE ME, I DID. AND IT CAME DOWN TO THIS...
IN THE MOMENT WHEN I TRULY UNDERSTAND MY ENEMY, UNDERSTAND HIM WELL ENOUGH TO DEFEAT HIM, THEN IN THAT VERY MOMENT I ALSO LOVE HIM.
AND THEN, IN THAT VERY MOMENT WHEN I LOVE THEM--
YOU BEAT THEM.
NO, YOU DON'T UNDERSTAND. I DESTROY THEM. I MAKE IT IMPOSSIBLE FOR THEM TO EVER HURT ME AGAIN. I GRIND THEM AND GRIND THEM UNTIL THEY DON'T EXIST.
I'VE REALLY HURT SOME PEOPLE, VAL. I'M NOT MAKING THIS UP.
OF COURSE YOU DON'T.
I KNOW, ENDER.
SEE WHAT I'M BECOMING, VAL? EVEN YOU'RE AFRAID OF ME.
I'M NOT.
YOU SHOULD BE.
YOU'VE BEEN DISCOVERING SOME OF THE DESTROYER IN YOURSELF, ENDER. SO HAVE I. PETER DIDN'T HAVE A MONOPOLY ON THAT, WHATEVER THE TESTERS THOUGHT.
WE AREN'T JUST ORDINARY CHILDREN, ARE WE? NONE OF US.
DON'T YOU SOMETIMES WISH WE WERE?
IT WOULD BE SO DULL.
I DON'T THINK SO.

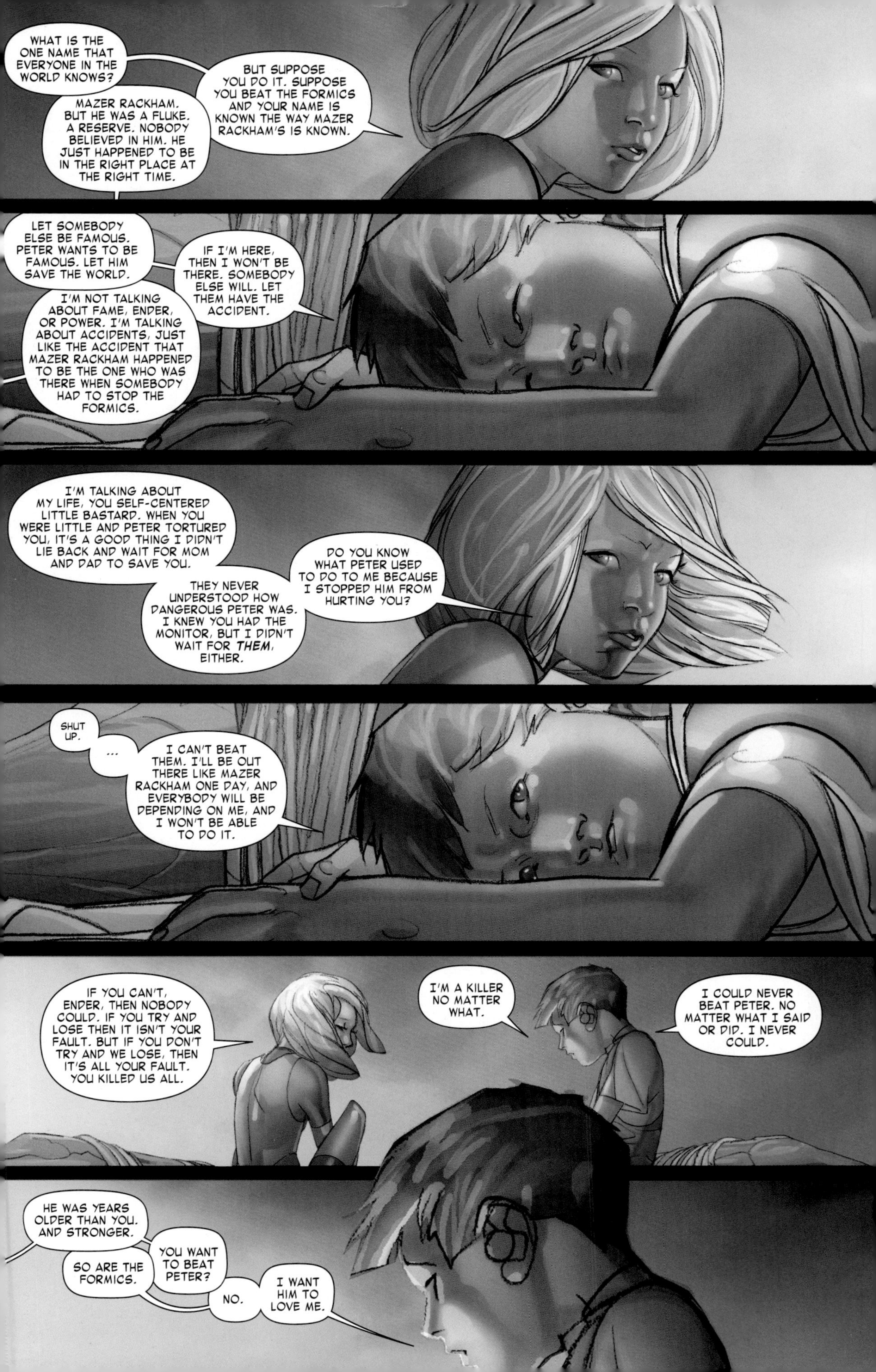
WHAT IS THE ONE NAME THAT EVERYONE IN THE WORLD KNOWS?
MAZER RACKHAM. BUT HE WAS A FLUKE. A RESERVE. NOBODY BELIEVED IN HIM. HE JUST HAPPENED TO BE IN THE RIGHT PLACE AT THE RIGHT TIME.
BUT SUPPOSE YOU DO IT. SUPPOSE YOU BEAT THE FORMICS AND YOUR NAME IS KNOWN THE WAY MAZER RACKHAM'S IS KNOWN.
LET SOMEBODY ELSE BE FAMOUS. PETER WANTS TO BE FAMOUS. LET HIM SAVE THE WORLD.
I'M NOT TALKING ABOUT FAME, ENDER, OR POWER. I'M TALKING ABOUT ACCIDENTS, JUST LIKE THE ACCIDENT THAT MAZER RACKHAM HAPPENED TO BE THE ONE WHO WAS THERE WHEN SOMEBODY HAD TO STOP THE FORMICS.
IF I'M HERE, THEN I WON'T BE THERE. SOMEBODY ELSE WILL. LET THEM HAVE THE ACCIDENT.
I'M TALKING ABOUT MY LIFE, YOU SELF-CENTERED LITTLE BASTARD. WHEN YOU WERE LITTLE AND PETER TORTURED YOU, IT'S A GOOD THING I DIDN'T LIE BACK AND WAIT FOR MOM AND DAD TO SAVE YOU.
THEY NEVER UNDERSTOOD HOW DANGEROUS PETER WAS. I KNEW YOU HAD THE MONITOR, BUT I DIDN'T WAIT FOR *THEM*, EITHER.
DO YOU KNOW WHAT PETER USED TO DO TO ME BECAUSE I STOPPED HIM FROM HURTING YOU?
SHUT UP.
...
I CAN'T BEAT THEM. I'LL BE OUT THERE LIKE MAZER RACKHAM ONE DAY, AND EVERYBODY WILL BE DEPENDING ON ME, AND I WON'T BE ABLE TO DO IT.
IF YOU CAN'T, ENDER, THEN NOBODY COULD. IF YOU TRY AND LOSE THEN IT ISN'T YOUR FAULT. BUT IF YOU DON'T TRY AND WE LOSE, THEN IT'S ALL YOUR FAULT. YOU KILLED US ALL.
I'M A KILLER NO MATTER WHAT.
I COULD NEVER BEAT PETER. NO MATTER WHAT I SAID OR DID. I NEVER COULD.
HE WAS YEARS OLDER THAN YOU. AND STRONGER.
SO ARE THE FORMICS.
YOU WANT TO BEAT PETER?
NO.
I WANT HIM TO LOVE ME.

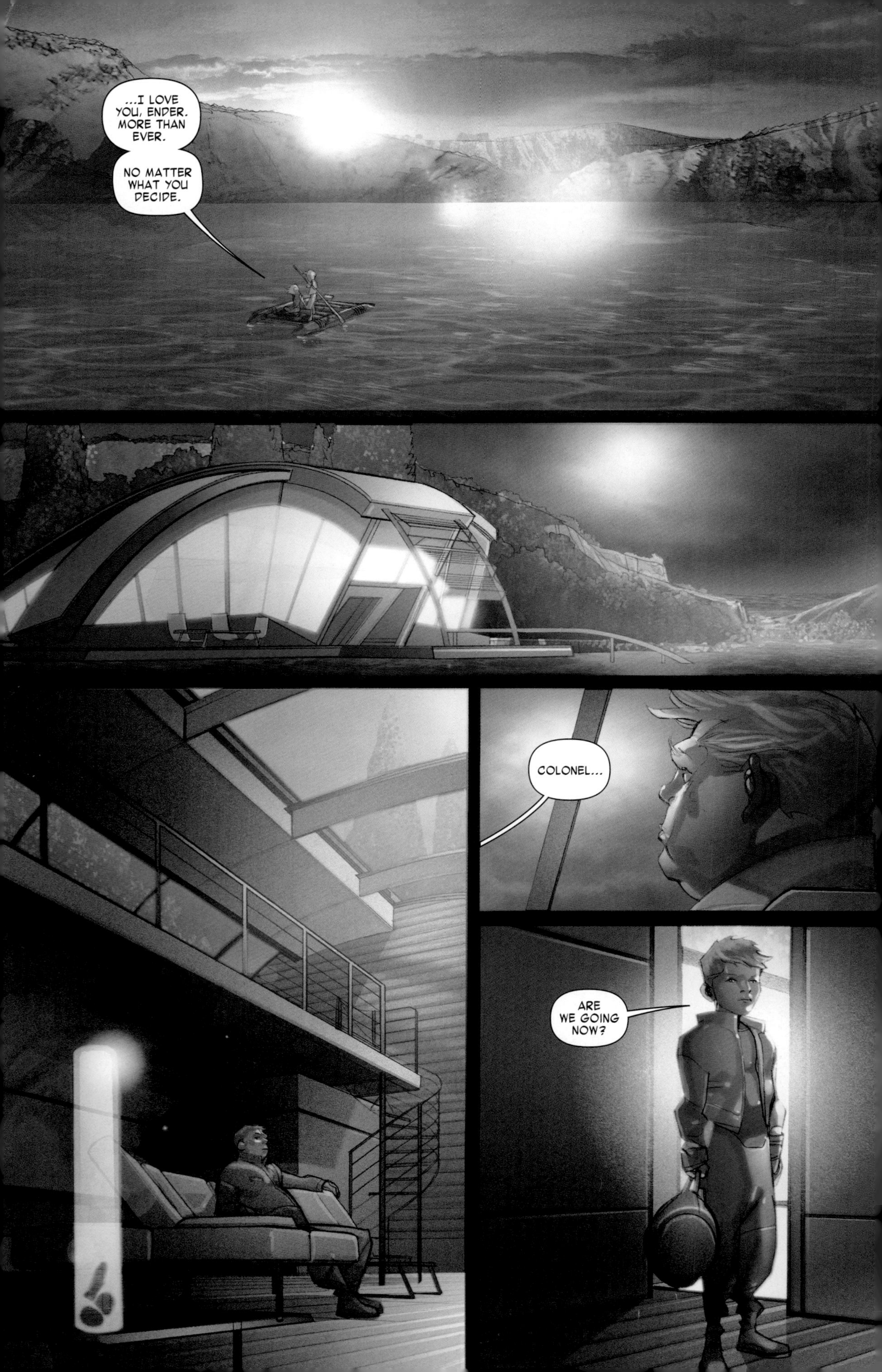
...I LOVE YOU, ENDER. MORE THAN EVER.
NO MATTER WHAT YOU DECIDE.
COLONEL...
ARE WE GOING NOW?

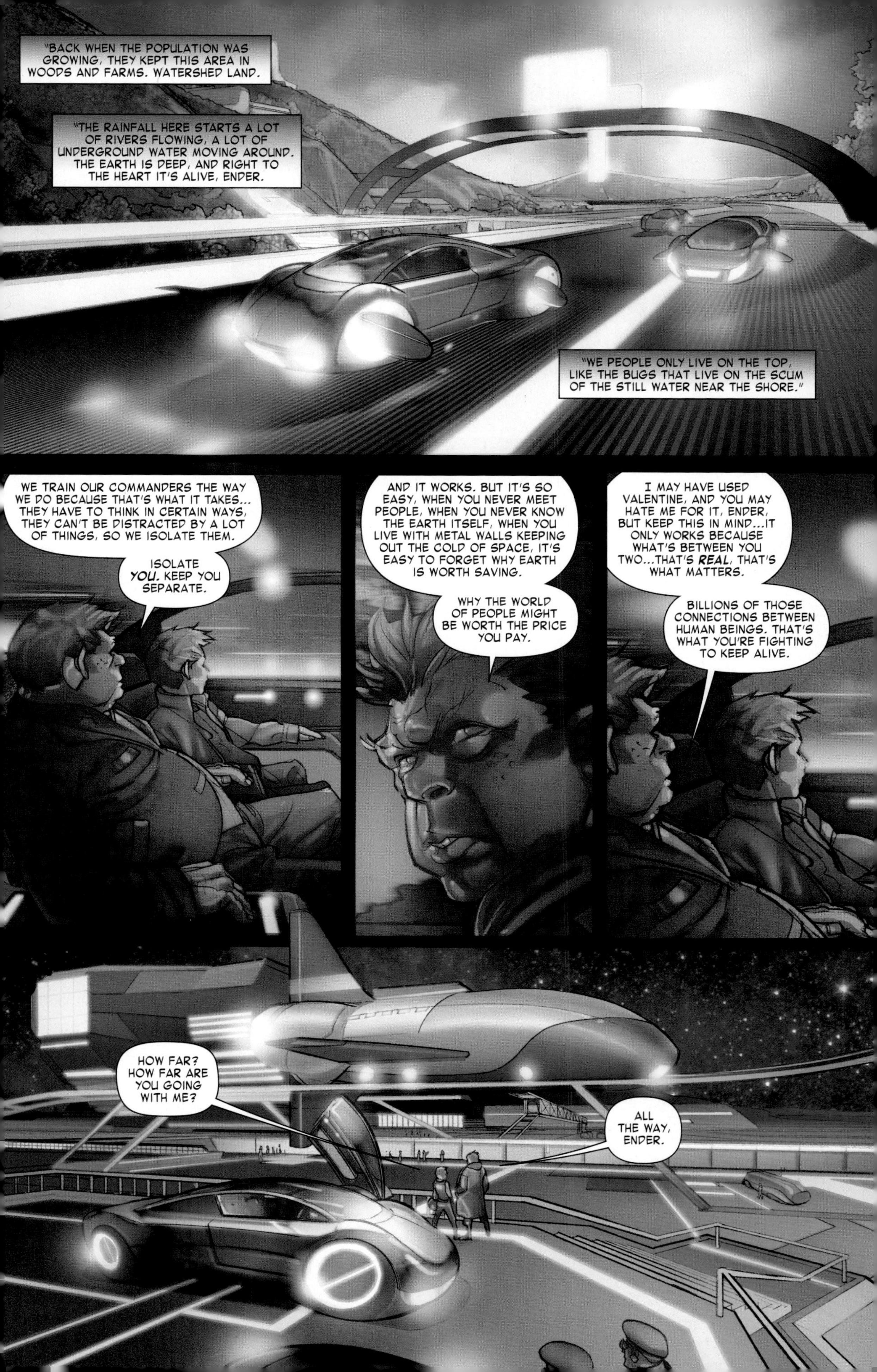
"BACK WHEN THE POPULATION WAS GROWING, THEY KEPT THIS AREA IN WOODS AND FARMS. WATERSHED LAND.
"THE RAINFALL HERE STARTS A LOT OF RIVERS FLOWING, A LOT OF UNDERGROUND WATER MOVING AROUND. THE EARTH IS DEEP, AND RIGHT TO THE HEART IT'S ALIVE, ENDER.
"WE PEOPLE ONLY LIVE ON THE TOP, LIKE THE BUGS THAT LIVE ON THE SCUM OF THE STILL WATER NEAR THE SHORE."
WE TRAIN OUR COMMANDERS THE WAY WE DO BECAUSE THAT'S WHAT IT TAKES... THEY HAVE TO THINK IN CERTAIN WAYS, THEY CAN'T BE DISTRACTED BY A LOT OF THINGS, SO WE ISOLATE THEM.
ISOLATE *YOU.* KEEP YOU SEPARATE.
AND IT WORKS. BUT IT'S SO EASY, WHEN YOU NEVER MEET PEOPLE, WHEN YOU NEVER KNOW THE EARTH ITSELF, WHEN YOU LIVE WITH METAL WALLS KEEPING OUT THE COLD OF SPACE, IT'S EASY TO FORGET WHY EARTH IS WORTH SAVING.
WHY THE WORLD OF PEOPLE MIGHT BE WORTH THE PRICE YOU PAY.
I MAY HAVE USED VALENTINE, AND YOU MAY HATE ME FOR IT, ENDER, BUT KEEP THIS IN MIND...IT ONLY WORKS BECAUSE WHAT'S BETWEEN YOU TWO...THAT'S ***REAL***, THAT'S WHAT MATTERS.
BILLIONS OF THOSE CONNECTIONS BETWEEN HUMAN BEINGS. THAT'S WHAT YOU'RE FIGHTING TO KEEP ALIVE.
HOW FAR? HOW FAR ARE YOU GOING WITH ME?
ALL THE WAY, ENDER.

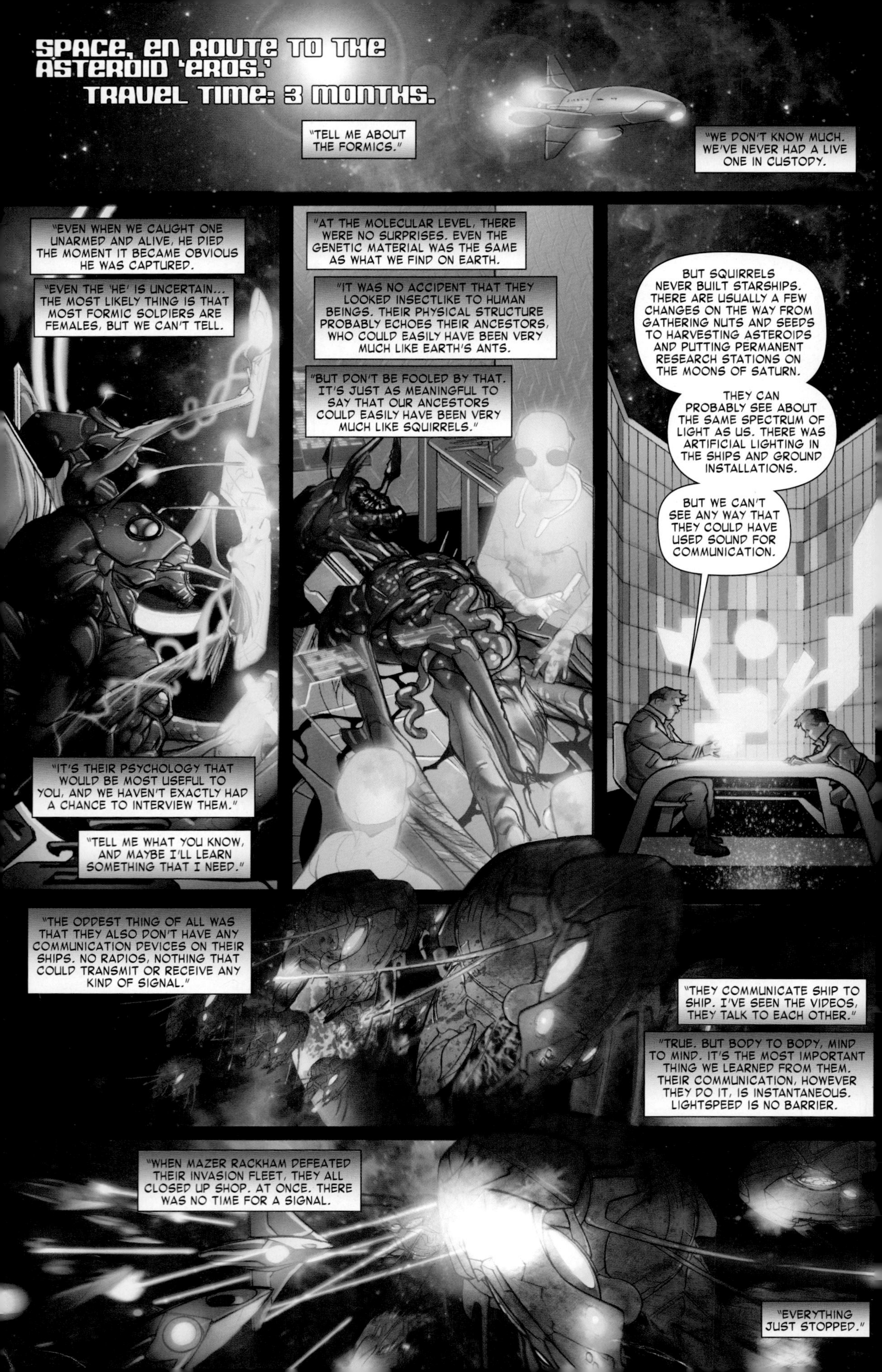
SPACE, EN ROUTE TO THE ASTEROID 'EROS.'
TRAVEL TIME: 3 MONTHS.
"TELL ME ABOUT THE FORMICS."
"WE DON'T KNOW MUCH. WE'VE NEVER HAD A LIVE ONE IN CUSTODY.
"EVEN WHEN WE CAUGHT ONE UNARMED AND ALIVE, HE DIED THE MOMENT IT BECAME OBVIOUS HE WAS CAPTURED.
"EVEN THE 'HE' IS UNCERTAIN... THE MOST LIKELY THING IS THAT MOST FORMIC SOLDIERS ARE FEMALES, BUT WE CAN'T TELL.
"IT'S THEIR PSYCHOLOGY THAT WOULD BE MOST USEFUL TO YOU, AND WE HAVEN'T EXACTLY HAD A CHANCE TO INTERVIEW THEM."
"TELL ME WHAT YOU KNOW, AND MAYBE I'LL LEARN SOMETHING THAT I NEED."
"AT THE MOLECULAR LEVEL, THERE WERE NO SURPRISES. EVEN THE GENETIC MATERIAL WAS THE SAME AS WHAT WE FIND ON EARTH.
"IT WAS NO ACCIDENT THAT THEY LOOKED INSECTLIKE TO HUMAN BEINGS. THEIR PHYSICAL STRUCTURE PROBABLY ECHOES THEIR ANCESTORS, WHO COULD EASILY HAVE BEEN VERY MUCH LIKE EARTH'S ANTS.
"BUT DON'T BE FOOLED BY THAT. IT'S JUST AS MEANINGFUL TO SAY THAT OUR ANCESTORS COULD EASILY HAVE BEEN VERY MUCH LIKE SQUIRRELS."
BUT SQUIRRELS NEVER BUILT STARSHIPS. THERE ARE USUALLY A FEW CHANGES ON THE WAY FROM GATHERING NUTS AND SEEDS TO HARVESTING ASTEROIDS AND PUTTING PERMANENT RESEARCH STATIONS ON THE MOONS OF SATURN.
THEY CAN PROBABLY SEE ABOUT THE SAME SPECTRUM OF LIGHT AS US. THERE WAS ARTIFICIAL LIGHTING IN THE SHIPS AND GROUND INSTALLATIONS.
BUT WE CAN'T SEE ANY WAY THAT THEY COULD HAVE USED SOUND FOR COMMUNICATION.
"THE ODDEST THING OF ALL WAS THAT THEY ALSO DON'T HAVE ANY COMMUNICATION DEVICES ON THEIR SHIPS. NO RADIOS, NOTHING THAT COULD TRANSMIT OR RECEIVE ANY KIND OF SIGNAL."
"THEY COMMUNICATE SHIP TO SHIP. I'VE SEEN THE VIDEOS, THEY TALK TO EACH OTHER."
"TRUE. BUT BODY TO BODY, MIND TO MIND. IT'S THE MOST IMPORTANT THING WE LEARNED FROM THEM. THEIR COMMUNICATION, HOWEVER THEY DO IT, IS INSTANTANEOUS. LIGHTSPEED IS NO BARRIER.
"WHEN MAZER RACKHAM DEFEATED THEIR INVASION FLEET, THEY ALL CLOSED UP SHOP. AT ONCE. THERE WAS NO TIME FOR A SIGNAL.
"EVERYTHING JUST STOPPED."

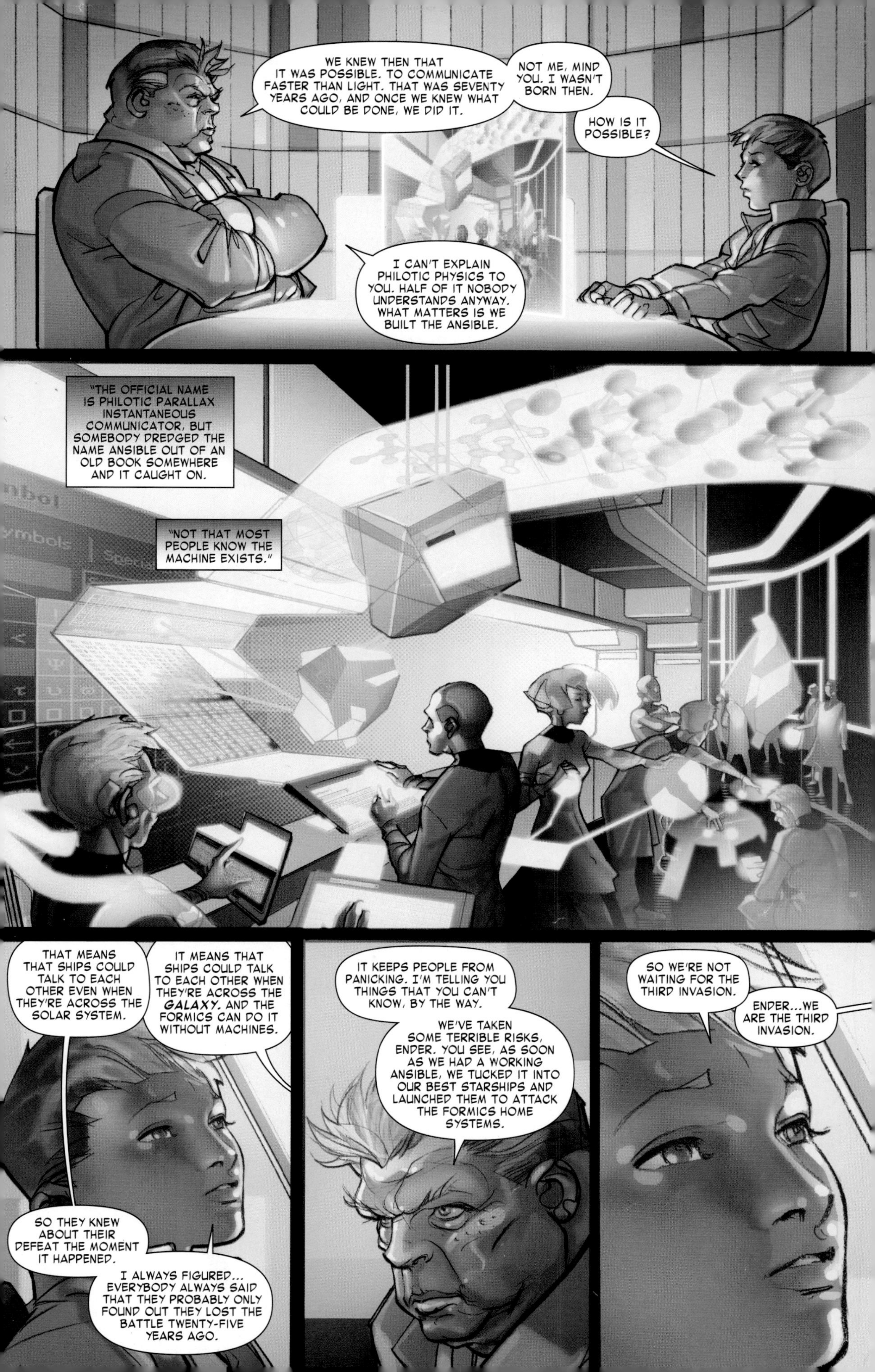
WE KNEW THEN THAT IT WAS POSSIBLE. TO COMMUNICATE FASTER THAN LIGHT. THAT WAS SEVENTY YEARS AGO, AND ONCE WE KNEW WHAT COULD BE DONE, WE DID IT.
NOT ME, MIND YOU. I WASN'T BORN THEN.
HOW IS IT POSSIBLE?
I CAN'T EXPLAIN PHILOTIC PHYSICS TO YOU. HALF OF IT NOBODY UNDERSTANDS ANYWAY. WHAT MATTERS IS WE BUILT THE ANSIBLE.
"THE OFFICIAL NAME IS PHILOTIC PARALLAX INSTANTANEOUS COMMUNICATOR, BUT SOMEBODY DREDGED THE NAME ANSIBLE OUT OF AN OLD BOOK SOMEWHERE AND IT CAUGHT ON.
"NOT THAT MOST PEOPLE KNOW THE MACHINE EXISTS."
THAT MEANS THAT SHIPS COULD TALK TO EACH OTHER EVEN WHEN THEY'RE ACROSS THE SOLAR SYSTEM.
IT MEANS THAT SHIPS COULD TALK TO EACH OTHER WHEN THEY'RE ACROSS THE *GALAXY.* AND THE FORMICS CAN DO IT WITHOUT MACHINES.
SO THEY KNEW ABOUT THEIR DEFEAT THE MOMENT IT HAPPENED.
I ALWAYS FIGURED... EVERYBODY ALWAYS SAID THAT THEY PROBABLY ONLY FOUND OUT THEY LOST THE BATTLE TWENTY-FIVE YEARS AGO.
IT KEEPS PEOPLE FROM PANICKING. I'M TELLING YOU THINGS THAT YOU CAN'T KNOW, BY THE WAY.
WE'VE TAKEN SOME TERRIBLE RISKS, ENDER. YOU SEE, AS SOON AS WE HAD A WORKING ANSIBLE, WE TUCKED IT INTO OUR BEST STARSHIPS AND LAUNCHED THEM TO ATTACK THE FORMICS HOME SYSTEMS.
SO WE'RE NOT WAITING FOR THE THIRD INVASION.
ENDER...WE ARE THE THIRD INVASION.

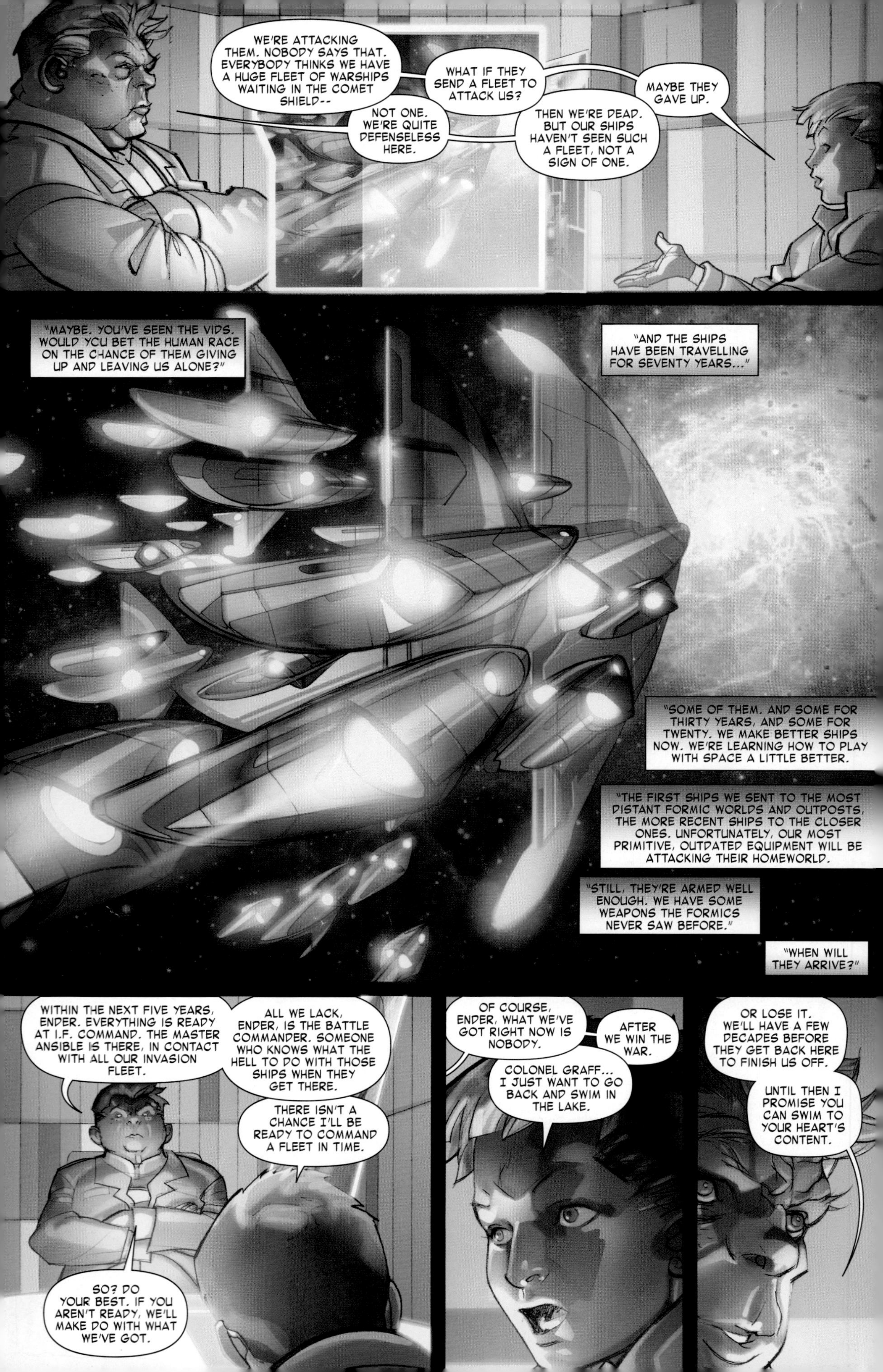
WE'RE ATTACKING THEM. NOBODY SAYS THAT. EVERYBODY THINKS WE HAVE A HUGE FLEET OF WARSHIPS WAITING IN THE COMET SHIELD--
NOT ONE. WE'RE QUITE DEFENSELESS HERE.
WHAT IF THEY SEND A FLEET TO ATTACK US?
THEN WE'RE DEAD. BUT OUR SHIPS HAVEN'T SEEN SUCH A FLEET, NOT A SIGN OF ONE.
MAYBE THEY GAVE UP.
"MAYBE. YOU'VE SEEN THE VIDS. WOULD YOU BET THE HUMAN RACE ON THE CHANCE OF THEM GIVING UP AND LEAVING US ALONE?"
"AND THE SHIPS HAVE BEEN TRAVELLING FOR SEVENTY YEARS..."
"SOME OF THEM. AND SOME FOR THIRTY YEARS, AND SOME FOR TWENTY. WE MAKE BETTER SHIPS NOW. WE'RE LEARNING HOW TO PLAY WITH SPACE A LITTLE BETTER.
"THE FIRST SHIPS WE SENT TO THE MOST DISTANT FORMIC WORLDS AND OUTPOSTS, THE MORE RECENT SHIPS TO THE CLOSER ONES. UNFORTUNATELY, OUR MOST PRIMITIVE, OUTDATED EQUIPMENT WILL BE ATTACKING THEIR HOMEWORLD.
"STILL, THEY'RE ARMED WELL ENOUGH. WE HAVE SOME WEAPONS THE FORMICS NEVER SAW BEFORE."
"WHEN WILL THEY ARRIVE?"
WITHIN THE NEXT FIVE YEARS, ENDER. EVERYTHING IS READY AT I.F. COMMAND. THE MASTER ANSIBLE IS THERE, IN CONTACT WITH ALL OUR INVASION FLEET.
ALL WE LACK, ENDER, IS THE BATTLE COMMANDER. SOMEONE WHO KNOWS WHAT THE HELL TO DO WITH THOSE SHIPS WHEN THEY GET THERE.
THERE ISN'T A CHANCE I'LL BE READY TO COMMAND A FLEET IN TIME.
SO? DO YOUR BEST. IF YOU AREN'T READY, WE'LL MAKE DO WITH WHAT WE'VE GOT.
OF COURSE, ENDER, WHAT WE'VE GOT RIGHT NOW IS NOBODY.
COLONEL GRAFF... I JUST WANT TO GO BACK AND SWIM IN THE LAKE.
AFTER WE WIN THE WAR.
OR LOSE IT. WE'LL HAVE A FEW DECADES BEFORE THEY GET BACK HERE TO FINISH US OFF.
UNTIL THEN I PROMISE YOU CAN SWIM TO YOUR HEART'S CONTENT.

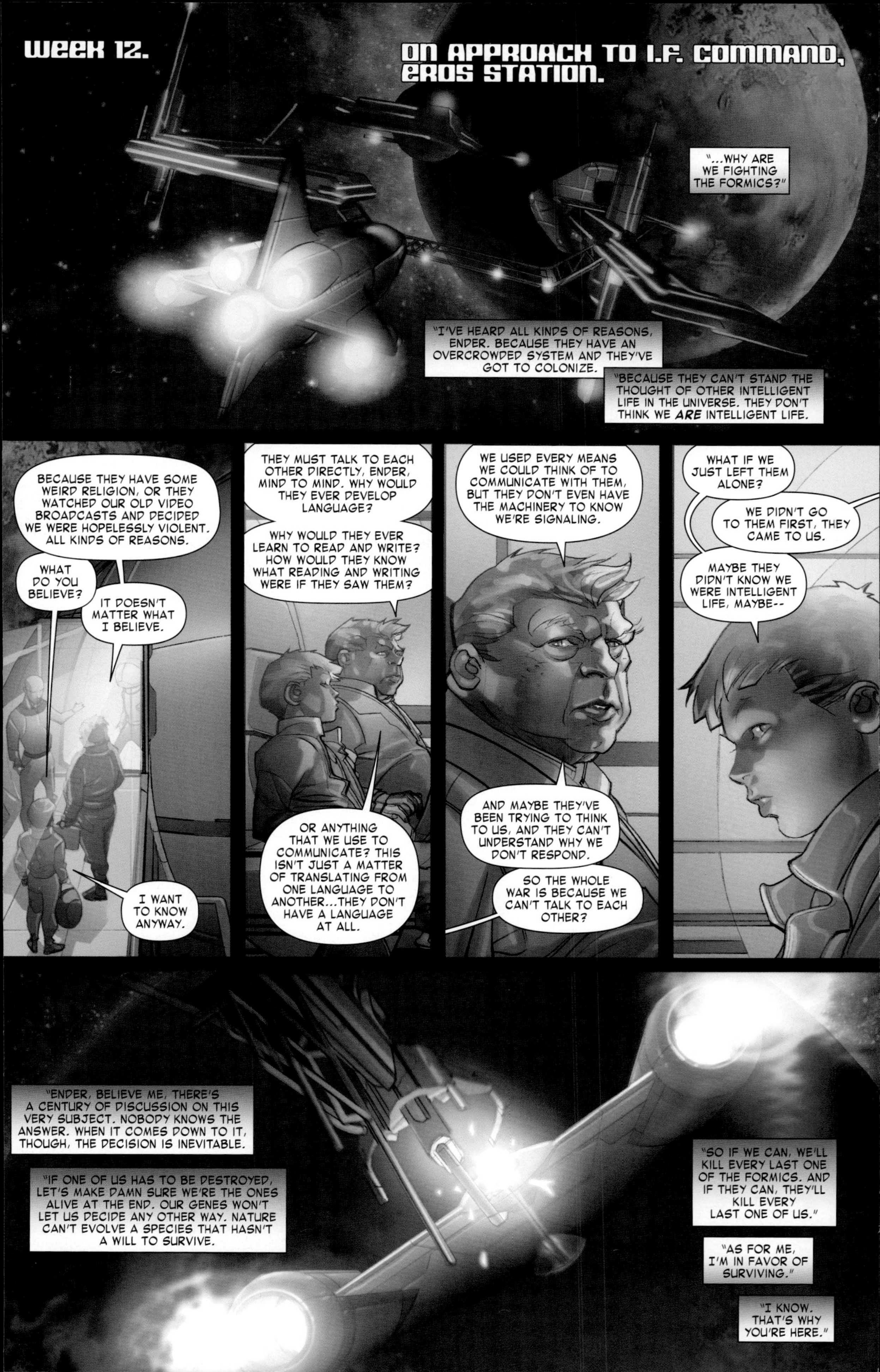
WEEK 12.
ON APPROACH TO I.F. COMMAND, EROS STATION.
"...WHY ARE WE FIGHTING THE FORMICS?"
"I'VE HEARD ALL KINDS OF REASONS, ENDER. BECAUSE THEY HAVE AN OVERCROWDED SYSTEM AND THEY'VE GOT TO COLONIZE.
"BECAUSE THEY CAN'T STAND THE THOUGHT OF OTHER INTELLIGENT LIFE IN THE UNIVERSE. THEY DON'T THINK WE ARE INTELLIGENT LIFE.
BECAUSE THEY HAVE SOME WEIRD RELIGION, OR THEY WATCHED OUR OLD VIDEO BROADCASTS AND DECIDED WE WERE HOPELESSLY VIOLENT. ALL KINDS OF REASONS.
WHAT DO YOU BELIEVE?
IT DOESN'T MATTER WHAT I BELIEVE.
I WANT TO KNOW ANYWAY.
THEY MUST TALK TO EACH OTHER DIRECTLY, ENDER, MIND TO MIND. WHY WOULD THEY EVER DEVELOP LANGUAGE?
WHY WOULD THEY EVER LEARN TO READ AND WRITE? HOW WOULD THEY KNOW WHAT READING AND WRITING WERE IF THEY SAW THEM?
OR ANYTHING THAT WE USE TO COMMUNICATE? THIS ISN'T JUST A MATTER OF TRANSLATING FROM ONE LANGUAGE TO ANOTHER...THEY DON'T HAVE A LANGUAGE AT ALL.
WE USED EVERY MEANS WE COULD THINK OF TO COMMUNICATE WITH THEM, BUT THEY DON'T EVEN HAVE THE MACHINERY TO KNOW WE'RE SIGNALING.
AND MAYBE THEY'VE BEEN TRYING TO THINK TO US, AND THEY CAN'T UNDERSTAND WHY WE DON'T RESPOND.
SO THE WHOLE WAR IS BECAUSE WE CAN'T TALK TO EACH OTHER?
WHAT IF WE JUST LEFT THEM ALONE?
WE DIDN'T GO TO THEM FIRST, THEY CAME TO US.
MAYBE THEY DIDN'T KNOW WE WERE INTELLIGENT LIFE, MAYBE--
"ENDER, BELIEVE ME, THERE'S A CENTURY OF DISCUSSION ON THIS VERY SUBJECT. NOBODY KNOWS THE ANSWER. WHEN IT COMES DOWN TO IT, THOUGH, THE DECISION IS INEVITABLE.
"IF ONE OF US HAS TO BE DESTROYED, LET'S MAKE DAMN SURE WE'RE THE ONES ALIVE AT THE END. OUR GENES WON'T LET US DECIDE ANY OTHER WAY. NATURE CAN'T EVOLVE A SPECIES THAT HASN'T A WILL TO SURVIVE.
"SO IF WE CAN, WE'LL KILL EVERY LAST ONE OF THE FORMICS. AND IF THEY CAN, THEY'LL KILL EVERY LAST ONE OF US."
"AS FOR ME, I'M IN FAVOR OF SURVIVING."
"I KNOW. THAT'S WHY YOU'RE HERE."

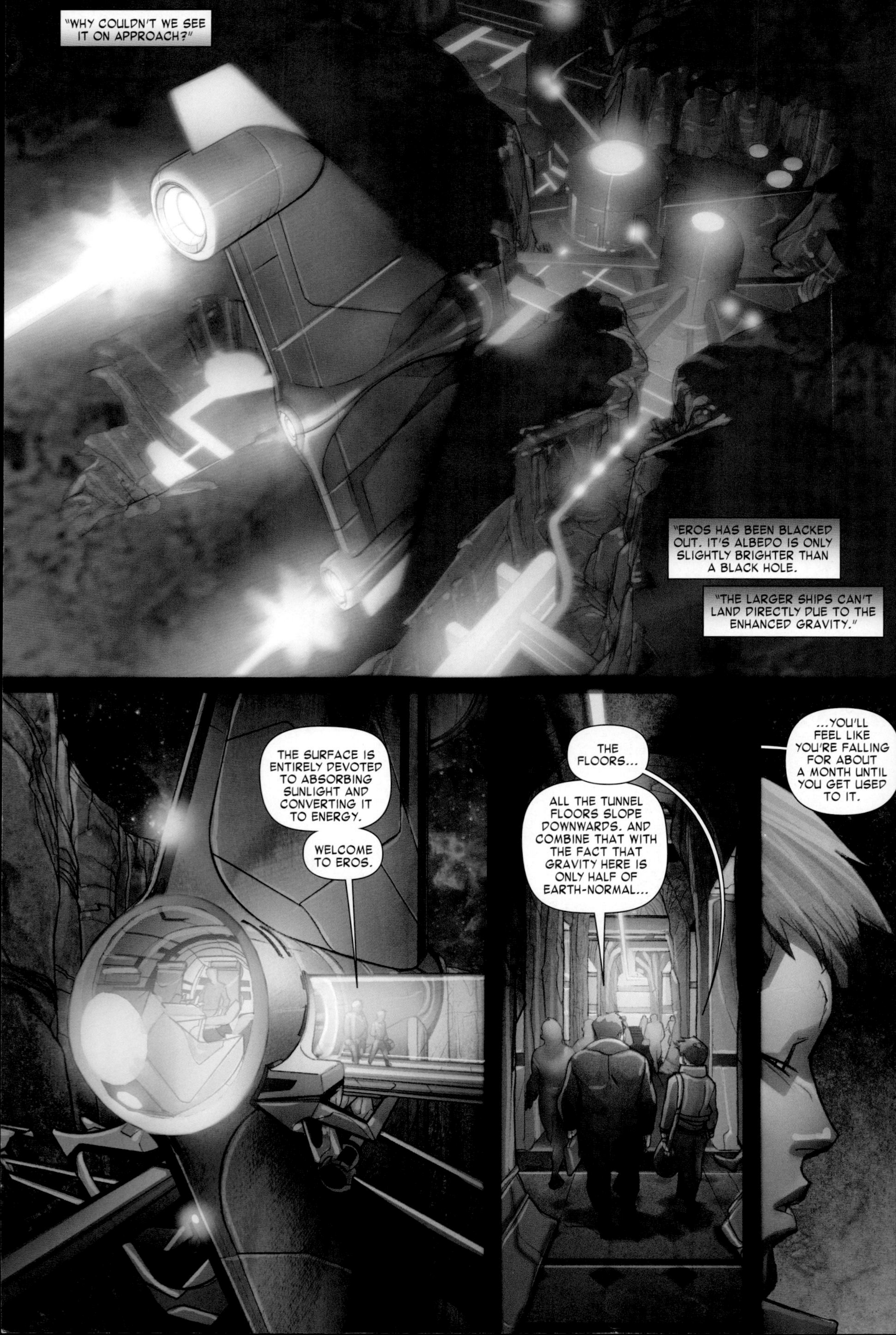
"WHY COULDN'T WE SEE IT ON APPROACH?"
"EROS HAS BEEN BLACKED OUT. IT'S ALBEDO IS ONLY SLIGHTLY BRIGHTER THAN A BLACK HOLE.
"THE LARGER SHIPS CAN'T LAND DIRECTLY DUE TO THE ENHANCED GRAVITY."
THE SURFACE IS ENTIRELY DEVOTED TO ABSORBING SUNLIGHT AND CONVERTING IT TO ENERGY.
WELCOME TO EROS.
THE FLOORS...
ALL THE TUNNEL FLOORS SLOPE DOWNWARDS. AND COMBINE THAT WITH THE FACT THAT GRAVITY HERE IS ONLY HALF OF EARTH-NORMAL...
...YOU'LL FEEL LIKE YOU'RE FALLING FOR ABOUT A MONTH UNTIL YOU GET USED TO IT.

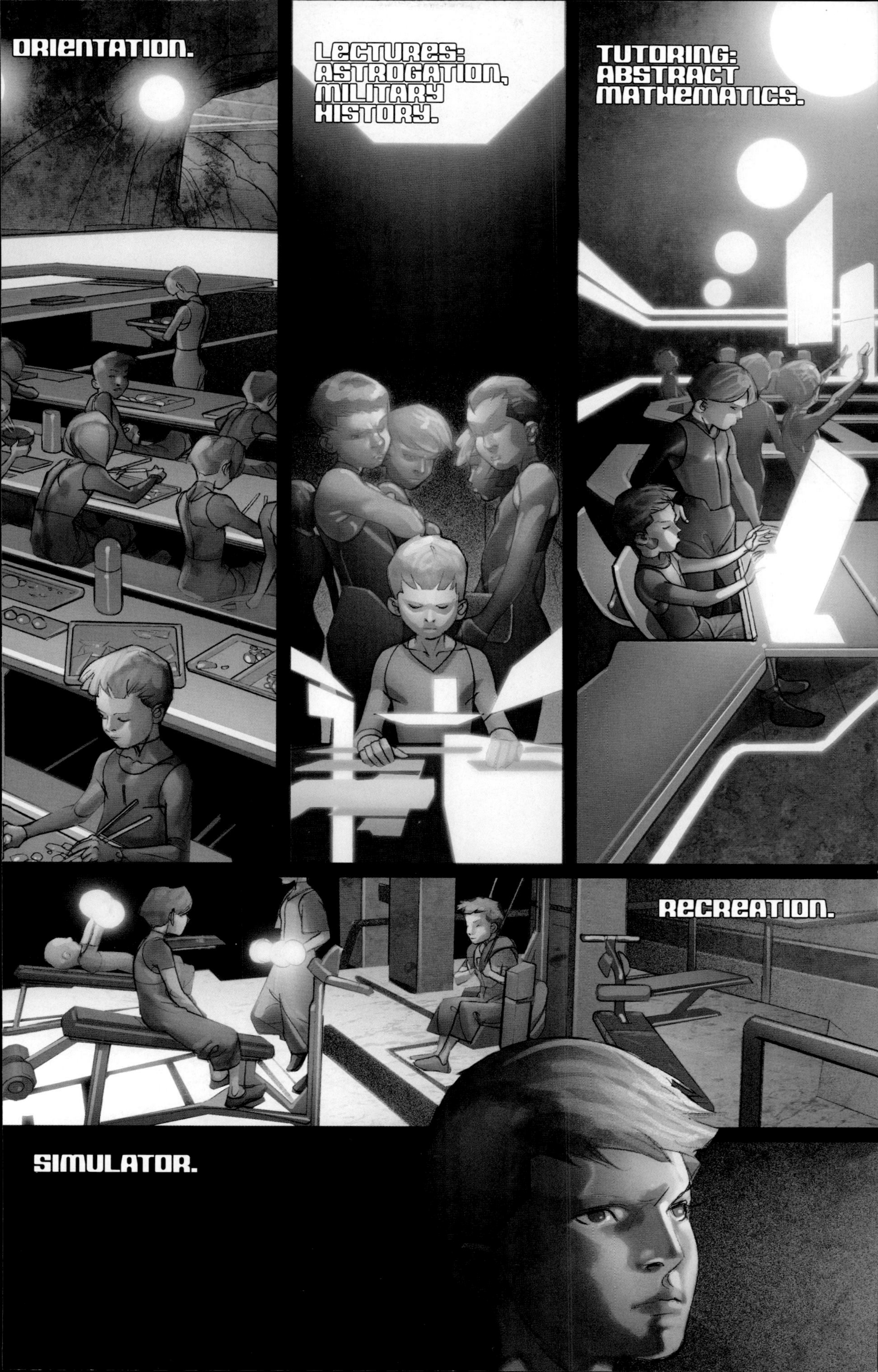
ORIENTATION.
LECTURES: ASTROGATION, MILITARY HISTORY.
TUTORING: ABSTRACT MATHEMATICS.
RECREATION.
SIMULATOR.

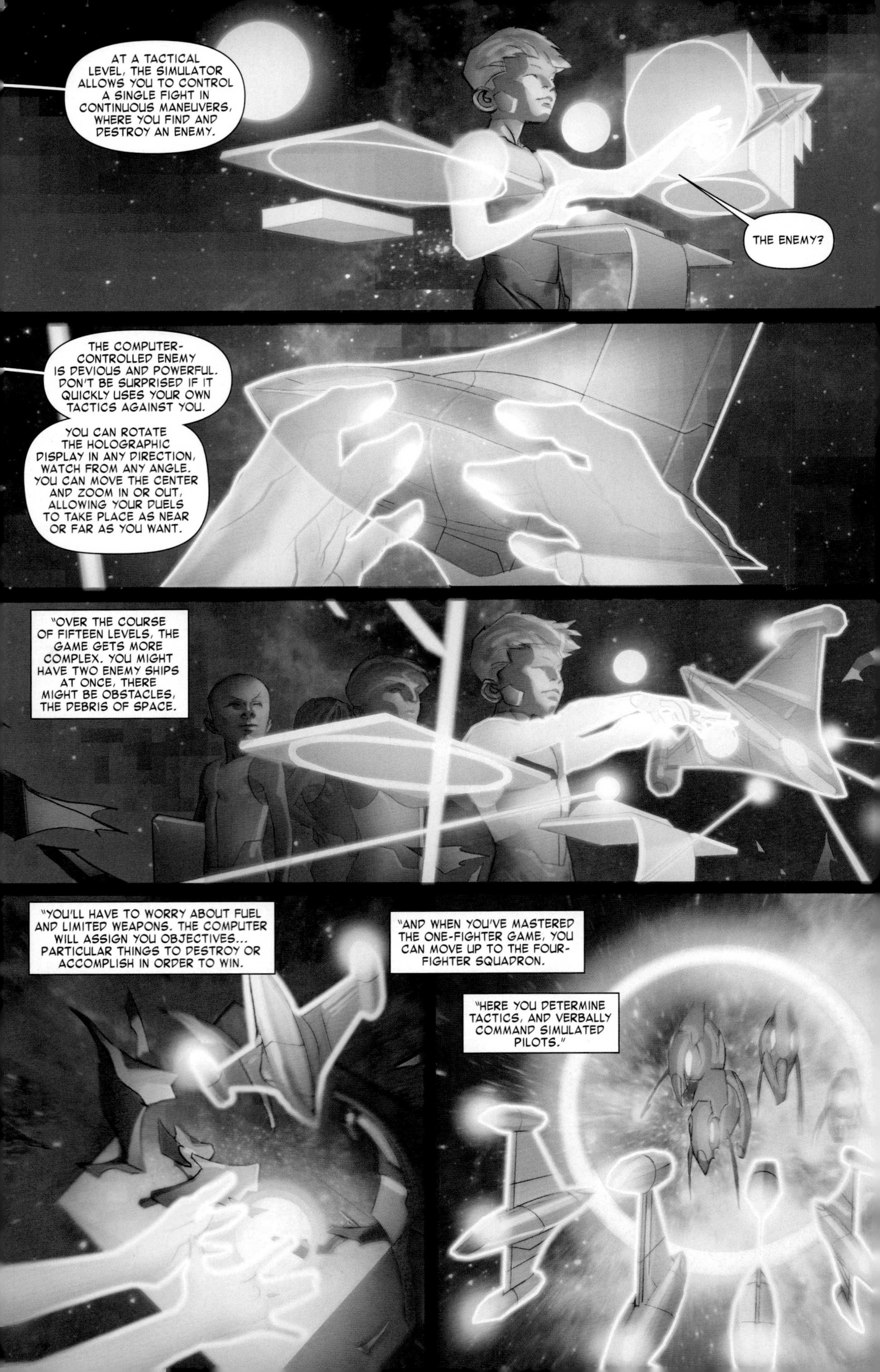
AT A TACTICAL LEVEL, THE SIMULATOR ALLOWS YOU TO CONTROL A SINGLE FIGHT IN CONTINUOUS MANEUVERS, WHERE YOU FIND AND DESTROY AN ENEMY.
THE ENEMY?
THE COMPUTER-CONTROLLED ENEMY IS DEVIOUS AND POWERFUL. DON'T BE SURPRISED IF IT QUICKLY USES YOUR OWN TACTICS AGAINST YOU.
YOU CAN ROTATE THE HOLOGRAPHIC DISPLAY IN ANY DIRECTION, WATCH FROM ANY ANGLE. YOU CAN MOVE THE CENTER AND ZOOM IN OR OUT, ALLOWING YOUR DUELS TO TAKE PLACE AS NEAR OR FAR AS YOU WANT.
"OVER THE COURSE OF FIFTEEN LEVELS, THE GAME GETS MORE COMPLEX. YOU MIGHT HAVE TWO ENEMY SHIPS AT ONCE, THERE MIGHT BE OBSTACLES, THE DEBRIS OF SPACE.
"YOU'LL HAVE TO WORRY ABOUT FUEL AND LIMITED WEAPONS. THE COMPUTER WILL ASSIGN YOU OBJECTIVES... PARTICULAR THINGS TO DESTROY OR ACCOMPLISH IN ORDER TO WIN.
"AND WHEN YOU'VE MASTERED THE ONE-FIGHTER GAME, YOU CAN MOVE UP TO THE FOUR-FIGHTER SQUADRON.
"HERE YOU DETERMINE TACTICS, AND VERBALLY COMMAND SIMULATED PILOTS."

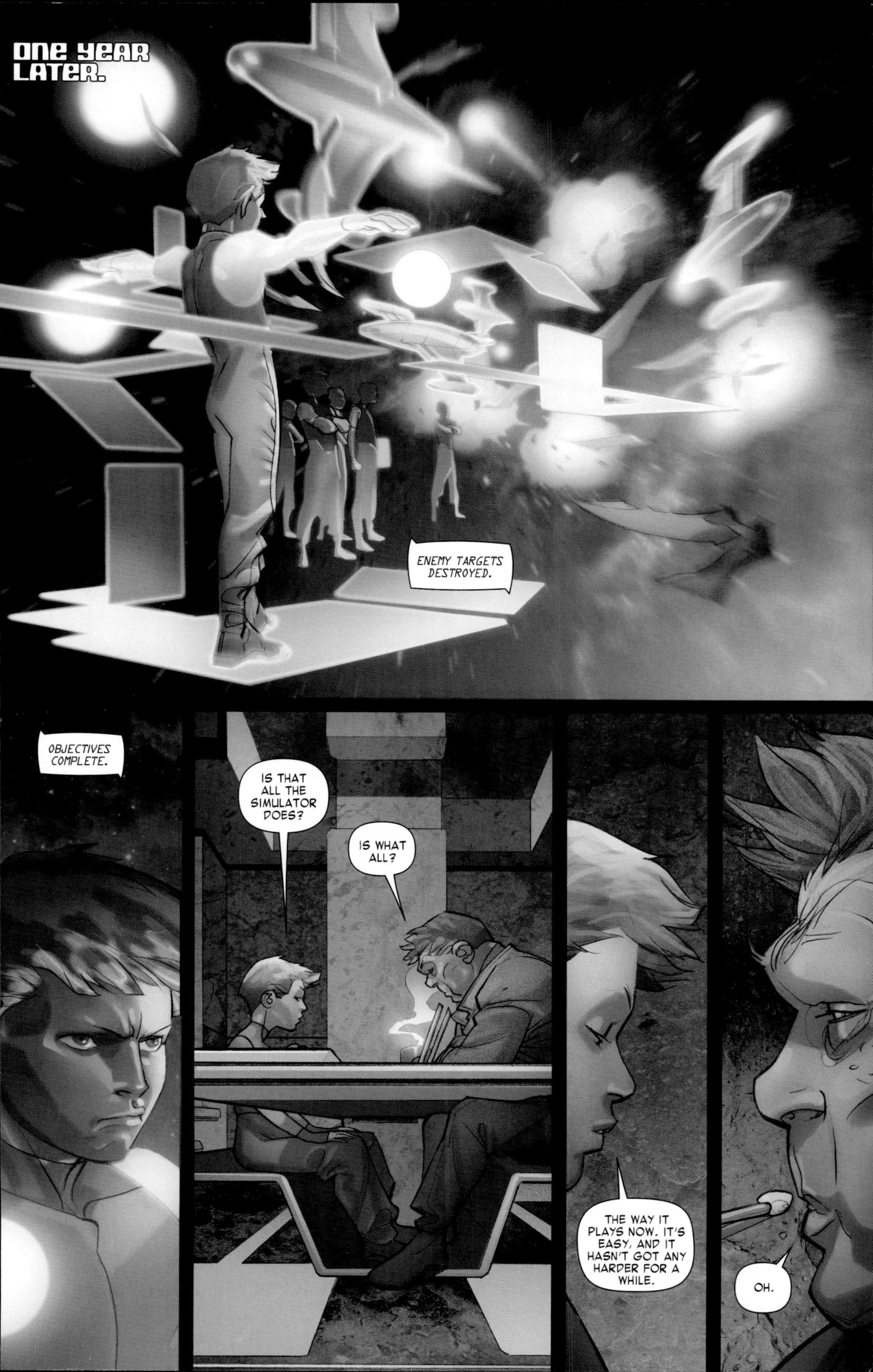
ONE YEAR LATER.
ENEMY TARGETS DESTROYED.
OBJECTIVES COMPLETE.
IS THAT ALL THE SIMULATOR DOES?
IS WHAT ALL?
THE WAY IT PLAYS NOW. IT'S EASY, AND IT HASN'T GOT ANY HARDER FOR A WHILE.
OH.

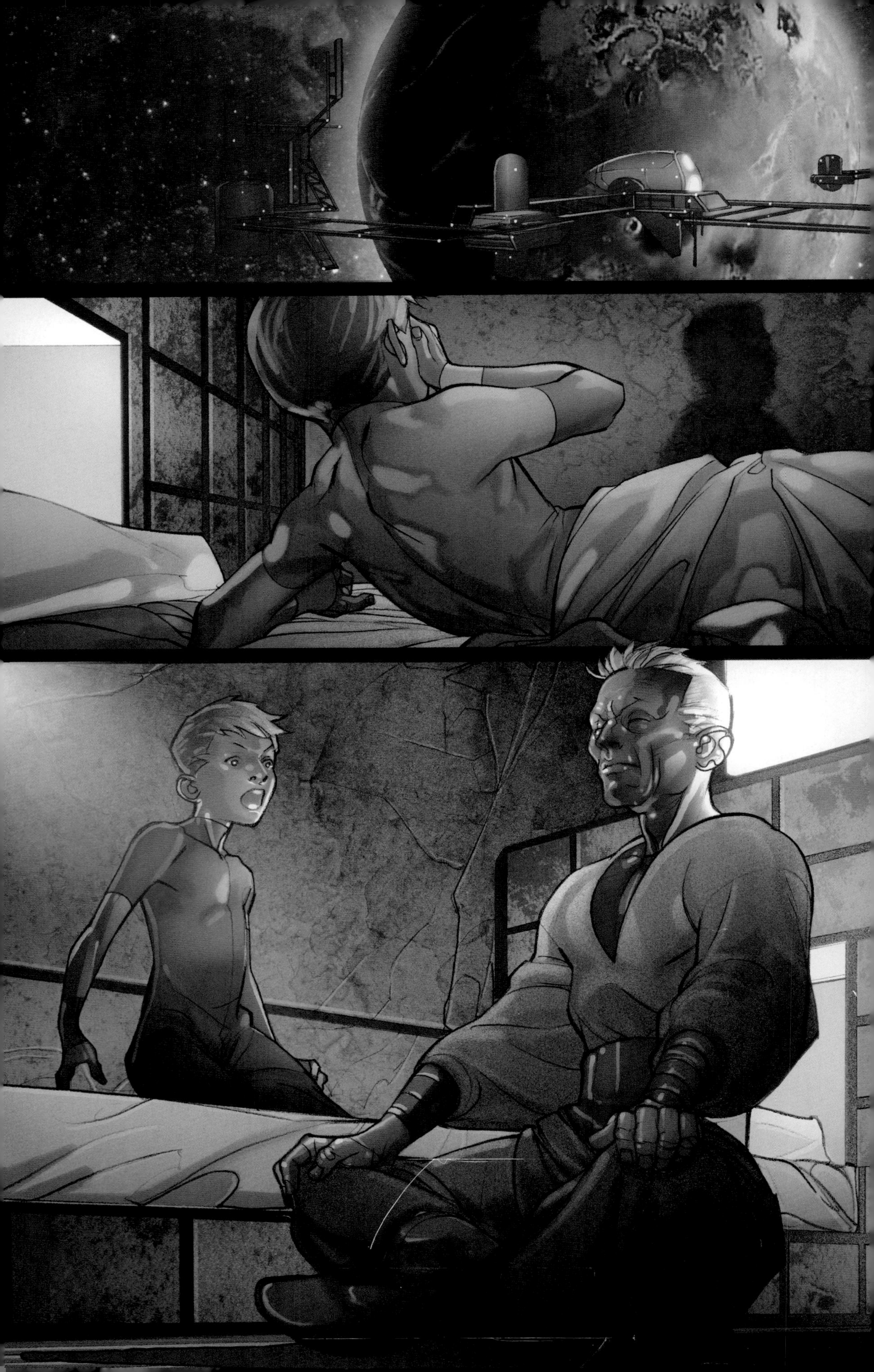

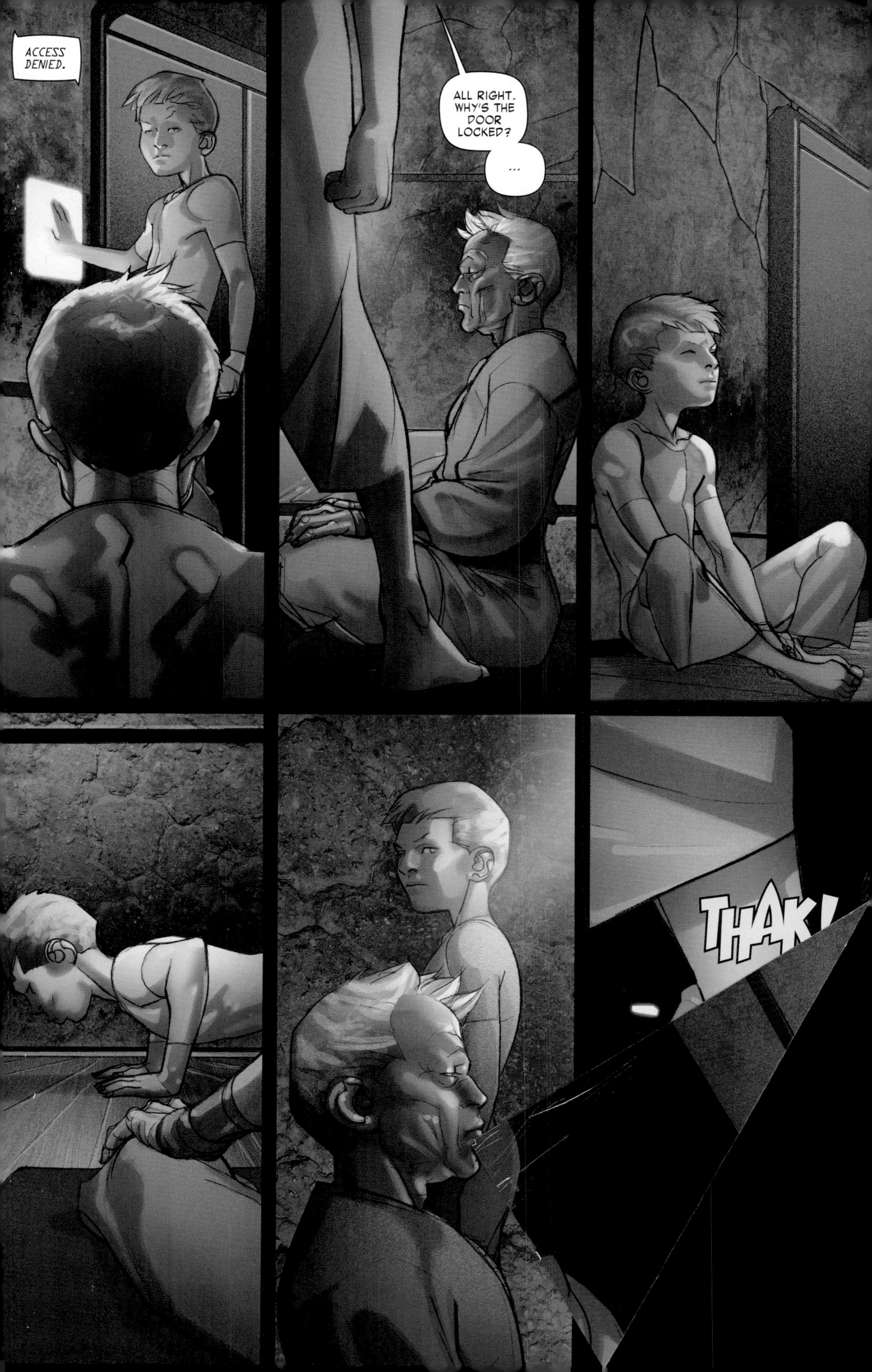
ACCESS DENIED.
ALL RIGHT. WHY'S THE DOOR LOCKED?
...
THAK!

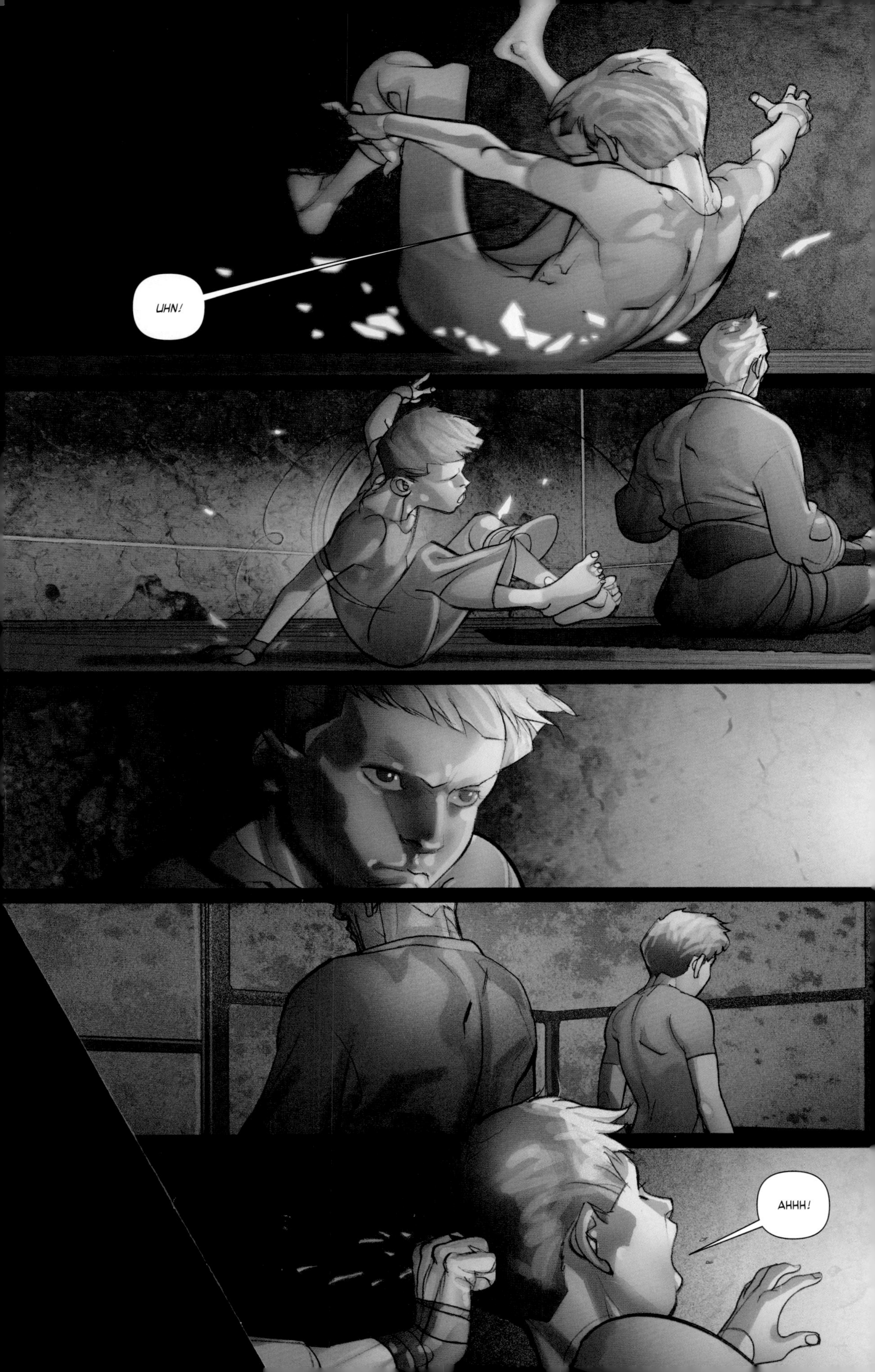
UHN!
AHHH!

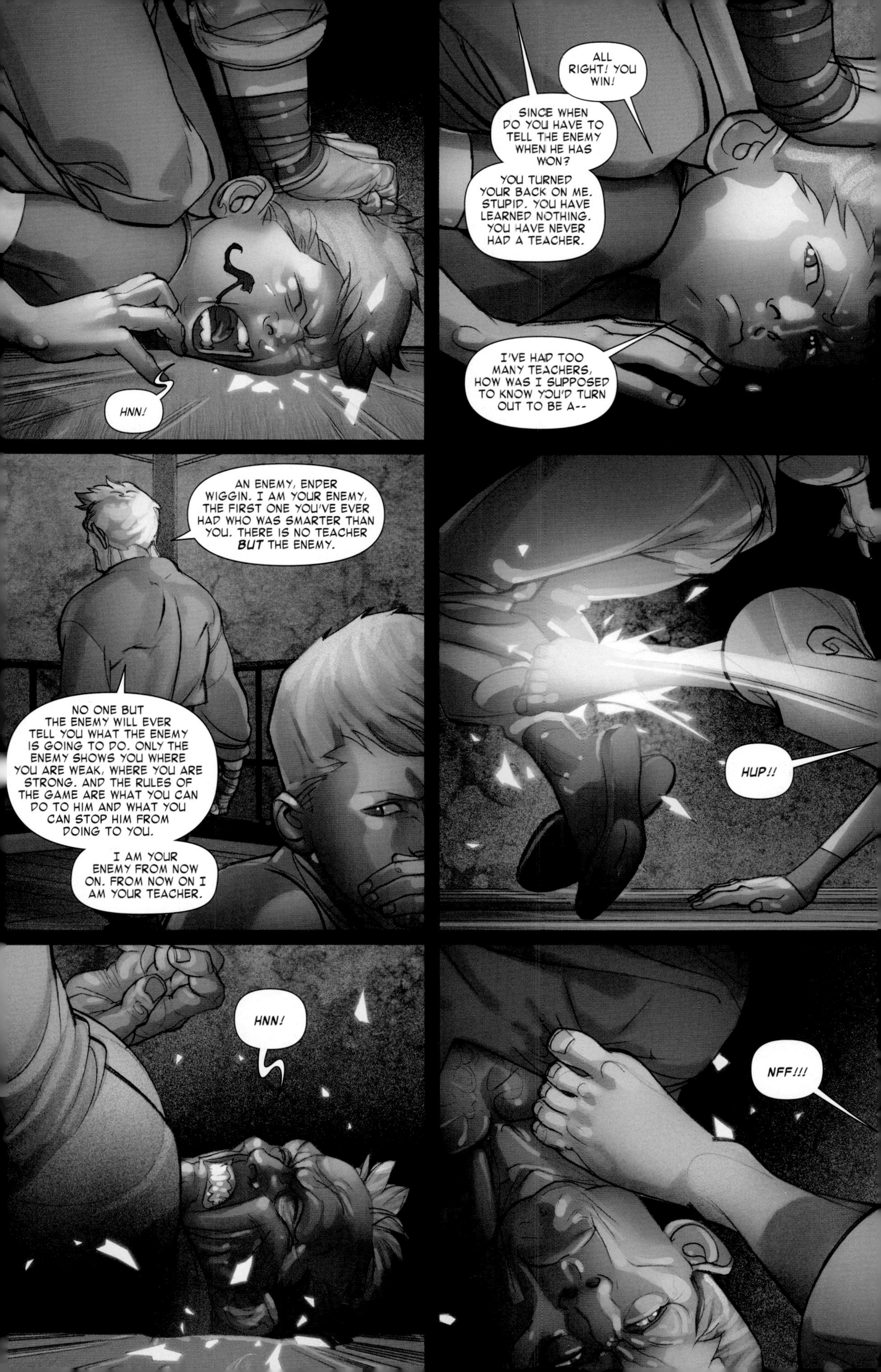
HNN!
ALL RIGHT! YOU WIN!
SINCE WHEN DO YOU HAVE TO TELL THE ENEMY WHEN HE HAS WON?
YOU TURNED YOUR BACK ON ME. STUPID. YOU HAVE LEARNED NOTHING. YOU HAVE NEVER HAD A TEACHER.
I'VE HAD TOO MANY TEACHERS, HOW WAS I SUPPOSED TO KNOW YOU'D TURN OUT TO BE A--
AN ENEMY, ENDER WIGGIN. I AM YOUR ENEMY, THE FIRST ONE YOU'VE EVER HAD WHO WAS SMARTER THAN YOU. THERE IS NO TEACHER *BUT* THE ENEMY.
NO ONE BUT THE ENEMY WILL EVER TELL YOU WHAT THE ENEMY IS GOING TO DO. ONLY THE ENEMY SHOWS YOU WHERE YOU ARE WEAK, WHERE YOU ARE STRONG. AND THE RULES OF THE GAME ARE WHAT YOU CAN DO TO HIM AND WHAT YOU CAN STOP HIM FROM DOING TO YOU.
I AM YOUR ENEMY FROM NOW ON. FROM NOW ON I AM YOUR TEACHER.
HUP!!
HNN!
NFF!!!

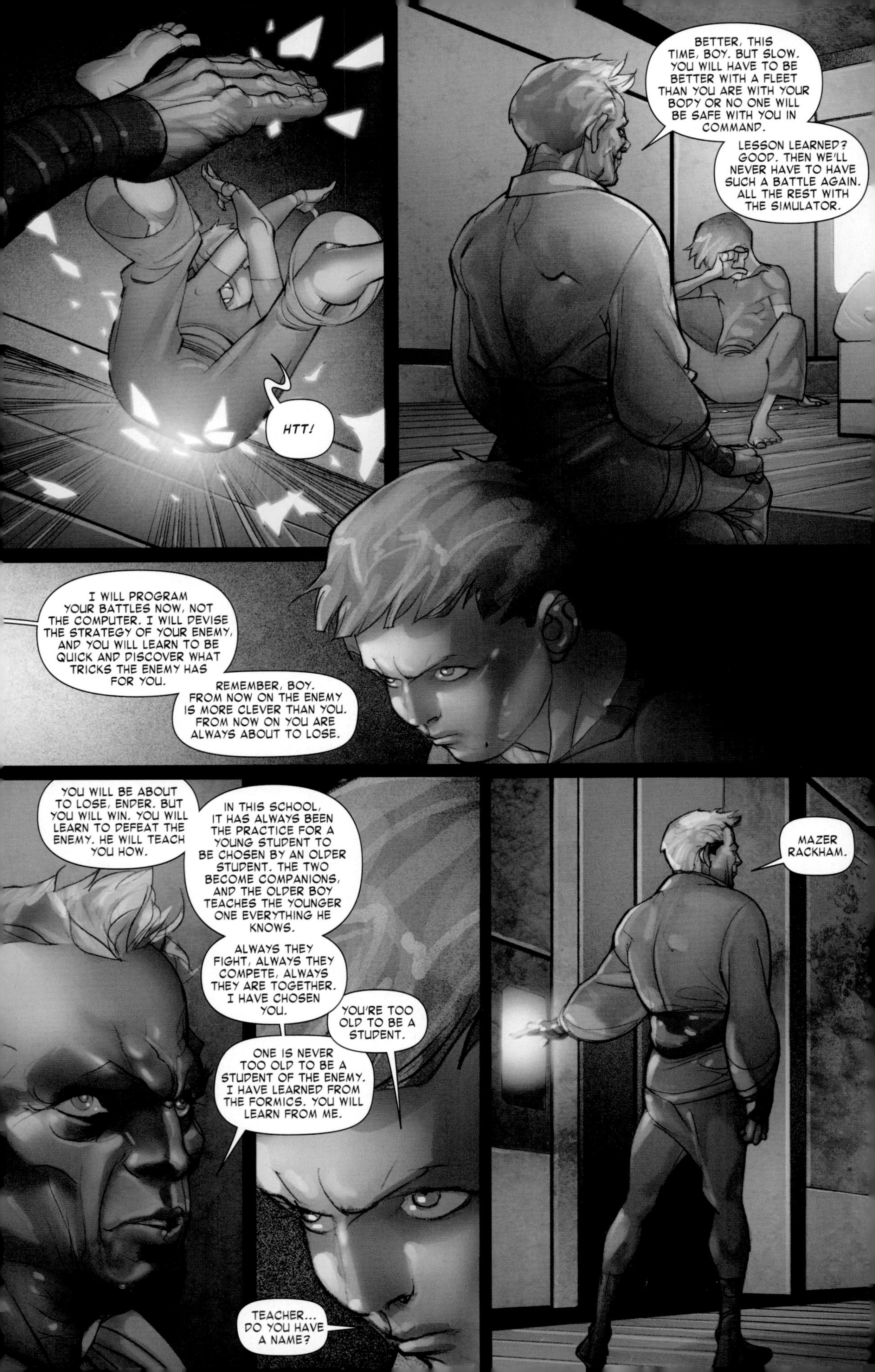
HTT!
BETTER, THIS TIME, BOY. BUT SLOW. YOU WILL HAVE TO BE BETTER WITH A FLEET THAN YOU ARE WITH YOUR BODY OR NO ONE WILL BE SAFE WITH YOU IN COMMAND.
LESSON LEARNED? GOOD. THEN WE'LL NEVER HAVE TO HAVE SUCH A BATTLE AGAIN. ALL THE REST WITH THE SIMULATOR.
I WILL PROGRAM YOUR BATTLES NOW, NOT THE COMPUTER. I WILL DEVISE THE STRATEGY OF YOUR ENEMY, AND YOU WILL LEARN TO BE QUICK AND DISCOVER WHAT TRICKS THE ENEMY HAS FOR YOU.
REMEMBER, BOY. FROM NOW ON THE ENEMY IS MORE CLEVER THAN YOU. FROM NOW ON YOU ARE ALWAYS ABOUT TO LOSE.
YOU WILL BE ABOUT TO LOSE, ENDER. BUT YOU WILL WIN. YOU WILL LEARN TO DEFEAT THE ENEMY. HE WILL TEACH YOU HOW.
IN THIS SCHOOL, IT HAS ALWAYS BEEN THE PRACTICE FOR A YOUNG STUDENT TO BE CHOSEN BY AN OLDER STUDENT. THE TWO BECOME COMPANIONS, AND THE OLDER BOY TEACHES THE YOUNGER ONE EVERYTHING HE KNOWS.
ALWAYS THEY FIGHT, ALWAYS THEY COMPETE, ALWAYS THEY ARE TOGETHER. I HAVE CHOSEN YOU.
YOU'RE TOO OLD TO BE A STUDENT.
ONE IS NEVER TOO OLD TO BE A STUDENT OF THE ENEMY. I HAVE LEARNED FROM THE FORMICS. YOU WILL LEARN FROM ME.
TEACHER... DO YOU HAVE A NAME?
MAZER RACKHAM.

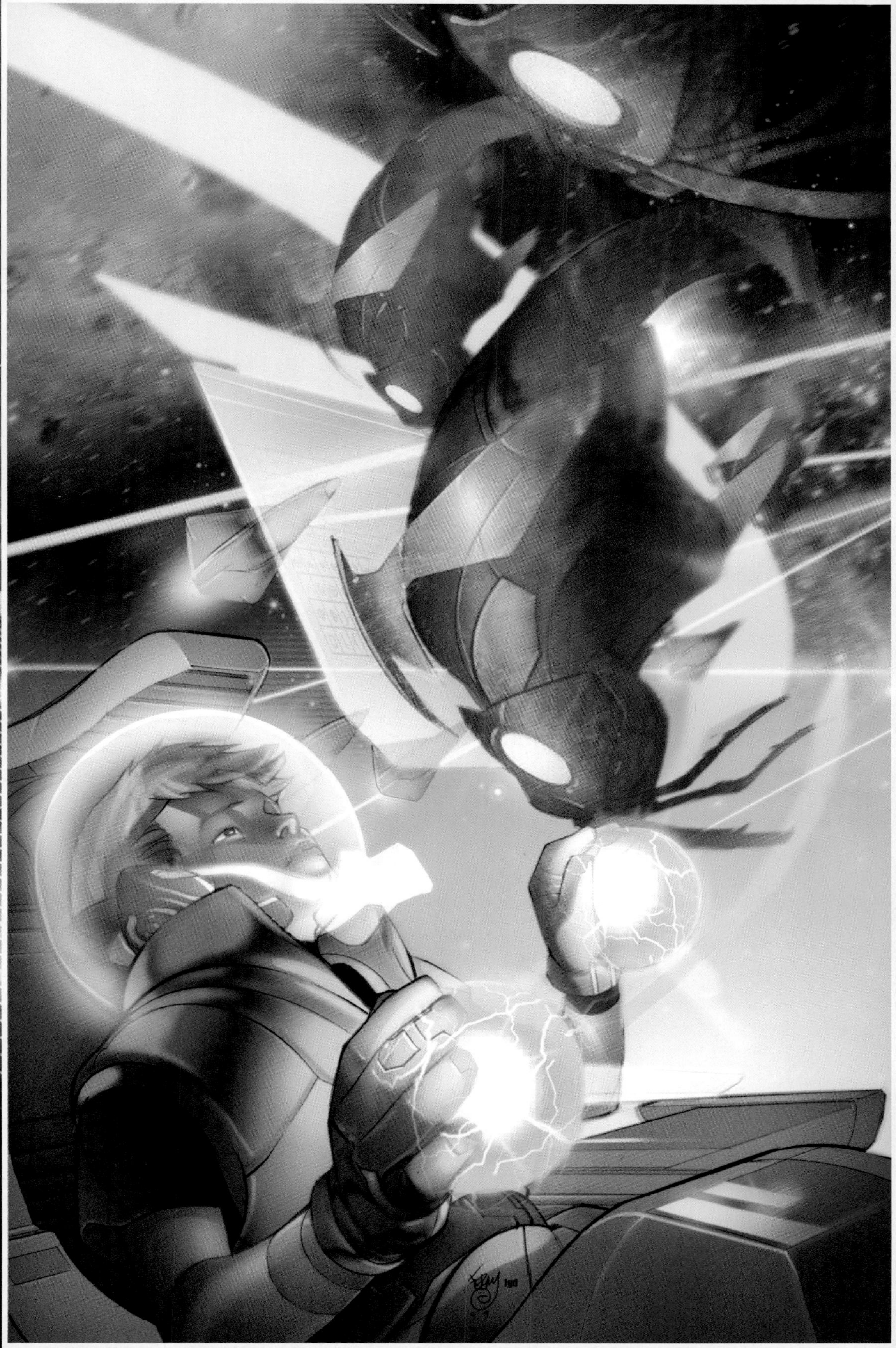

F I V E

INTERNATIONAL FLEET MONITORED COMMUNICATIONS
PARTICIPANTS: RACKHAM, M. AND WIGGIN, A.
REF ID # 94024-2-391, KEYWORD SEARCH: 'RACKHAM'

<<<THIS IS A PARTIAL TRANSCRIPT OF A CONVERSATION HELD ON EROS DURING REVIEW OF FORMIC/I.F. ARCHIVE FOOTAGE>>>

WIGGIN: Why aren't you dead? You fought your battle seventy years ago. I don't think you're even sixty years old.

RACKHAM: The miracle of relativity. They kept me here for twenty years after the battle, even though I begged them to let me command one of the starships they launched against the Formic home planet and their colonies.

They came to realize I was still the only person able to understand the things I understood about the Formics. I was the only person who had ever defeated the Formics by intelligence rather than luck. They needed me here to...teach the person who WOULD command the fleet.

W: So they sent you out in a starship, got you up to relativistic speed–

R: And then I turned around and came home. A very dull voyage, Ender. Fifty years in space. Officially, only eight years passed for me, but it felt like five hundred. All so I could teach the next commander everything I knew.

W: Am I to be commander, then?

R: Let's say that you're our best bet at the present.

W: There are others being prepared, too?

R: No.

W: That makes me the only choice, then, doesn't it? [NO RESPONSE] Except you. You're still alive, aren't you? [NO RESPONSE] Why not you? You won before.

R: I cannot be the commander for good and sufficient reasons.

W: Show me how you beat the Formics, Mazer.

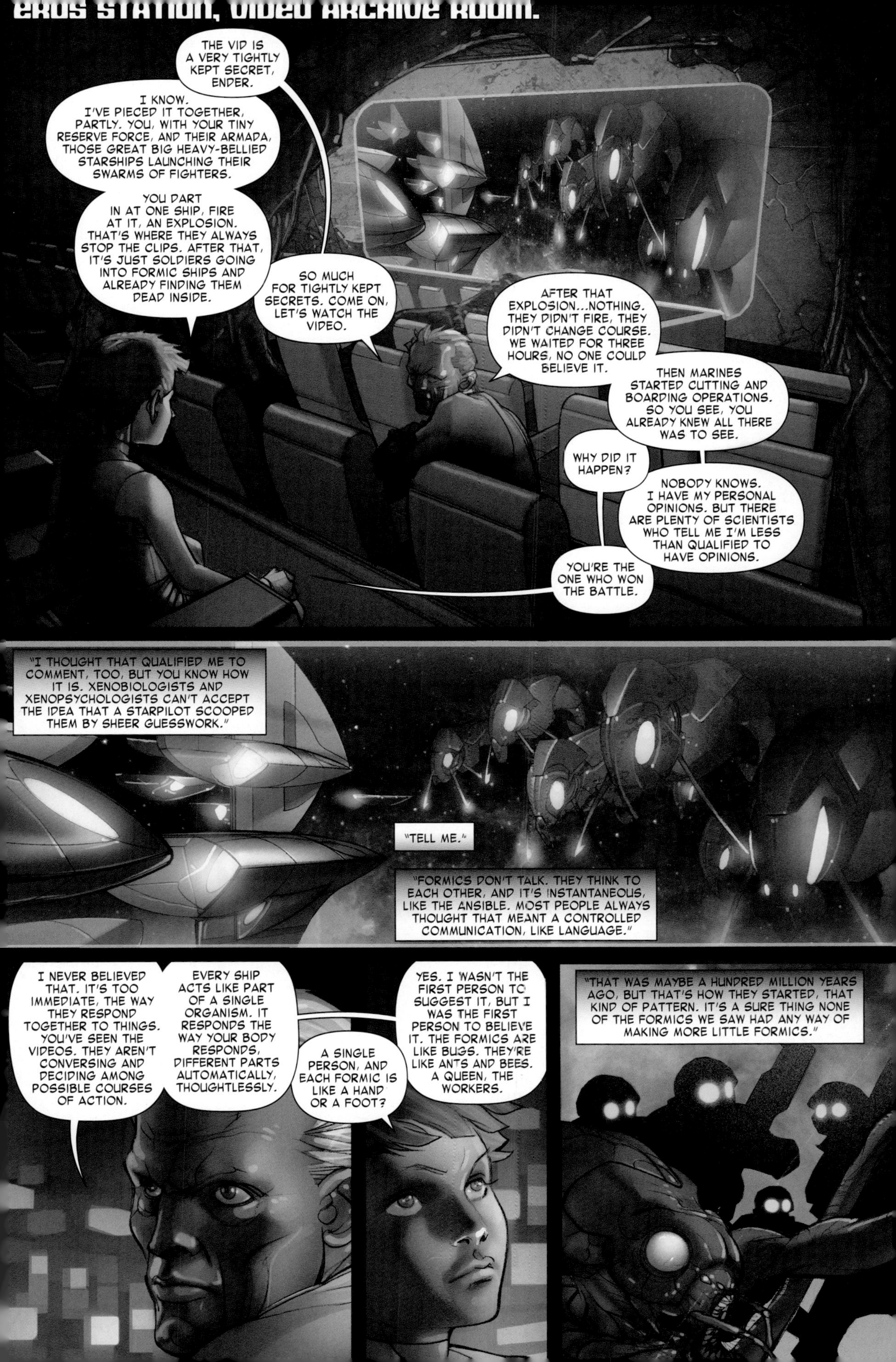
EROS STATION, VIDEO ARCHIVE ROOM.
THE VID IS A VERY TIGHTLY KEPT SECRET, ENDER.
I KNOW. I'VE PIECED IT TOGETHER, PARTLY. YOU, WITH YOUR TINY RESERVE FORCE, AND THEIR ARMADA, THOSE GREAT BIG HEAVY-BELLIED STARSHIPS LAUNCHING THEIR SWARMS OF FIGHTERS.
YOU DART IN AT ONE SHIP, FIRE AT IT, AN EXPLOSION. THAT'S WHERE THEY ALWAYS STOP THE CLIPS. AFTER THAT, IT'S JUST SOLDIERS GOING INTO FORMIC SHIPS AND ALREADY FINDING THEM DEAD INSIDE.
SO MUCH FOR TIGHTLY KEPT SECRETS. COME ON, LET'S WATCH THE VIDEO.
AFTER THAT EXPLOSION...NOTHING. THEY DIDN'T FIRE, THEY DIDN'T CHANGE COURSE. WE WAITED FOR THREE HOURS, NO ONE COULD BELIEVE IT.
THEN MARINES STARTED CUTTING AND BOARDING OPERATIONS. SO YOU SEE, YOU ALREADY KNEW ALL THERE WAS TO SEE.
WHY DID IT HAPPEN?
NOBODY KNOWS. I HAVE MY PERSONAL OPINIONS. BUT THERE ARE PLENTY OF SCIENTISTS WHO TELL ME I'M LESS THAN QUALIFIED TO HAVE OPINIONS.
YOU'RE THE ONE WHO WON THE BATTLE.
"I THOUGHT THAT QUALIFIED ME TO COMMENT, TOO, BUT YOU KNOW HOW IT IS. XENOBIOLOGISTS AND XENOPSYCHOLOGISTS CAN'T ACCEPT THE IDEA THAT A STARPILOT SCOOPED THEM BY SHEER GUESSWORK."
"TELL ME."
"FORMICS DON'T TALK. THEY THINK TO EACH OTHER, AND IT'S INSTANTANEOUS, LIKE THE ANSIBLE. MOST PEOPLE ALWAYS THOUGHT THAT MEANT A CONTROLLED COMMUNICATION, LIKE LANGUAGE."
I NEVER BELIEVED THAT. IT'S TOO IMMEDIATE, THE WAY THEY RESPOND TOGETHER TO THINGS. YOU'VE SEEN THE VIDEOS. THEY AREN'T CONVERSING AND DECIDING AMONG POSSIBLE COURSES OF ACTION.
EVERY SHIP ACTS LIKE PART OF A SINGLE ORGANISM. IT RESPONDS THE WAY YOUR BODY RESPONDS, DIFFERENT PARTS AUTOMATICALLY, THOUGHTLESSLY.
A SINGLE PERSON, AND EACH FORMIC IS LIKE A HAND OR A FOOT?
YES. I WASN'T THE FIRST PERSON TO SUGGEST IT, BUT I WAS THE FIRST PERSON TO BELIEVE IT. THE FORMICS ARE LIKE BUGS. THEY'RE LIKE ANTS AND BEES. A QUEEN, THE WORKERS.
"THAT WAS MAYBE A HUNDRED MILLION YEARS AGO, BUT THAT'S HOW THEY STARTED, THAT KIND OF PATTERN. IT'S A SURE THING NONE OF THE FORMICS WE SAW HAD ANY WAY OF MAKING MORE LITTLE FORMICS."

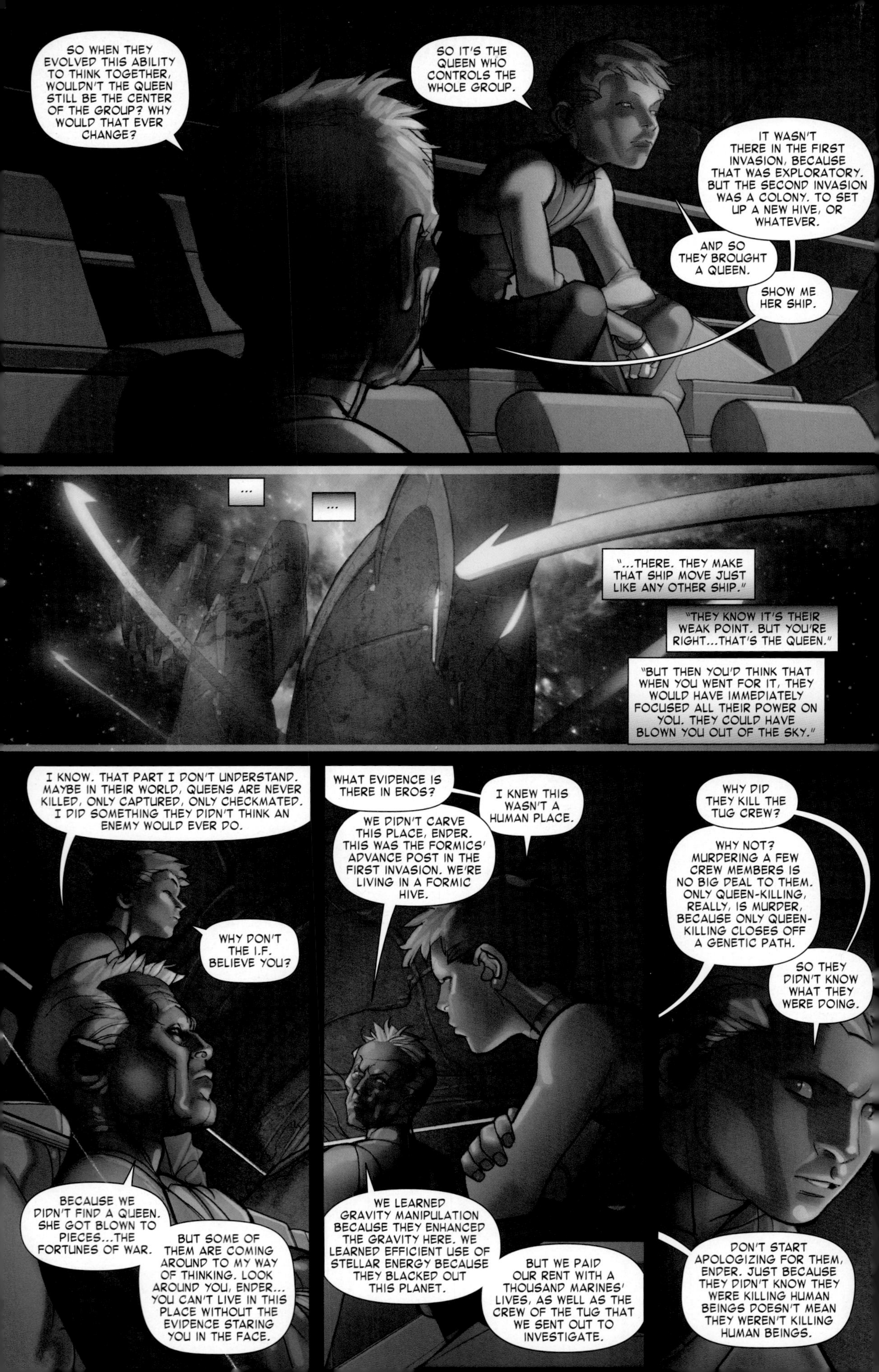

SO WHEN THEY EVOLVED THIS ABILITY TO THINK TOGETHER, WOULDN'T THE QUEEN STILL BE THE CENTER OF THE GROUP? WHY WOULD THAT EVER CHANGE?
SO IT'S THE QUEEN WHO CONTROLS THE WHOLE GROUP.
IT WASN'T THERE IN THE FIRST INVASION, BECAUSE THAT WAS EXPLORATORY. BUT THE SECOND INVASION WAS A COLONY. TO SET UP A NEW HIVE, OR WHATEVER.
AND SO THEY BROUGHT A QUEEN.
SHOW ME HER SHIP.
...
...
"...THERE. THEY MAKE THAT SHIP MOVE JUST LIKE ANY OTHER SHIP."
"THEY KNOW IT'S THEIR WEAK POINT. BUT YOU'RE RIGHT...THAT'S THE QUEEN."
"BUT THEN YOU'D THINK THAT WHEN YOU WENT FOR IT, THEY WOULD HAVE IMMEDIATELY FOCUSED ALL THEIR POWER ON YOU. THEY COULD HAVE BLOWN YOU OUT OF THE SKY."
I KNOW. THAT PART I DON'T UNDERSTAND. MAYBE IN THEIR WORLD, QUEENS ARE NEVER KILLED, ONLY CAPTURED, ONLY CHECKMATED. I DID SOMETHING THEY DIDN'T THINK AN ENEMY WOULD EVER DO.
WHY DON'T THE I.F. BELIEVE YOU?
BECAUSE WE DIDN'T FIND A QUEEN. SHE GOT BLOWN TO PIECES...THE FORTUNES OF WAR.
BUT SOME OF THEM ARE COMING AROUND TO MY WAY OF THINKING. LOOK AROUND YOU, ENDER... YOU CAN'T LIVE IN THIS PLACE WITHOUT THE EVIDENCE STARING YOU IN THE FACE.
WHAT EVIDENCE IS THERE IN EROS?
I KNEW THIS WASN'T A HUMAN PLACE.
WE DIDN'T CARVE THIS PLACE, ENDER. THIS WAS THE FORMICS' ADVANCE POST IN THE FIRST INVASION. WE'RE LIVING IN A FORMIC HIVE.
WE LEARNED GRAVITY MANIPULATION BECAUSE THEY ENHANCED THE GRAVITY HERE. WE LEARNED EFFICIENT USE OF STELLAR ENERGY BECAUSE THEY BLACKED OUT THIS PLANET.
BUT WE PAID OUR RENT WITH A THOUSAND MARINES' LIVES, AS WELL AS THE CREW OF THE TUG THAT WE SENT OUT TO INVESTIGATE.
WHY DID THEY KILL THE TUG CREW?
WHY NOT? MURDERING A FEW CREW MEMBERS IS NO BIG DEAL TO THEM. ONLY QUEEN-KILLING, REALLY, IS MURDER, BECAUSE ONLY QUEEN-KILLING CLOSES OFF A GENETIC PATH.
SO THEY DIDN'T KNOW WHAT THEY WERE DOING.
DON'T START APOLOGIZING FOR THEM, ENDER. JUST BECAUSE THEY DIDN'T KNOW THEY WERE KILLING HUMAN BEINGS DOESN'T MEAN THEY WEREN'T KILLING HUMAN BEINGS.

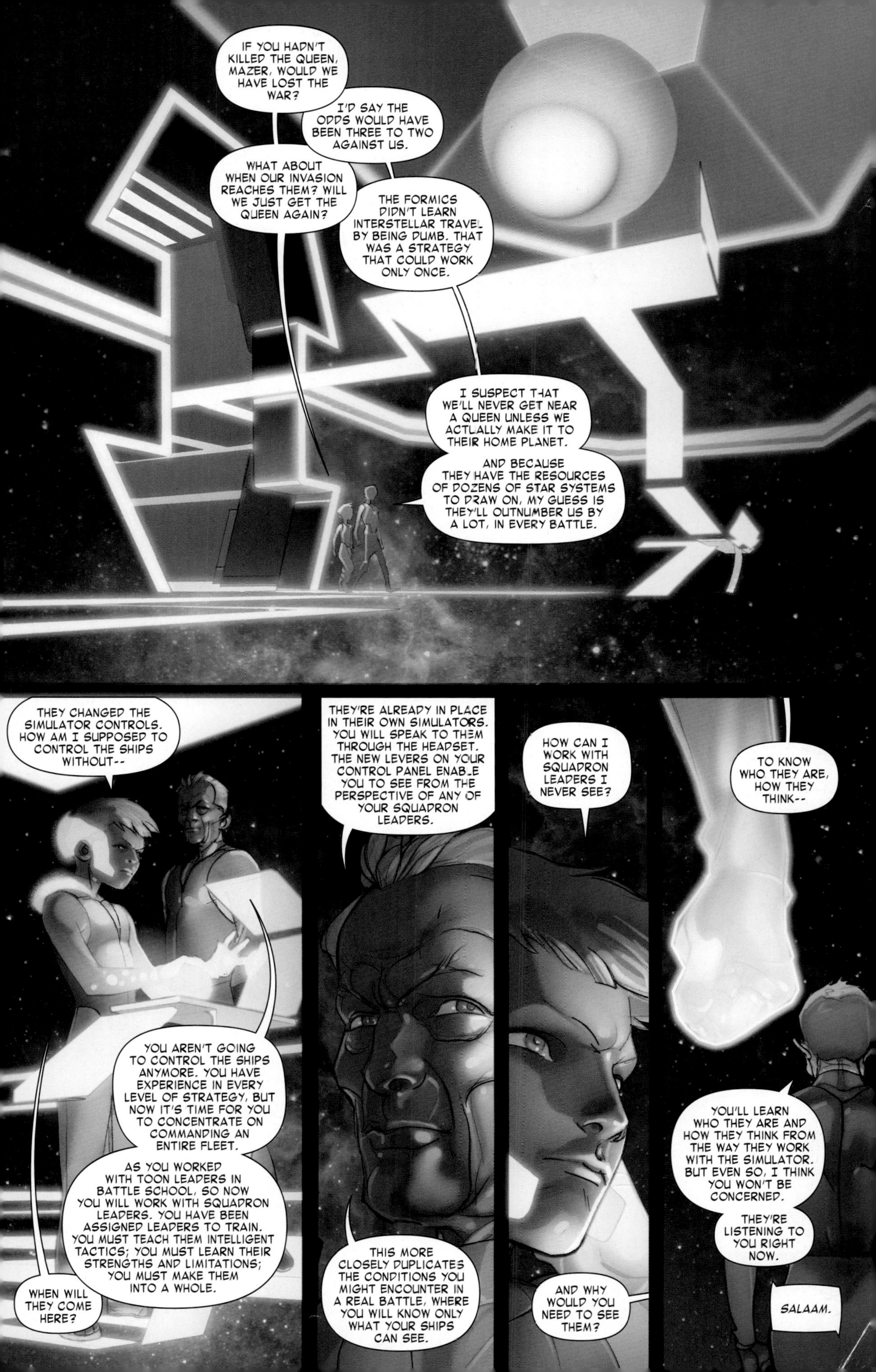
IF YOU HADN'T KILLED THE QUEEN, MAZER, WOULD WE HAVE LOST THE WAR?
I'D SAY THE ODDS WOULD HAVE BEEN THREE TO TWO AGAINST US.
WHAT ABOUT WHEN OUR INVASION REACHES THEM? WILL WE JUST GET THE QUEEN AGAIN?
THE FORMICS DIDN'T LEARN INTERSTELLAR TRAVEL BY BEING DUMB. THAT WAS A STRATEGY THAT COULD WORK ONLY ONCE.
I SUSPECT THAT WE'LL NEVER GET NEAR A QUEEN UNLESS WE ACTUALLY MAKE IT TO THEIR HOME PLANET.
AND BECAUSE THEY HAVE THE RESOURCES OF DOZENS OF STAR SYSTEMS TO DRAW ON, MY GUESS IS THEY'LL OUTNUMBER US BY A LOT, IN EVERY BATTLE.
THEY CHANGED THE SIMULATOR CONTROLS. HOW AM I SUPPOSED TO CONTROL THE SHIPS WITHOUT--
YOU AREN'T GOING TO CONTROL THE SHIPS ANYMORE. YOU HAVE EXPERIENCE IN EVERY LEVEL OF STRATEGY, BUT NOW IT'S TIME FOR YOU TO CONCENTRATE ON COMMANDING AN ENTIRE FLEET.
AS YOU WORKED WITH TOON LEADERS IN BATTLE SCHOOL, SO NOW YOU WILL WORK WITH SQUADRON LEADERS. YOU HAVE BEEN ASSIGNED LEADERS TO TRAIN. YOU MUST TEACH THEM INTELLIGENT TACTICS; YOU MUST LEARN THEIR STRENGTHS AND LIMITATIONS; YOU MUST MAKE THEM INTO A WHOLE.
WHEN WILL THEY COME HERE?
THEY'RE ALREADY IN PLACE IN THEIR OWN SIMULATORS. YOU WILL SPEAK TO THEM THROUGH THE HEADSET. THE NEW LEVERS ON YOUR CONTROL PANEL ENABLE YOU TO SEE FROM THE PERSPECTIVE OF ANY OF YOUR SQUADRON LEADERS.
THIS MORE CLOSELY DUPLICATES THE CONDITIONS YOU MIGHT ENCOUNTER IN A REAL BATTLE, WHERE YOU WILL KNOW ONLY WHAT YOUR SHIPS CAN SEE.
HOW CAN I WORK WITH SQUADRON LEADERS I NEVER SEE?
AND WHY WOULD YOU NEED TO SEE THEM?
TO KNOW WHO THEY ARE, HOW THEY THINK--
YOU'LL LEARN WHO THEY ARE AND HOW THEY THINK FROM THE WAY THEY WORK WITH THE SIMULATOR. BUT EVEN SO, I THINK YOU WON'T BE CONCERNED.
THEY'RE LISTENING TO YOU RIGHT NOW.
SALAAM.

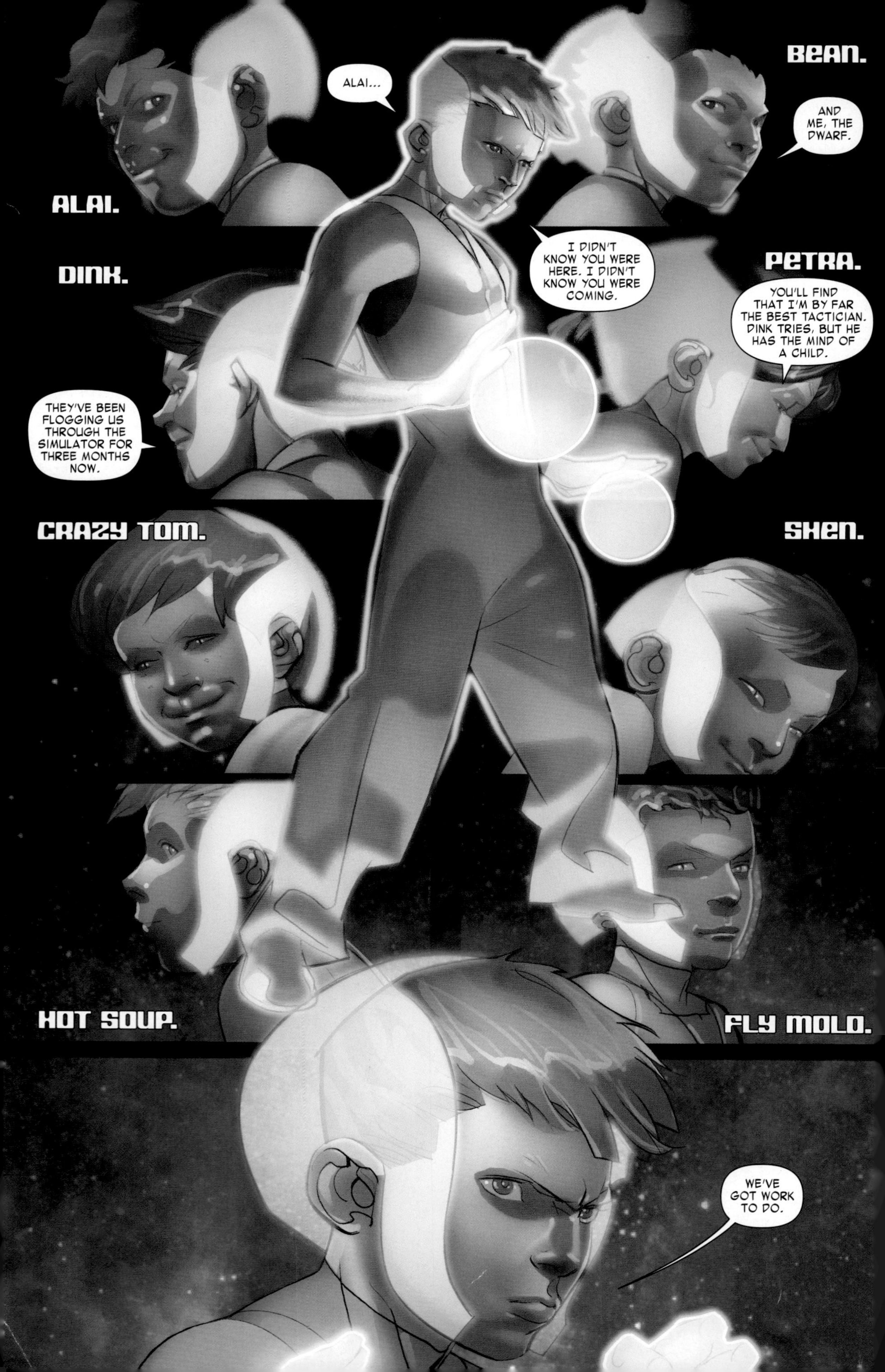
ALAI...
BEAN.
AND ME, THE DWARF.
ALAI.
I DIDN'T KNOW YOU WERE HERE. I DIDN'T KNOW YOU WERE COMING.
DINK.
PETRA.
YOU'LL FIND THAT I'M BY FAR THE BEST TACTICIAN. DINK TRIES, BUT HE HAS THE MIND OF A CHILD.
THEY'VE BEEN FLOGGING US THROUGH THE SIMULATOR FOR THREE MONTHS NOW.
CRAZY TOM.
SHEN.
HOT SOUP.
FLY MOLO.
WE'VE GOT WORK TO DO.

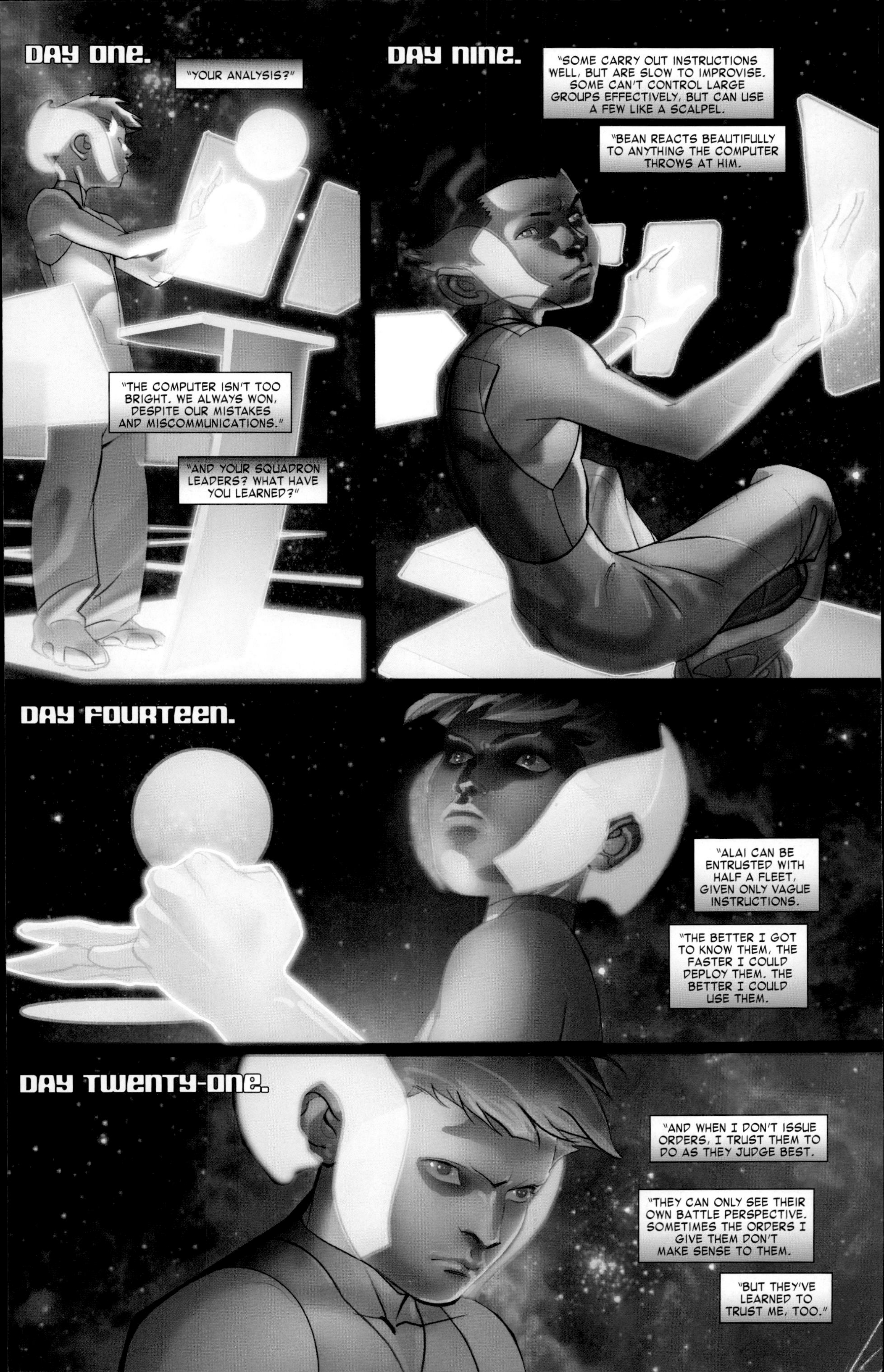
DAY ONE.
"YOUR ANALYSIS?"
"THE COMPUTER ISN'T TOO BRIGHT. WE ALWAYS WON, DESPITE OUR MISTAKES AND MISCOMMUNICATIONS."
"AND YOUR SQUADRON LEADERS? WHAT HAVE YOU LEARNED?"
DAY NINE.
"SOME CARRY OUT INSTRUCTIONS WELL, BUT ARE SLOW TO IMPROVISE. SOME CAN'T CONTROL LARGE GROUPS EFFECTIVELY, BUT CAN USE A FEW LIKE A SCALPEL.
"BEAN REACTS BEAUTIFULLY TO ANYTHING THE COMPUTER THROWS AT HIM.
DAY FOURTEEN.
"ALAI CAN BE ENTRUSTED WITH HALF A FLEET, GIVEN ONLY VAGUE INSTRUCTIONS.
"THE BETTER I GOT TO KNOW THEM, THE FASTER I COULD DEPLOY THEM. THE BETTER I COULD USE THEM.
DAY TWENTY-ONE.
"AND WHEN I DON'T ISSUE ORDERS, I TRUST THEM TO DO AS THEY JUDGE BEST.
"THEY CAN ONLY SEE THEIR OWN BATTLE PERSPECTIVE. SOMETIMES THE ORDERS I GIVE THEM DON'T MAKE SENSE TO THEM.
"BUT THEY'VE LEARNED TO TRUST ME, TOO."

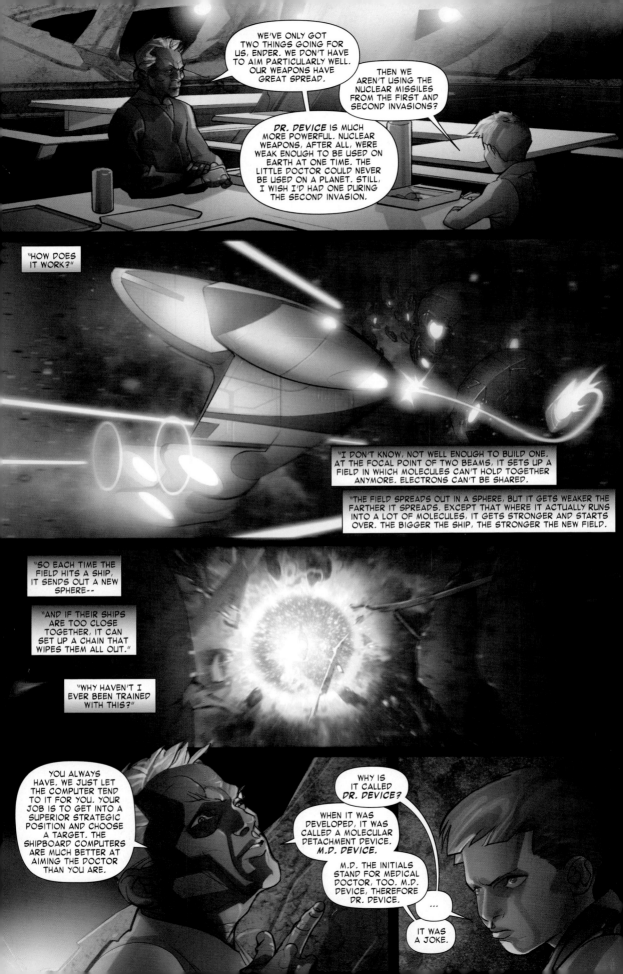

WE'VE ONLY GOT TWO THINGS GOING FOR US, ENDER. WE DON'T HAVE TO AIM PARTICULARLY WELL. OUR WEAPONS HAVE GREAT SPREAD.

THEN WE AREN'T USING THE NUCLEAR MISSILES FROM THE FIRST AND SECOND INVASIONS?

DR. DEVICE IS MUCH MORE POWERFUL. NUCLEAR WEAPONS, AFTER ALL, WERE WEAK ENOUGH TO BE USED ON EARTH AT ONE TIME. THE LITTLE DOCTOR COULD NEVER BE USED ON A PLANET. STILL, I WISH I'D HAD ONE DURING THE SECOND INVASION.

"HOW DOES IT WORK?"

"I DON'T KNOW, NOT WELL ENOUGH TO BUILD ONE. AT THE FOCAL POINT OF TWO BEAMS, IT SETS UP A FIELD IN WHICH MOLECULES CAN'T HOLD TOGETHER ANYMORE. ELECTRONS CAN'T BE SHARED.

"THE FIELD SPREADS OUT IN A SPHERE, BUT IT GETS WEAKER THE FARTHER IT SPREADS. EXCEPT THAT WHERE IT ACTUALLY RUNS INTO A LOT OF MOLECULES, IT GETS STRONGER AND STARTS OVER. THE BIGGER THE SHIP, THE STRONGER THE NEW FIELD.

"SO EACH TIME THE FIELD HITS A SHIP, IT SENDS OUT A NEW SPHERE--

"AND IF THEIR SHIPS ARE TOO CLOSE TOGETHER, IT CAN SET UP A CHAIN THAT WIPES THEM ALL OUT."

"WHY HAVEN'T I EVER BEEN TRAINED WITH THIS?"

YOU ALWAYS HAVE. WE JUST LET THE COMPUTER TEND TO IT FOR YOU. YOUR JOB IS TO GET INTO A SUPERIOR STRATEGIC POSITION AND CHOOSE A TARGET. THE SHIPBOARD COMPUTERS ARE MUCH BETTER AT AIMING THE DOCTOR THAN YOU ARE.

WHY IS IT CALLED DR. DEVICE?

WHEN IT WAS DEVELOPED, IT WAS CALLED A MOLECULAR DETACHMENT DEVICE. M.D. DEVICE.

M.D. THE INITIALS STAND FOR MEDICAL DOCTOR, TOO. M.D. DEVICE, THEREFORE DR. DEVICE.

...

IT WAS A JOKE.

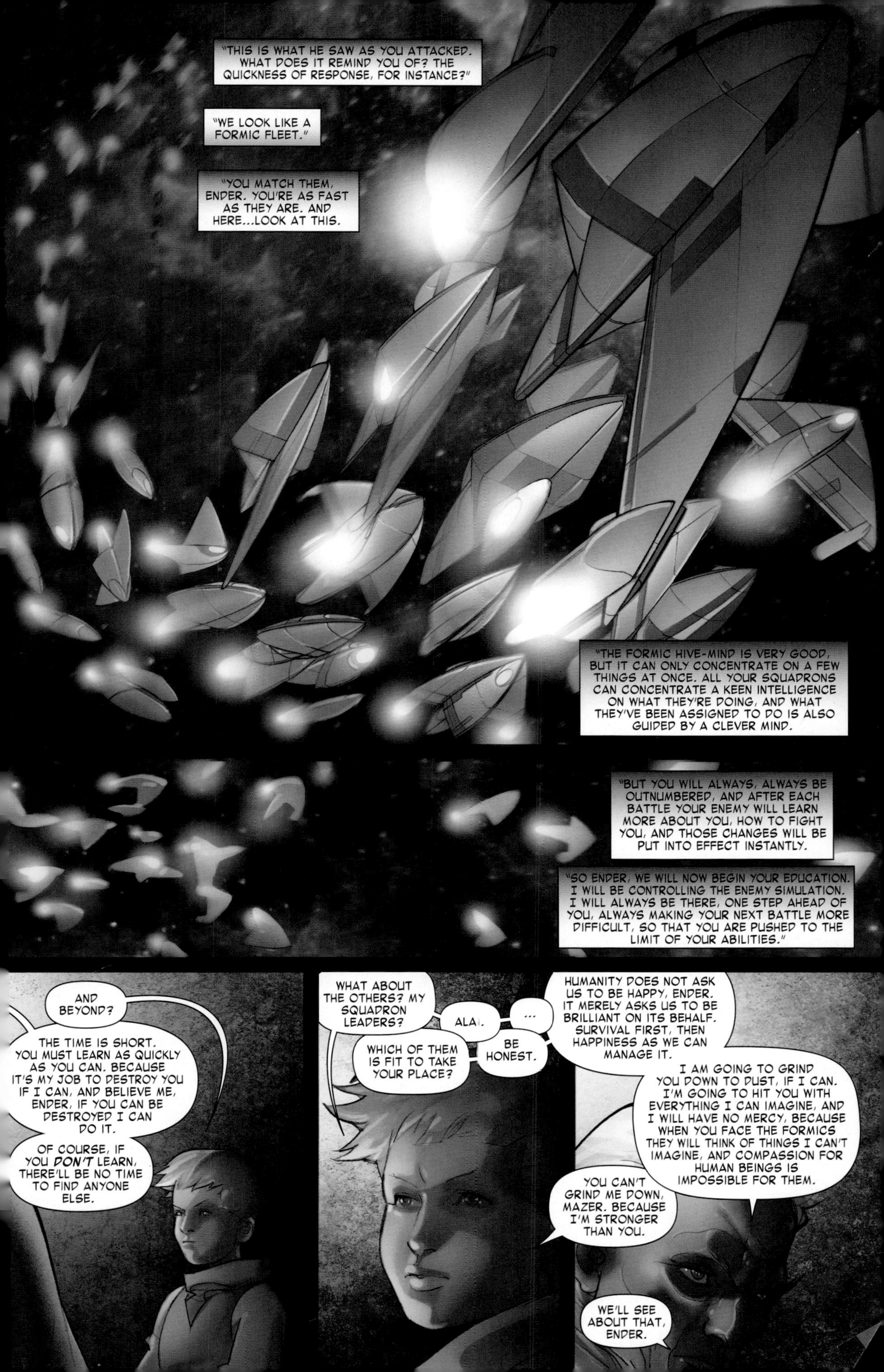

"THIS IS WHAT HE SAW AS YOU ATTACKED. WHAT DOES IT REMIND YOU OF? THE QUICKNESS OF RESPONSE, FOR INSTANCE?"
"WE LOOK LIKE A FORMIC FLEET."
"YOU MATCH THEM, ENDER. YOU'RE AS FAST AS THEY ARE. AND HERE...LOOK AT THIS.
"THE FORMIC HIVE-MIND IS VERY GOOD, BUT IT CAN ONLY CONCENTRATE ON A FEW THINGS AT ONCE. ALL YOUR SQUADRONS CAN CONCENTRATE A KEEN INTELLIGENCE ON WHAT THEY'RE DOING, AND WHAT THEY'VE BEEN ASSIGNED TO DO IS ALSO GUIDED BY A CLEVER MIND.
"BUT YOU WILL ALWAYS, ALWAYS BE OUTNUMBERED, AND AFTER EACH BATTLE YOUR ENEMY WILL LEARN MORE ABOUT YOU, HOW TO FIGHT YOU, AND THOSE CHANGES WILL BE PUT INTO EFFECT INSTANTLY.
"SO ENDER, WE WILL NOW BEGIN YOUR EDUCATION. I WILL BE CONTROLLING THE ENEMY SIMULATION. I WILL ALWAYS BE THERE, ONE STEP AHEAD OF YOU, ALWAYS MAKING YOUR NEXT BATTLE MORE DIFFICULT, SO THAT YOU ARE PUSHED TO THE LIMIT OF YOUR ABILITIES."
AND BEYOND?
THE TIME IS SHORT. YOU MUST LEARN AS QUICKLY AS YOU CAN. BECAUSE IT'S MY JOB TO DESTROY YOU IF I CAN, AND BELIEVE ME, ENDER, IF YOU CAN BE DESTROYED I CAN DO IT.
OF COURSE, IF YOU *DON'T* LEARN, THERE'LL BE NO TIME TO FIND ANYONE ELSE.
WHAT ABOUT THE OTHERS? MY SQUADRON LEADERS?
WHICH OF THEM IS FIT TO TAKE YOUR PLACE?
ALAI.
...
BE HONEST.
HUMANITY DOES NOT ASK US TO BE HAPPY, ENDER. IT MERELY ASKS US TO BE BRILLIANT ON ITS BEHALF. SURVIVAL FIRST, THEN HAPPINESS AS WE CAN MANAGE IT.
I AM GOING TO GRIND YOU DOWN TO DUST, IF I CAN. I'M GOING TO HIT YOU WITH EVERYTHING I CAN IMAGINE, AND I WILL HAVE NO MERCY, BECAUSE WHEN YOU FACE THE FORMICS THEY WILL THINK OF THINGS I CAN'T IMAGINE, AND COMPASSION FOR HUMAN BEINGS IS IMPOSSIBLE FOR THEM.
YOU CAN'T GRIND ME DOWN, MAZER. BECAUSE I'M STRONGER THAN YOU.
WE'LL SEE ABOUT THAT, ENDER.

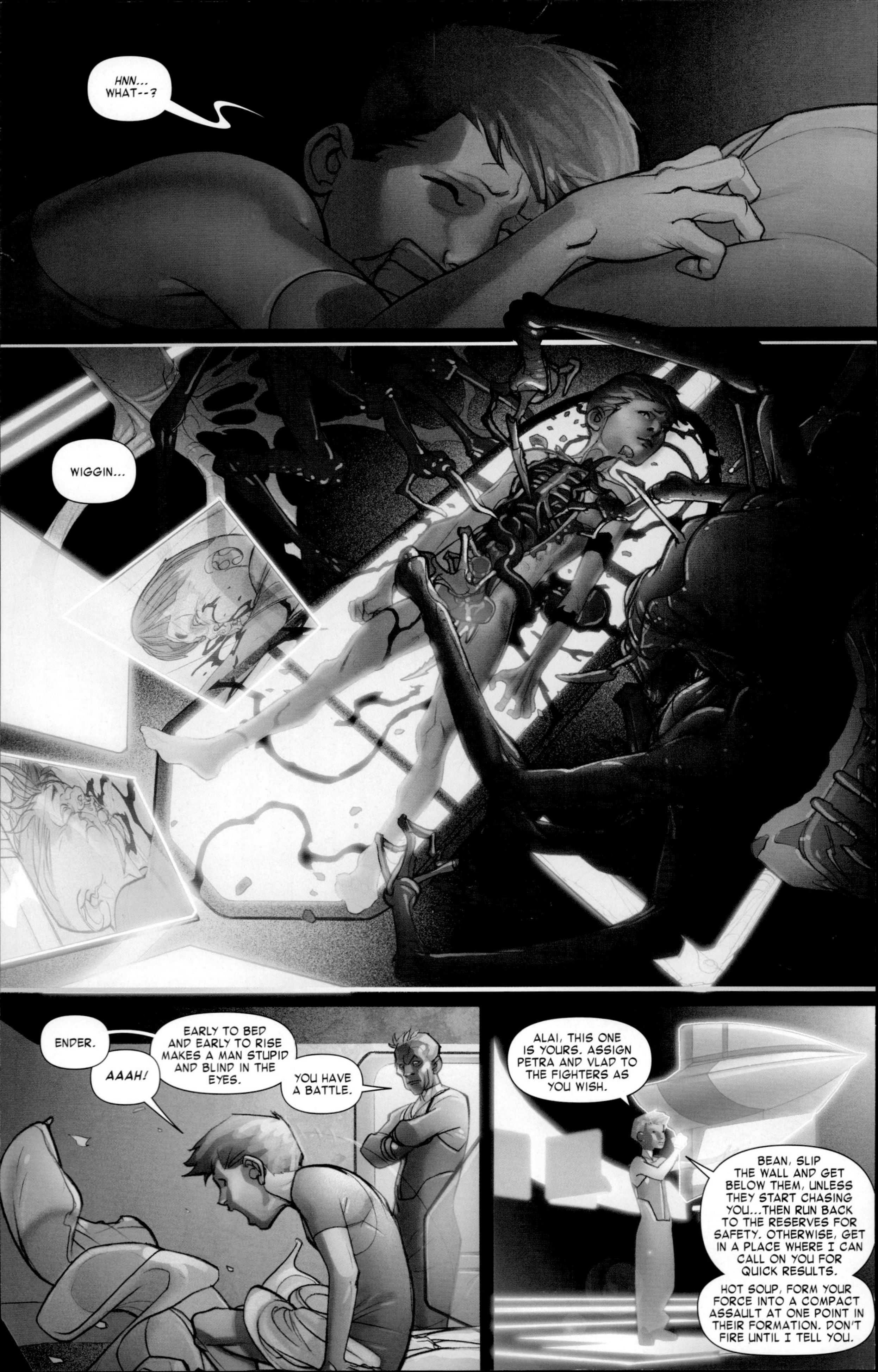
HNN... WHAT--?
WIGGIN...
ENDER.
AAAH!
EARLY TO BED AND EARLY TO RISE MAKES A MAN STUPID AND BLIND IN THE EYES.
YOU HAVE A BATTLE.
ALAI, THIS ONE IS YOURS. ASSIGN PETRA AND VLAD TO THE FIGHTERS AS YOU WISH.
BEAN, SLIP THE WALL AND GET BELOW THEM, UNLESS THEY START CHASING YOU...THEN RUN BACK TO THE RESERVES FOR SAFETY. OTHERWISE, GET IN A PLACE WHERE I CAN CALL ON YOU FOR QUICK RESULTS.
HOT SOUP, FORM YOUR FORCE INTO A COMPACT ASSAULT AT ONE POINT IN THEIR FORMATION. DON'T FIRE UNTIL I TELL YOU.

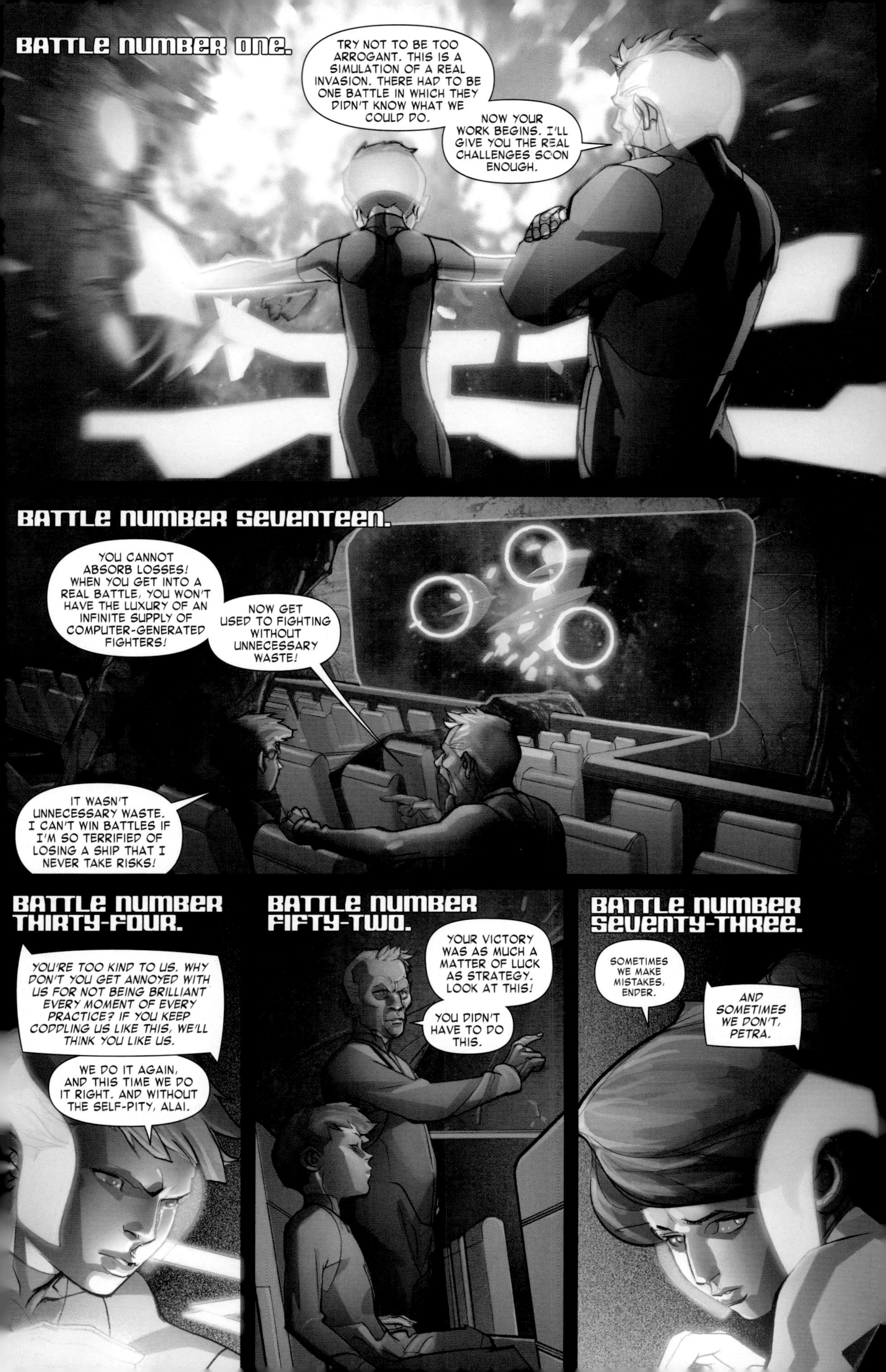
BATTLE NUMBER ONE.
TRY NOT TO BE TOO ARROGANT. THIS IS A SIMULATION OF A REAL INVASION. THERE HAD TO BE ONE BATTLE IN WHICH THEY DIDN'T KNOW WHAT WE COULD DO.
NOW YOUR WORK BEGINS. I'LL GIVE YOU THE REAL CHALLENGES SOON ENOUGH.
BATTLE NUMBER SEVENTEEN.
YOU CANNOT ABSORB LOSSES! WHEN YOU GET INTO A REAL BATTLE, YOU WON'T HAVE THE LUXURY OF AN INFINITE SUPPLY OF COMPUTER-GENERATED FIGHTERS!
NOW GET USED TO FIGHTING WITHOUT UNNECESSARY WASTE!
IT WASN'T UNNECESSARY WASTE. I CAN'T WIN BATTLES IF I'M SO TERRIFIED OF LOSING A SHIP THAT I NEVER TAKE RISKS!
BATTLE NUMBER THIRTY-FOUR.
YOU'RE TOO KIND TO US. WHY DON'T YOU GET ANNOYED WITH US FOR NOT BEING BRILLIANT EVERY MOMENT OF EVERY PRACTICE? IF YOU KEEP CODDLING US LIKE THIS, WE'LL THINK YOU LIKE US.
WE DO IT AGAIN, AND THIS TIME WE DO IT RIGHT. AND WITHOUT THE SELF-PITY, ALAI.
BATTLE NUMBER FIFTY-TWO.
YOUR VICTORY WAS AS MUCH A MATTER OF LUCK AS STRATEGY. LOOK AT THIS!
YOU DIDN'T HAVE TO DO THIS.
BATTLE NUMBER SEVENTY-THREE.
SOMETIMES WE MAKE MISTAKES, ENDER.
AND SOMETIMES WE DON'T, PETRA.

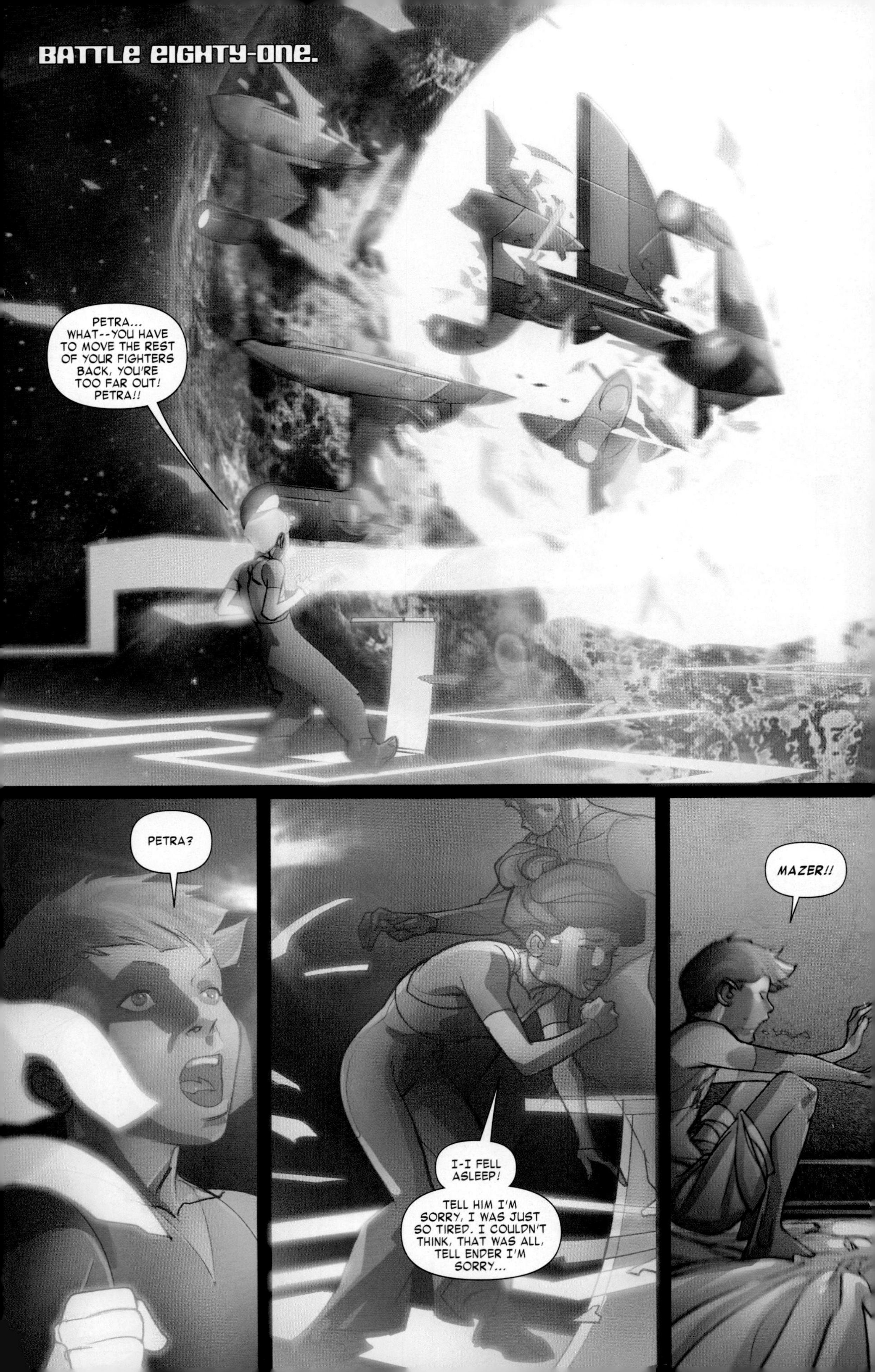
BATTLE EIGHTY-ONE.
PETRA... WHAT--YOU HAVE TO MOVE THE REST OF YOUR FIGHTERS BACK, YOU'RE TOO FAR OUT! PETRA!!
PETRA?
I-I FELL ASLEEP!
TELL HIM I'M SORRY, I WAS JUST SO TIRED. I COULDN'T THINK, THAT WAS ALL, TELL ENDER I'M SORRY...
MAZER!!

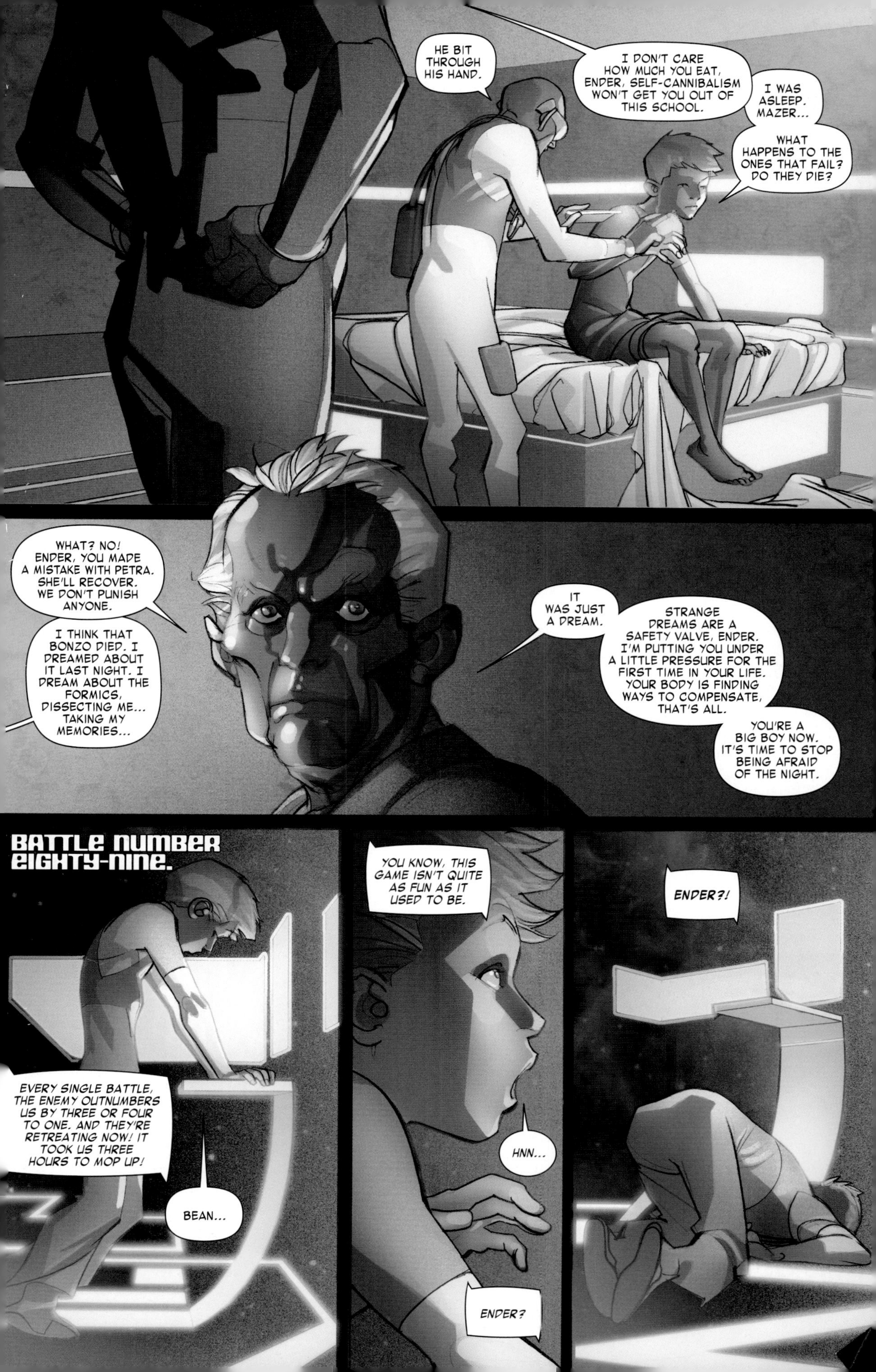
HE BIT THROUGH HIS HAND.
I DON'T CARE HOW MUCH YOU EAT, ENDER, SELF-CANNIBALISM WON'T GET YOU OUT OF THIS SCHOOL.
I WAS ASLEEP, MAZER...
WHAT HAPPENS TO THE ONES THAT FAIL? DO THEY DIE?
WHAT? NO! ENDER, YOU MADE A MISTAKE WITH PETRA. SHE'LL RECOVER. WE DON'T PUNISH ANYONE.
I THINK THAT BONZO DIED. I DREAMED ABOUT IT LAST NIGHT. I DREAM ABOUT THE FORMICS, DISSECTING ME... TAKING MY MEMORIES...
IT WAS JUST A DREAM.
STRANGE DREAMS ARE A SAFETY VALVE, ENDER. I'M PUTTING YOU UNDER A LITTLE PRESSURE FOR THE FIRST TIME IN YOUR LIFE. YOUR BODY IS FINDING WAYS TO COMPENSATE, THAT'S ALL.
YOU'RE A BIG BOY NOW. IT'S TIME TO STOP BEING AFRAID OF THE NIGHT.
BATTLE NUMBER EIGHTY-NINE.
EVERY SINGLE BATTLE, THE ENEMY OUTNUMBERS US BY THREE OR FOUR TO ONE. AND THEY'RE RETREATING NOW! IT TOOK US THREE HOURS TO MOP UP!
BEAN...
YOU KNOW, THIS GAME ISN'T QUITE AS FUN AS IT USED TO BE.
HNN...
ENDER?
ENDER?!

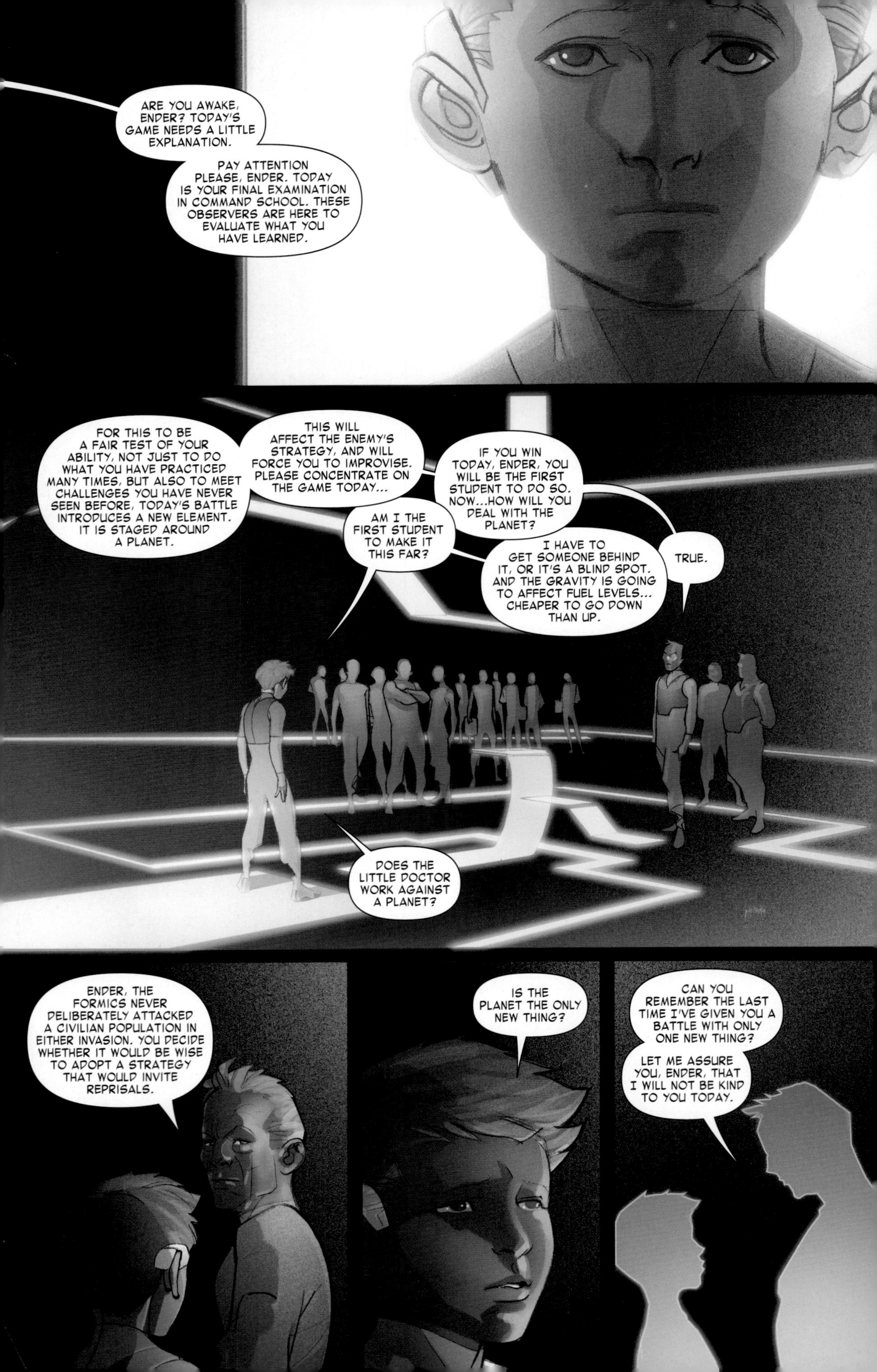
ARE YOU AWAKE, ENDER? TODAY'S GAME NEEDS A LITTLE EXPLANATION.
PAY ATTENTION PLEASE, ENDER. TODAY IS YOUR FINAL EXAMINATION IN COMMAND SCHOOL. THESE OBSERVERS ARE HERE TO EVALUATE WHAT YOU HAVE LEARNED.
FOR THIS TO BE A FAIR TEST OF YOUR ABILITY, NOT JUST TO DO WHAT YOU HAVE PRACTICED MANY TIMES, BUT ALSO TO MEET CHALLENGES YOU HAVE NEVER SEEN BEFORE, TODAY'S BATTLE INTRODUCES A NEW ELEMENT. IT IS STAGED AROUND A PLANET.
THIS WILL AFFECT THE ENEMY'S STRATEGY, AND WILL FORCE YOU TO IMPROVISE. PLEASE CONCENTRATE ON THE GAME TODAY...
AM I THE FIRST STUDENT TO MAKE IT THIS FAR?
IF YOU WIN TODAY, ENDER, YOU WILL BE THE FIRST STUDENT TO DO SO. NOW...HOW WILL YOU DEAL WITH THE PLANET?
I HAVE TO GET SOMEONE BEHIND IT, OR IT'S A BLIND SPOT. AND THE GRAVITY IS GOING TO AFFECT FUEL LEVELS... CHEAPER TO GO DOWN THAN UP.
TRUE.
DOES THE LITTLE DOCTOR WORK AGAINST A PLANET?
ENDER, THE FORMICS NEVER DELIBERATELY ATTACKED A CIVILIAN POPULATION IN EITHER INVASION. YOU DECIDE WHETHER IT WOULD BE WISE TO ADOPT A STRATEGY THAT WOULD INVITE REPRISALS.
IS THE PLANET THE ONLY NEW THING?
CAN YOU REMEMBER THE LAST TIME I'VE GIVEN YOU A BATTLE WITH ONLY ONE NEW THING?
LET ME ASSURE YOU, ENDER, THAT I WILL NOT BE KIND TO YOU TODAY.

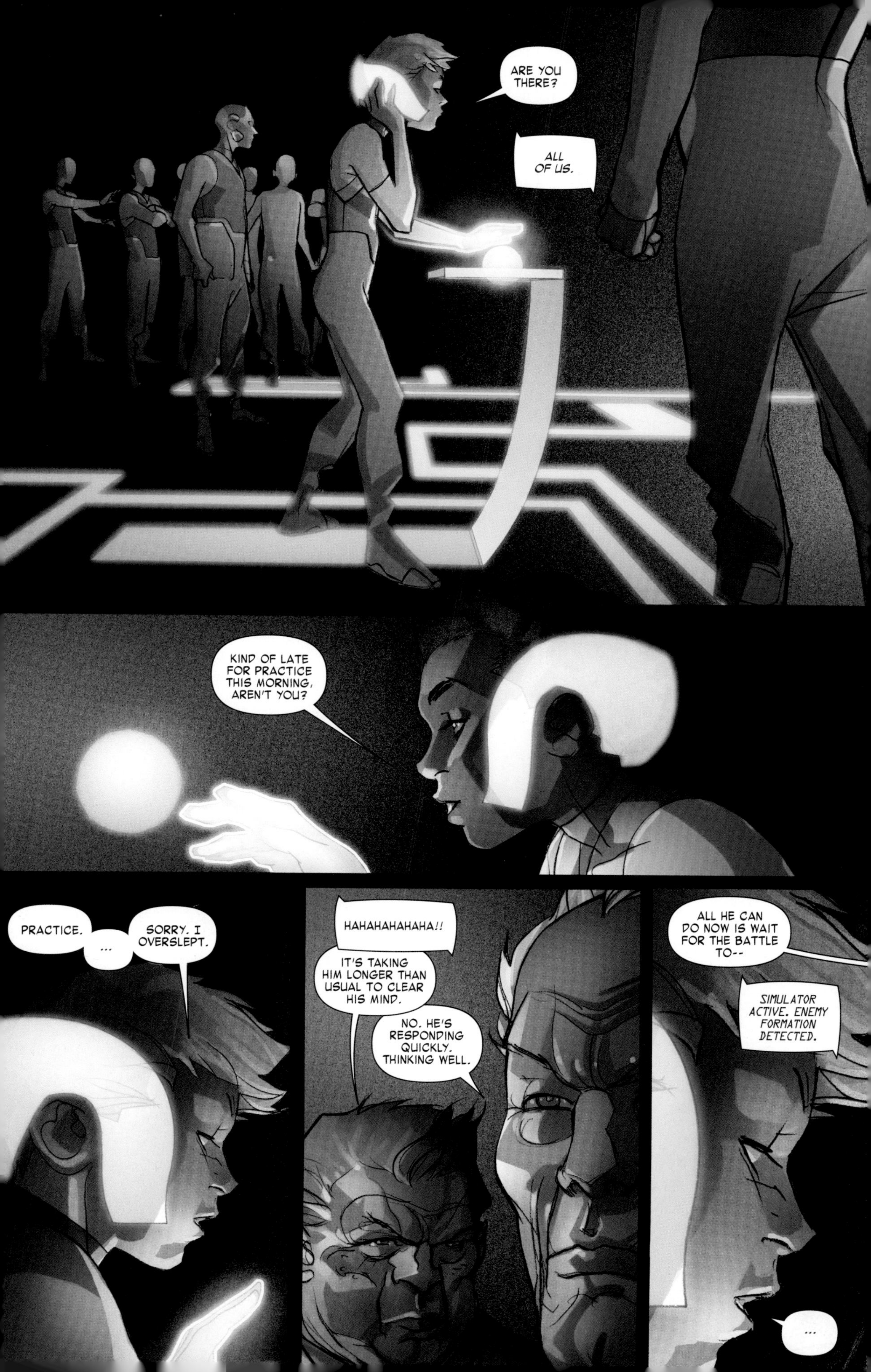
ARE YOU THERE?
ALL OF US.
KIND OF LATE FOR PRACTICE THIS MORNING, AREN'T YOU?
PRACTICE.
...
SORRY. I OVERSLEPT.
HAHAHAHAHAHA!!
IT'S TAKING HIM LONGER THAN USUAL TO CLEAR HIS MIND.
NO. HE'S RESPONDING QUICKLY. THINKING WELL.
ALL HE CAN DO NOW IS WAIT FOR THE BATTLE TO--
SIMULATOR ACTIVE. ENEMY FORMATION DETECTED.
...

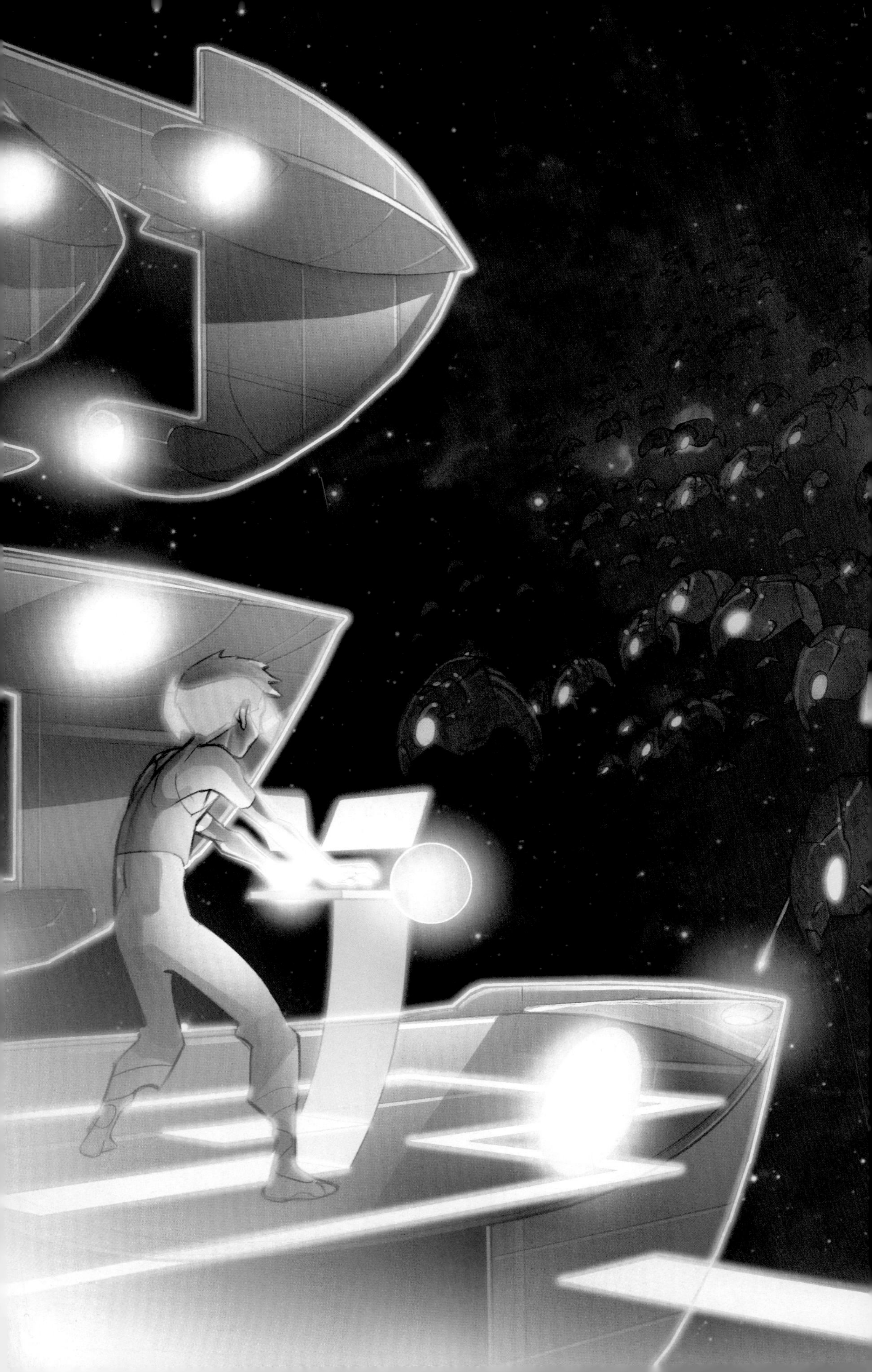

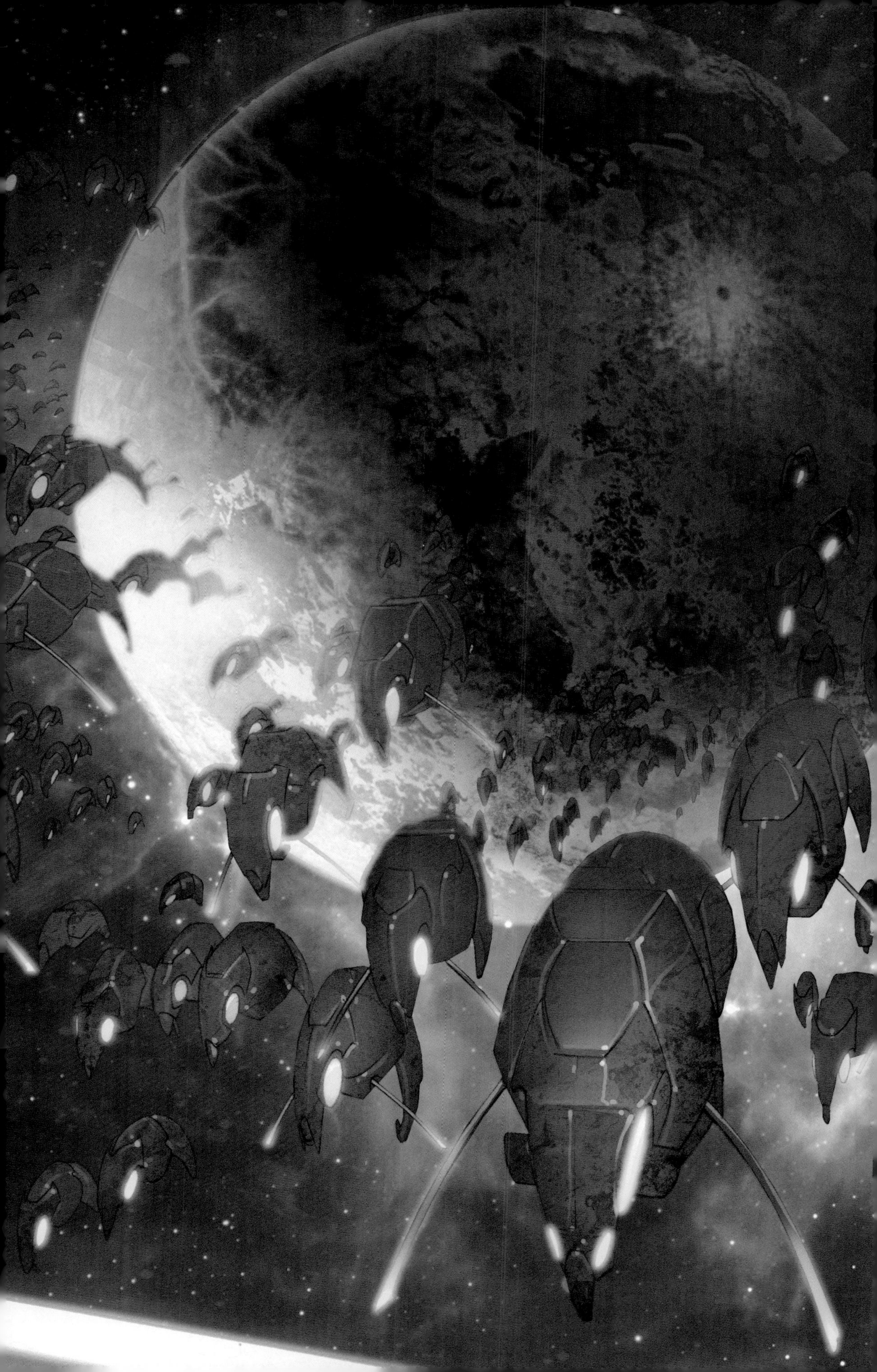

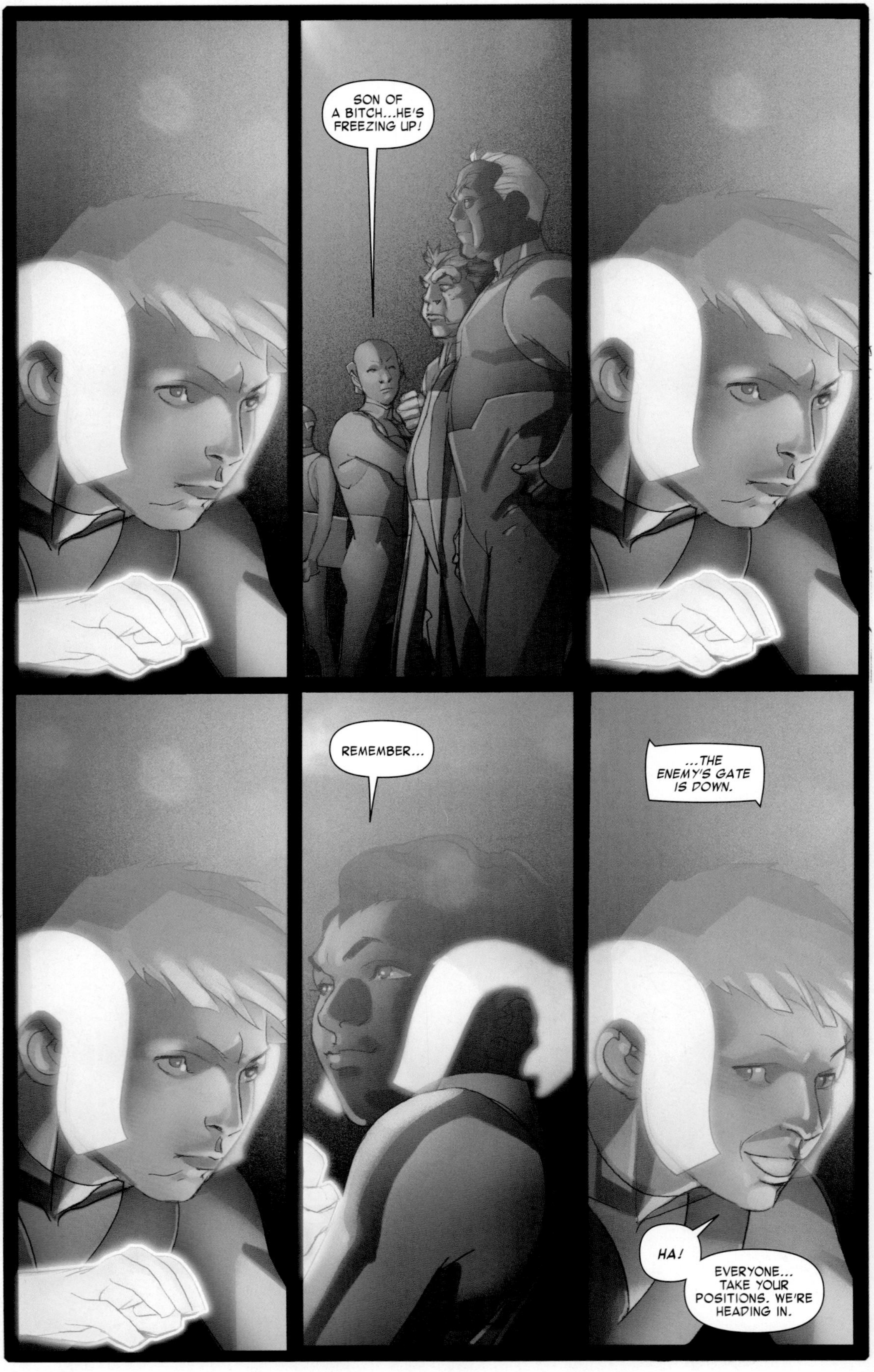
SON OF A BITCH...HE'S FREEZING UP!
REMEMBER...
...THE ENEMY'S GATE IS DOWN.
HA!
EVERYONE... TAKE YOUR POSITIONS. WE'RE HEADING IN.

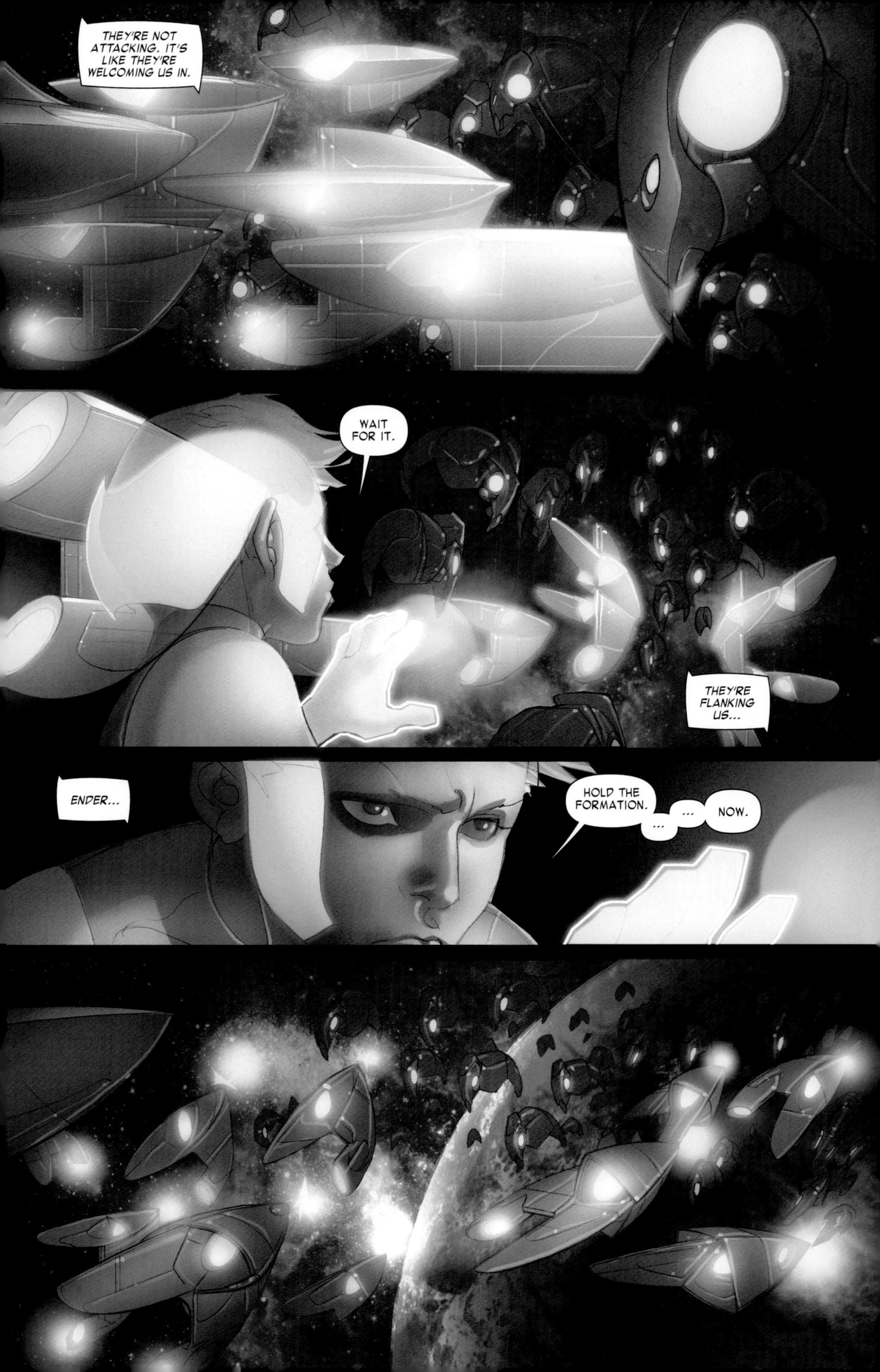
THEY'RE NOT ATTACKING. IT'S LIKE THEY'RE WELCOMING US IN.
WAIT FOR IT.
THEY'RE FLANKING US...
ENDER...
HOLD THE FORMATION.
...
...
NOW.

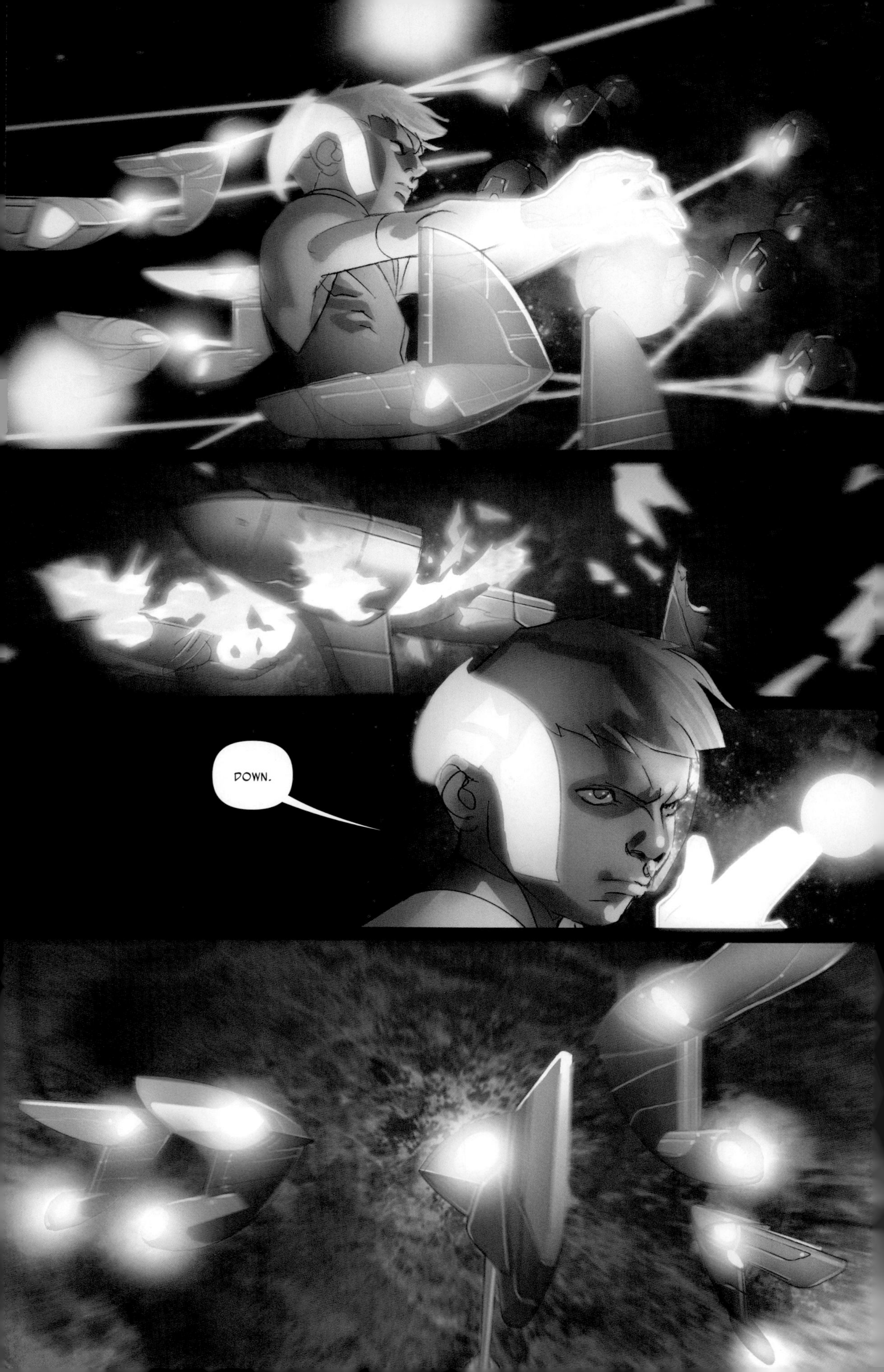
DOWN.

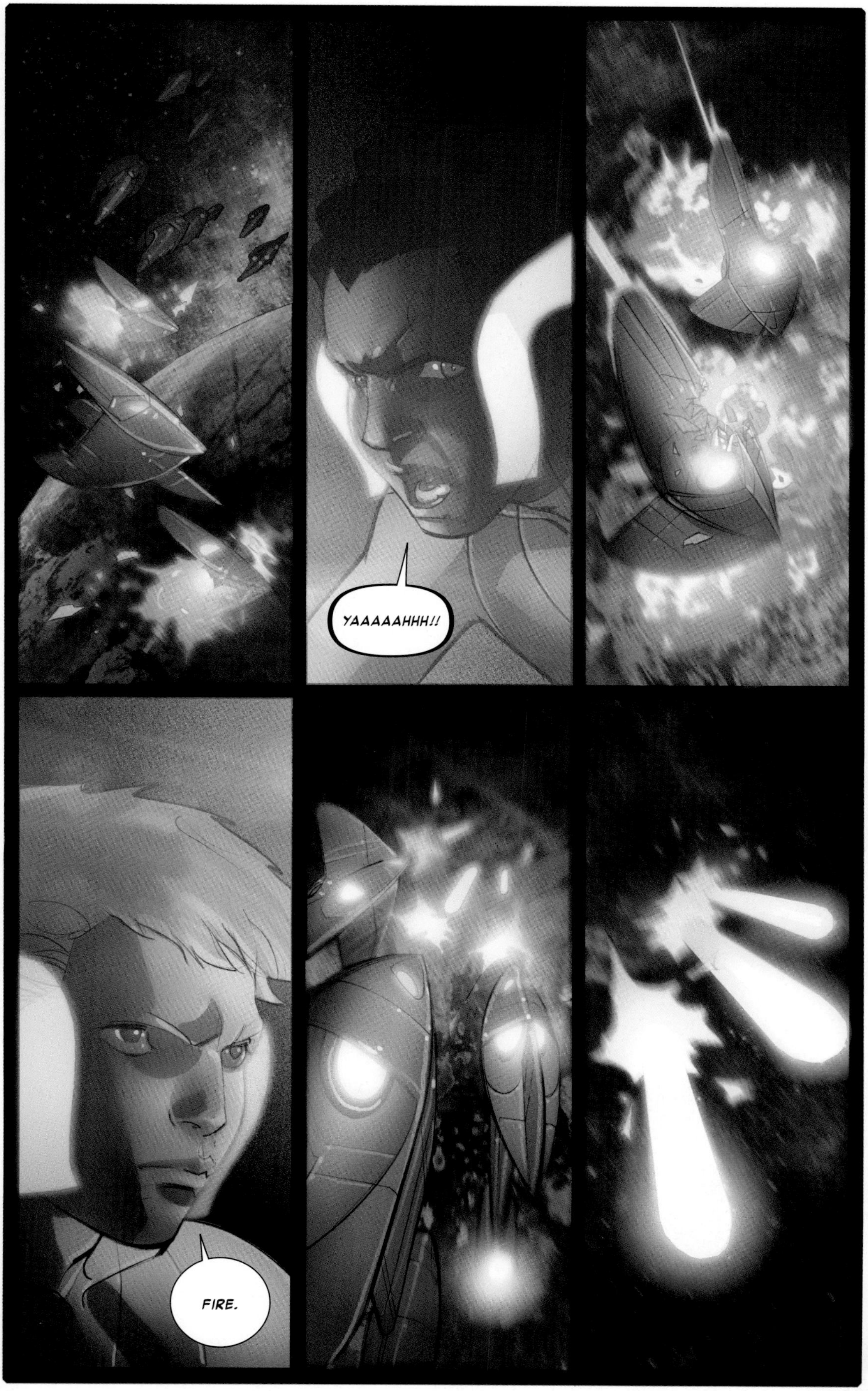
YAAAAAHHH!!
FIRE.

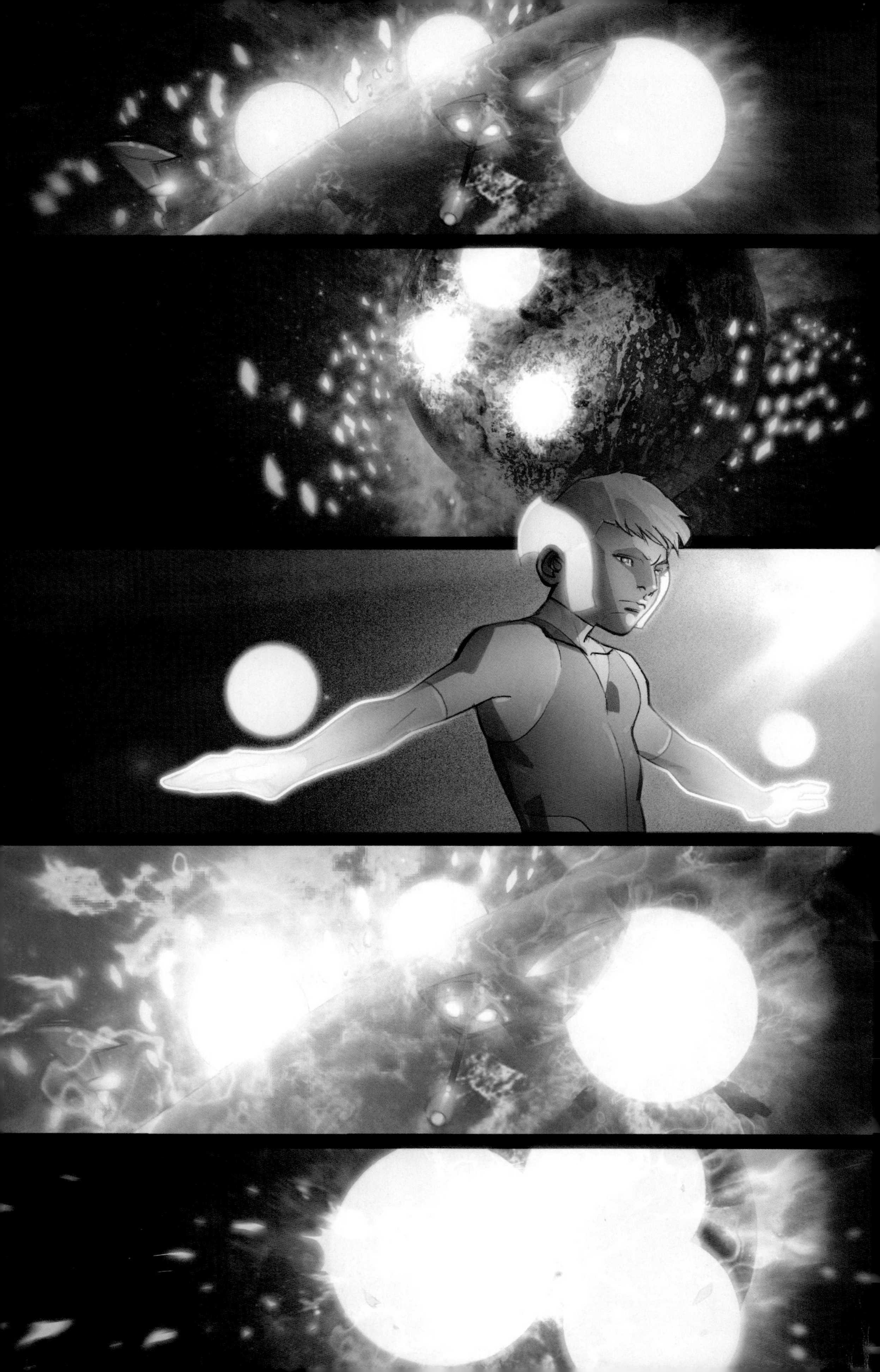

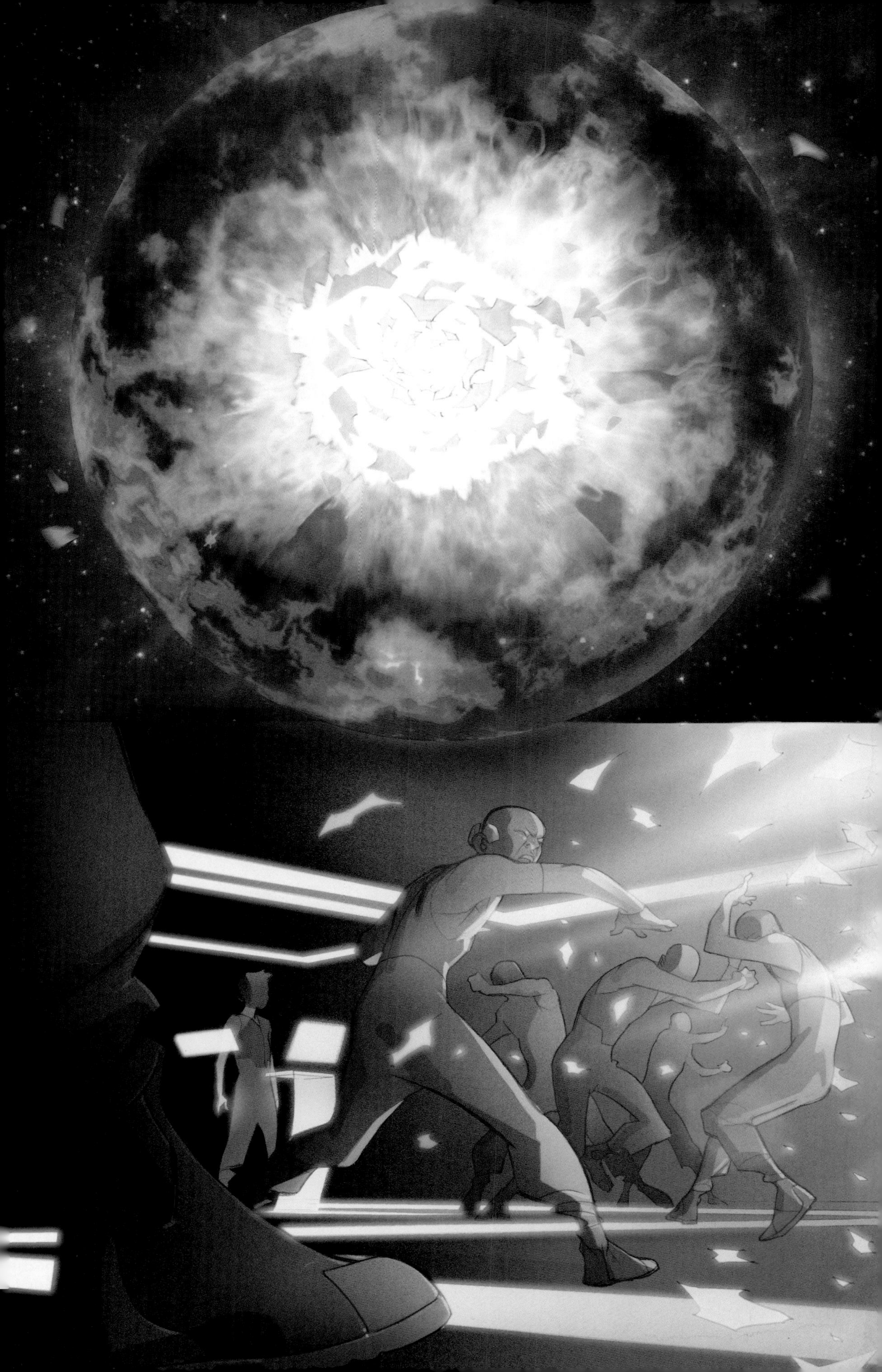

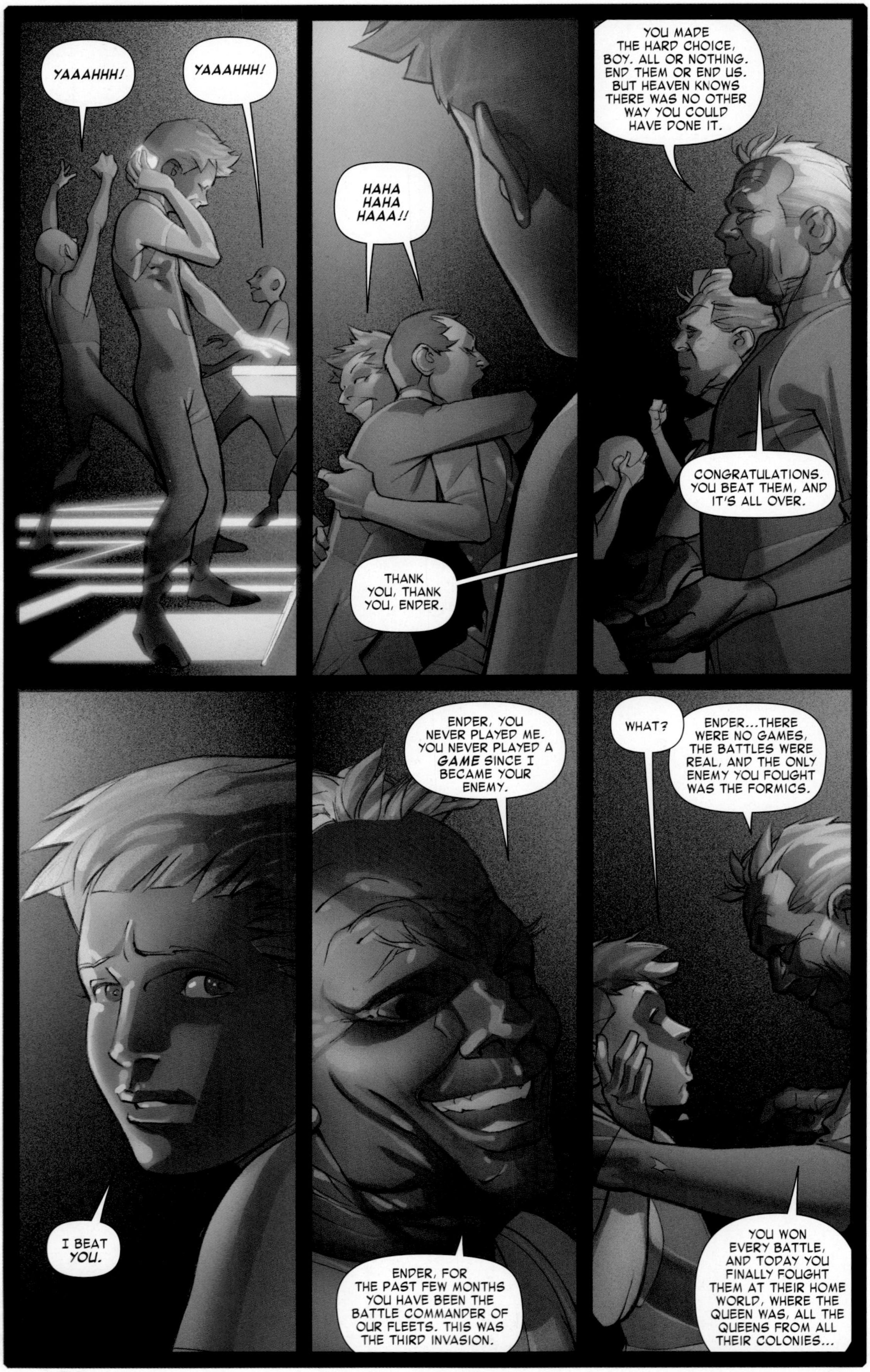
YAAAHHH!
YAAAHHH!
HAHA HAHA HAAA!!
THANK YOU, THANK YOU, ENDER.
YOU MADE THE HARD CHOICE, BOY. ALL OR NOTHING. END THEM OR END US. BUT HEAVEN KNOWS THERE WAS NO OTHER WAY YOU COULD HAVE DONE IT.
CONGRATULATIONS. YOU BEAT THEM, AND IT'S ALL OVER.
I BEAT *YOU*.
ENDER, YOU NEVER PLAYED ME. YOU NEVER PLAYED A *GAME* SINCE I BECAME YOUR ENEMY.
ENDER, FOR THE PAST FEW MONTHS YOU HAVE BEEN THE BATTLE COMMANDER OF OUR FLEETS. THIS WAS THE THIRD INVASION.
WHAT?
ENDER...THERE WERE NO GAMES, THE BATTLES WERE REAL, AND THE ONLY ENEMY YOU FOUGHT WAS THE FORMICS.
YOU WON EVERY BATTLE, AND TODAY YOU FINALLY FOUGHT THEM AT THEIR HOME WORLD, WHERE THE QUEEN WAS, ALL THE QUEENS FROM ALL THEIR COLONIES...

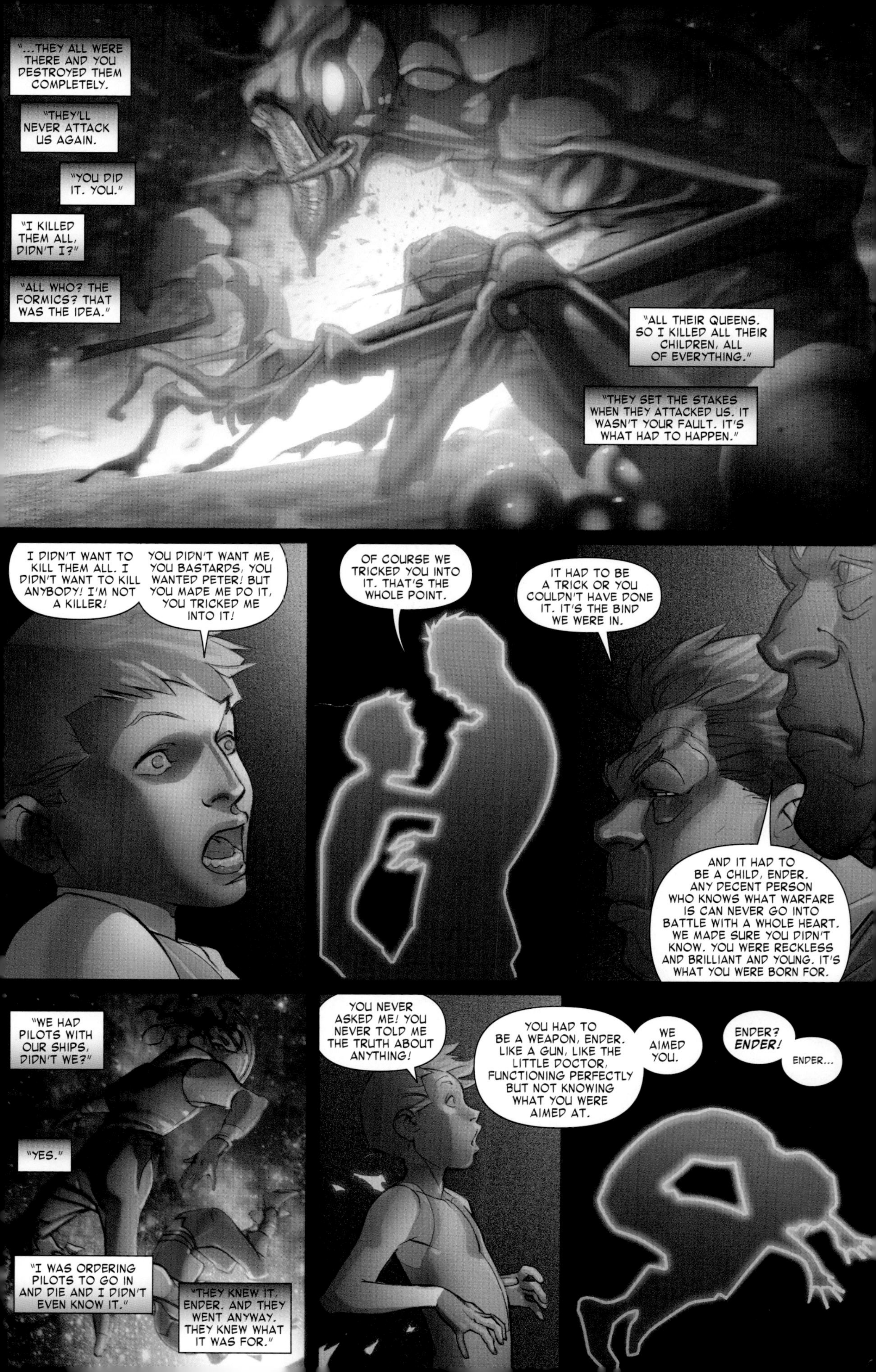
"...THEY ALL WERE THERE AND YOU DESTROYED THEM COMPLETELY.
"THEY'LL NEVER ATTACK US AGAIN.
"YOU DID IT. YOU."
"I KILLED THEM ALL, DIDN'T I?"
"ALL WHO? THE FORMICS? THAT WAS THE IDEA."
"ALL THEIR QUEENS. SO I KILLED ALL THEIR CHILDREN, ALL OF EVERYTHING."
"THEY SET THE STAKES WHEN THEY ATTACKED US. IT WASN'T YOUR FAULT. IT'S WHAT HAD TO HAPPEN."
I DIDN'T WANT TO KILL THEM ALL. I DIDN'T WANT TO KILL ANYBODY! I'M NOT A KILLER!
YOU DIDN'T WANT ME, YOU BASTARDS, YOU WANTED PETER! BUT YOU MADE ME DO IT, YOU TRICKED ME INTO IT!
OF COURSE WE TRICKED YOU INTO IT. THAT'S THE WHOLE POINT.
IT HAD TO BE A TRICK OR YOU COULDN'T HAVE DONE IT. IT'S THE BIND WE WERE IN.
AND IT HAD TO BE A CHILD, ENDER. ANY DECENT PERSON WHO KNOWS WHAT WARFARE IS CAN NEVER GO INTO BATTLE WITH A WHOLE HEART. WE MADE SURE YOU DIDN'T KNOW. YOU WERE RECKLESS AND BRILLIANT AND YOUNG. IT'S WHAT YOU WERE BORN FOR.
"WE HAD PILOTS WITH OUR SHIPS, DIDN'T WE?"
"YES."
"I WAS ORDERING PILOTS TO GO IN AND DIE AND I DIDN'T EVEN KNOW IT."
"THEY KNEW IT, ENDER. AND THEY WENT ANYWAY. THEY KNEW WHAT IT WAS FOR."
YOU NEVER ASKED ME! YOU NEVER TOLD ME THE TRUTH ABOUT ANYTHING!
YOU HAD TO BE A WEAPON, ENDER. LIKE A GUN, LIKE THE LITTLE DOCTOR, FUNCTIONING PERFECTLY BUT NOT KNOWING WHAT YOU WERE AIMED AT.
WE AIMED YOU.
ENDER? ***ENDER!***
ENDER...

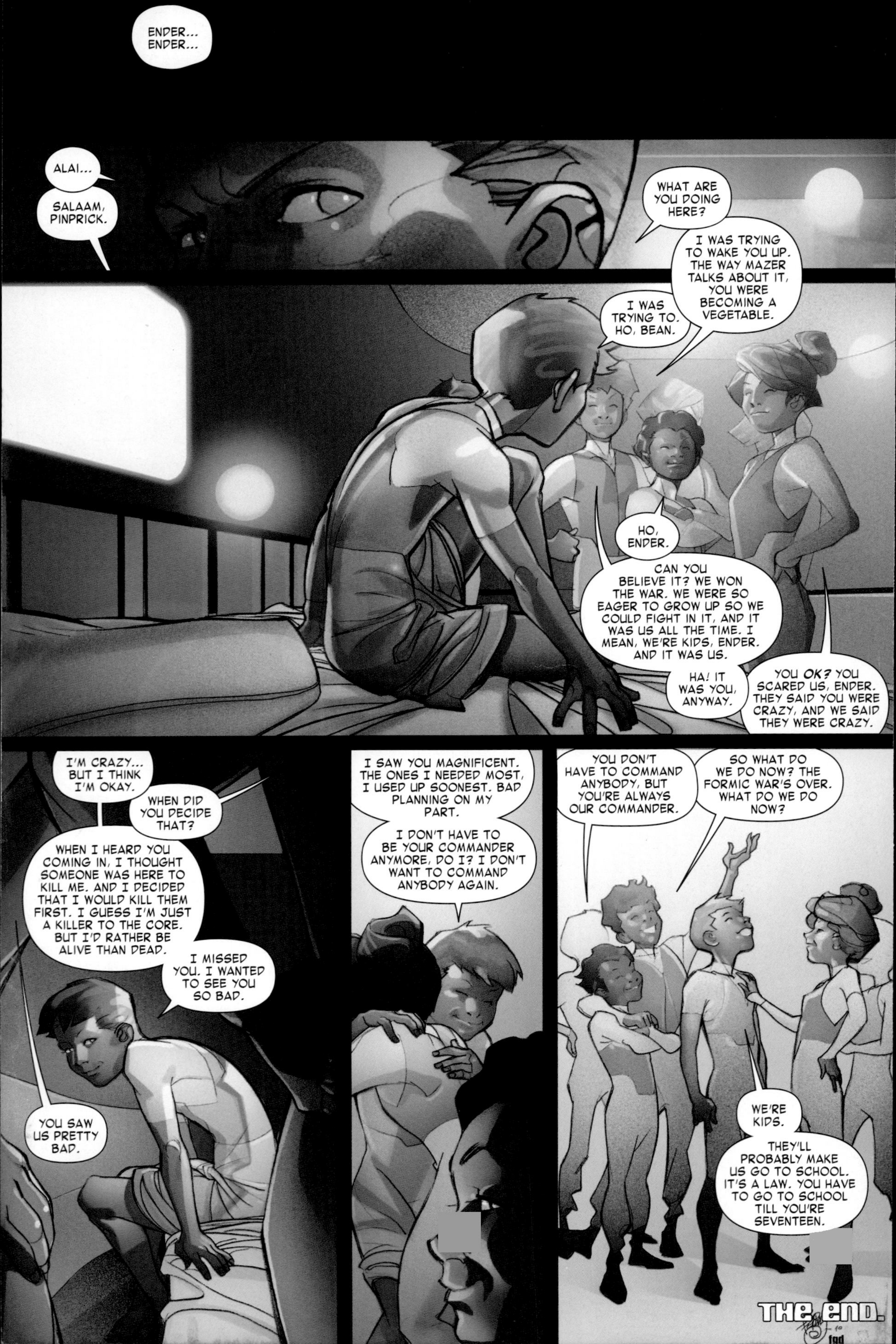
ENDER... ENDER...
ALAI...
SALAAM, PINPRICK.
WHAT ARE YOU DOING HERE?
I WAS TRYING TO WAKE YOU UP. THE WAY MAZER TALKS ABOUT IT, YOU WERE BECOMING A VEGETABLE.
I WAS TRYING TO. HO, BEAN.
HO, ENDER.
CAN YOU BELIEVE IT? WE WON THE WAR. WE WERE SO EAGER TO GROW UP SO WE COULD FIGHT IN IT, AND IT WAS US ALL THE TIME. I MEAN, WE'RE KIDS, ENDER. AND IT WAS US.
HA! IT WAS YOU, ANYWAY.
YOU OK? YOU SCARED US, ENDER. THEY SAID YOU WERE CRAZY, AND WE SAID THEY WERE CRAZY.
I'M CRAZY... BUT I THINK I'M OKAY.
WHEN DID YOU DECIDE THAT?
WHEN I HEARD YOU COMING IN, I THOUGHT SOMEONE WAS HERE TO KILL ME. AND I DECIDED THAT I WOULD KILL THEM FIRST. I GUESS I'M JUST A KILLER TO THE CORE. BUT I'D RATHER BE ALIVE THAN DEAD.
I MISSED YOU. I WANTED TO SEE YOU SO BAD.
YOU SAW US PRETTY BAD.
I SAW YOU MAGNIFICENT. THE ONES I NEEDED MOST, I USED UP SOONEST. BAD PLANNING ON MY PART.
I DON'T HAVE TO BE YOUR COMMANDER ANYMORE, DO I? I DON'T WANT TO COMMAND ANYBODY AGAIN.
YOU DON'T HAVE TO COMMAND ANYBODY, BUT YOU'RE ALWAYS OUR COMMANDER.
SO WHAT DO WE DO NOW? THE FORMIC WAR'S OVER. WHAT DO WE DO NOW?
WE'RE KIDS.
THEY'LL PROBABLY MAKE US GO TO SCHOOL. IT'S A LAW. YOU HAVE TO GO TO SCHOOL TILL YOU'RE SEVENTEEN.
THE END.

COVER SKETCHES BY PASQUAL FERRY

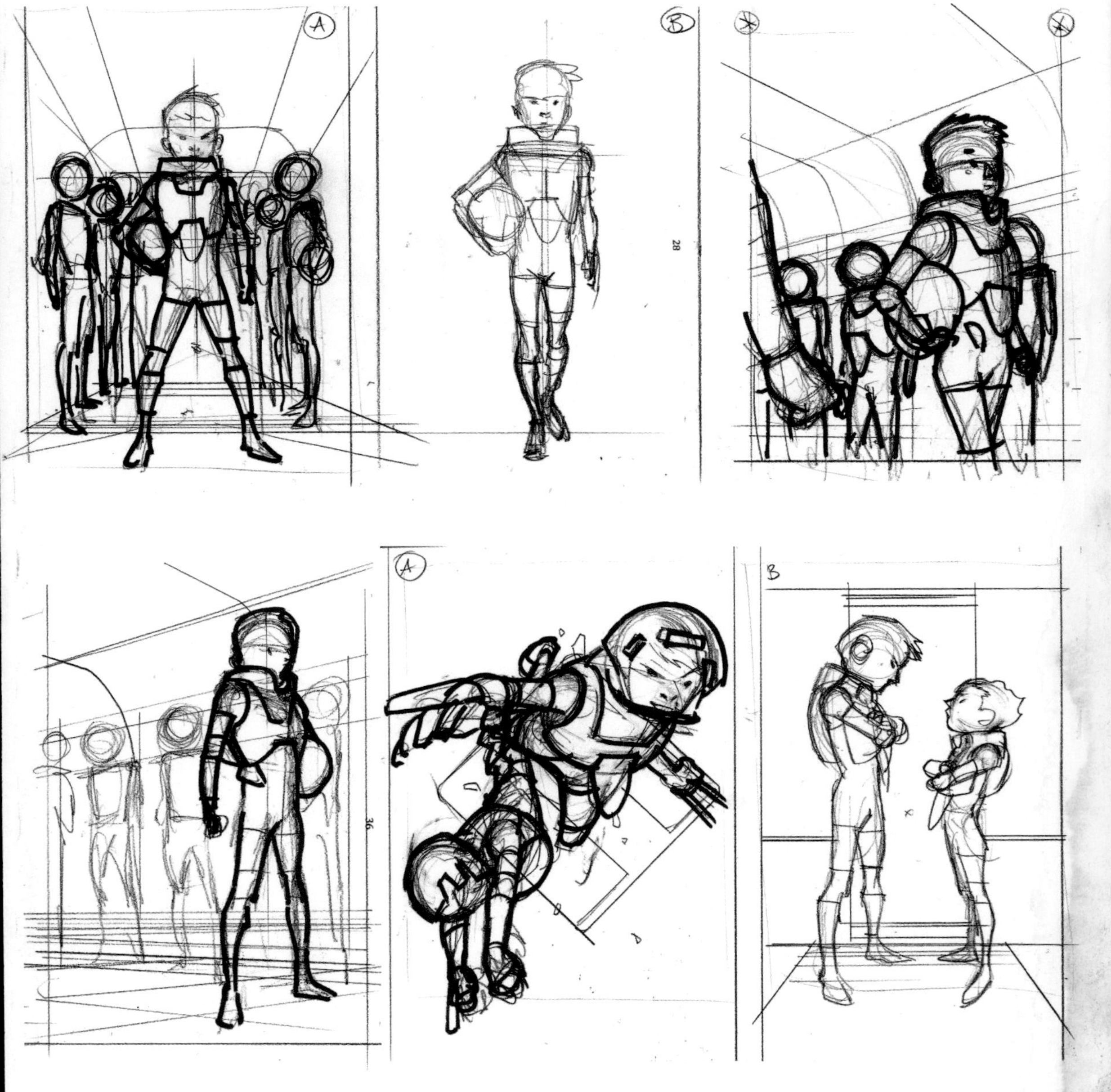
A
B
A
B

A (8)

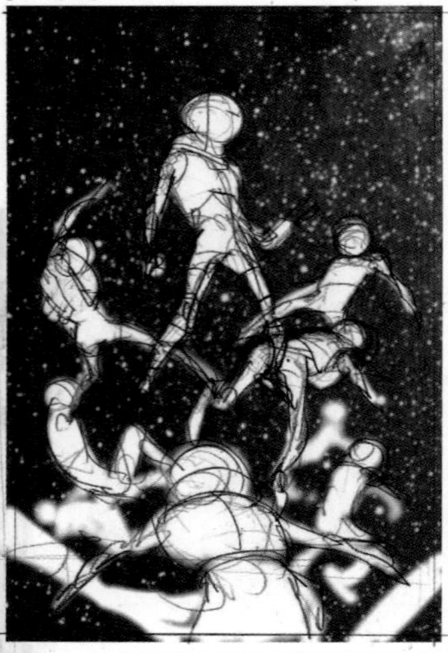

B (8)

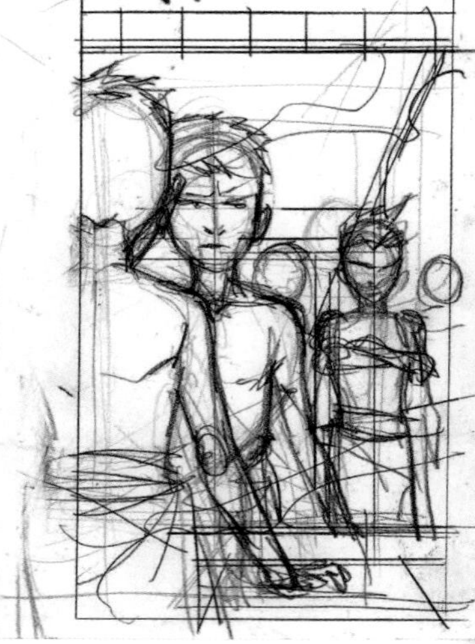

1 (9)

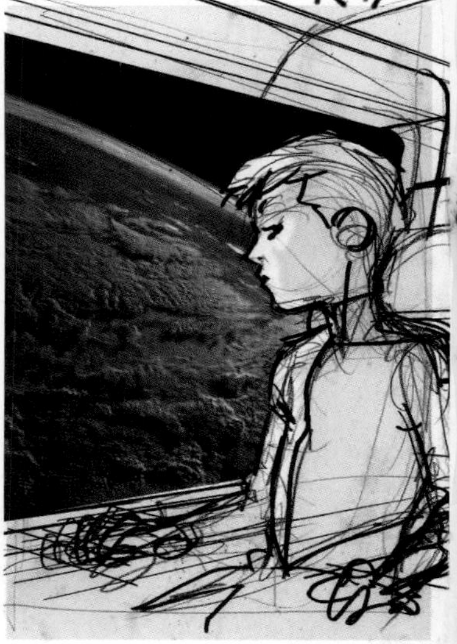

2 (9)

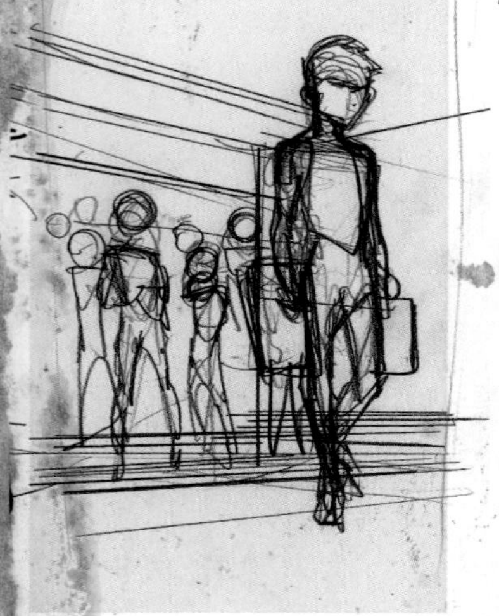

A

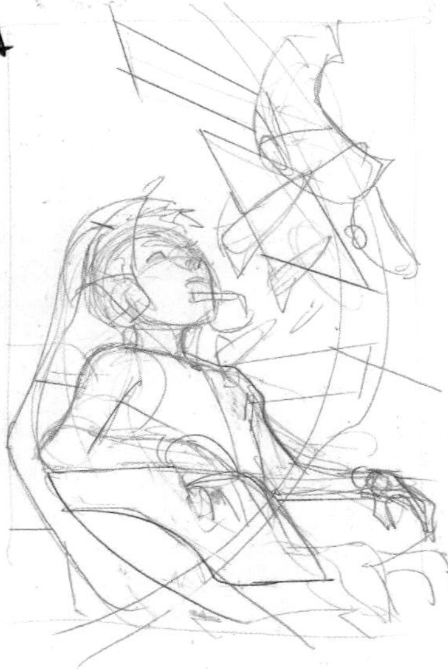

B

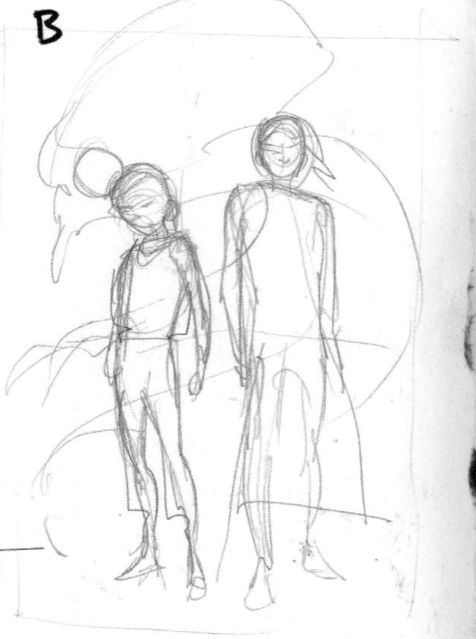

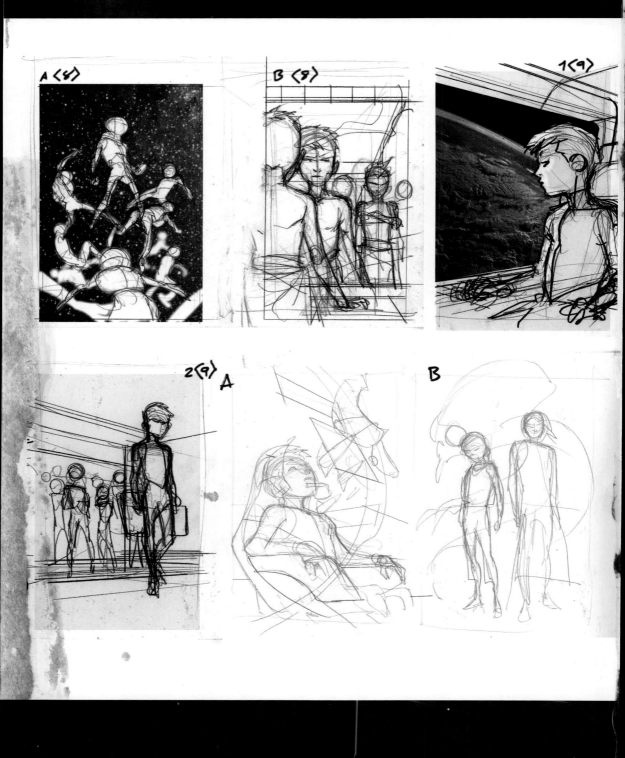